Dickens and the Myth o

This study explores the ways in which Dickens's published work and his thousands of letters intersect, to shape and promote particular myths of the reading experience, as well as redefining the status of the writer. It shows that the boundaries between private and public writing are subject to constant disruption and readjustment, as recipients of letters are asked to see themselves as privileged readers of coded text or to appropriate novels as personal letters to themselves. Imaginative hierarchies are both questioned and ultimately reinforced, as prefaces and letters function to create a mythical reader who is placed in imaginative communion with the writer of the text. But the written word itself becomes increasingly unstable, through its association in the later novels with evasion, fraud and even murder.

Carolyn W. de la L. Oulton is Professor of Victorian Literature and Director of the International Centre for Victorian Women Writers (ICVWW) at Canterbury Christ Church University, UK.

Dickens and the Myth of the Reader

Carolyn W. de la L. Oulton

LONDON AND NEW YORK

First published 2017 by Routledge

2 Park Square, Milton Park, Abingdon, Oxfordshire OX14 4RN
52 Vanderbilt Avenue, New York, NY 10017

Routledge is an imprint of the Taylor & Francis Group, an informa business

First issued in paperback 2018

Copyright © 2017 Carolyn W. de la L. Oulton

The right of Carolyn W. de la L. Oulton to be identified as author of this work has been asserted by her in accordance with sections 77 and 78 of the Copyright, Designs and Patents Act 1988.

All rights reserved. No part of this book may be reprinted or reproduced or utilised in any form or by any electronic, mechanical, or other means, now known or hereafter invented, including photocopying and recording, or in any information storage or retrieval system, without permission in writing from the publishers.

Notice:
Product or corporate names may be trademarks or registered trademarks, and are used only for identification and explanation without intent to infringe.

Library of Congress Cataloging-in-Publication Data

Names: Oulton, Carolyn, 1972- author.
Title: Dickens and the myth of the reader / by Carolyn W. de la L. Oulton.
Description: New York: Routledge, 2016. | Includes bibliographical references and index.
Identifiers: LCCN 2016026997 (print) | LCCN 2016044970 (ebook)
Subjects: LCSH: Dickens, Charles, 1812–1870—Criticism and interpretation. | Dickens, Charles, 1812–1870.—Language. | Authors and readers. | Reader-response criticism.
Classification: LCC PR4592.R36 O97 2016 (print) | LCC PR4592.R36 (ebook) | DDC 823/.8—dc23
LC record available at https://lccn.loc.gov/2016026997

ISBN: 978-1-138-23032-3 (hbk)
ISBN: 978-0-367-17567-2 (pbk)

Typeset in Sabon
by codeMantra

Contents

Acknowledgements   vii

Introduction: Creating the Reader and Writing the Writer   1

1 Reciprocal Readers and the 1830s–40s   27
2 The Hero of His Life   80
3 First-Person-Narrators and Editorial 'Conducting': Limited Intimacy and the Shared Imaginary   104
4 Decoding the Text   136
5 Afterlives   157

Bibliography   177
Index   183

Acknowledgements

Some material in Chapter Two has previously appeared in *Dickens Studies Annual* Vol. 43, as part of an article entitled '"Shall memory be the only thing to die?" Fictions of childhood in Dickens and Jerome K. Jerome.' This material is reproduced with thanks, by permission of AMS Press, Inc.

Introduction
Creating the Reader and Writing the Writer

At the very centre of Dickens's literary project lies a paradox – a strategic but apparently genuine invitation to readers to navigate imaginatively what cannot be fully articulated by the writer himself. Across his writing, words are used to deprecate the limitations of language in capturing experience, suggesting that their function is to drive the imagination beyond these limits.

In the fiction both writer and reader are invited to claim imaginative status in their respective roles as creator and interpreter of the text, apparently renegotiating accepted hierarchies in which the imaginative faculties of readers necessarily derive from the power of authorial language. However Dickens himself clearly drives the range of possible meanings, creating an 'ideal reader' across more than three decades of his work. This study is therefore concerned with two central questions: how does Dickens mythologise the practice of reading and writing and how are readers repositioned as 'readers of Dickens'? Specifically it explores the literary techniques through which he constructs his famously 'personal' relationship with readers, most obviously in his novels but also in early journalism and in letters. Analysis of the relationship between the *Sketches by Boz* and the early novels, the mature fiction and the thousands of letters that have survived will show how Dickens uses his writing across a range of genres to blur the lines between speech and writing, presence and absence, distance and intimacy, public and private.

This sense of indulging in a shared range of thought and emotion depends on the establishment of basic principles, which the reader has to accept in order to sustain the writer / reader relationship as devised by the writer himself. In the first place, the reader must accept that intimacy can exist between people who have never met, where the writer is both conscious of, and transcends, the limits of the page; in return, the writer trusts that a mutual exchange can be initiated where there is no guarantee of the words being read at all. Finally however, readers are constructed as a 'unified' entity who can be educated into reading the texts correctly and so allowing the writer to continue his work.

The relationship Dickens seeks with readers involves the mythologising of both himself and them, but this is never effected on equal terms. Even in setting up imaginative (or imagined) relations between readers, Dickens reminds them of his own status in the transaction. In a useful analysis of Dickens's impact in forging connections between readers and characters, Jonathan Grossman suggests that 'the novel as an art not only could enable his community, whose individuals were increasingly atomized, to come to know their manifold unseen connectedness, but also, more specifically, could help to produce its self-comprehension in terms of a crisscrossing journeying or characters simultaneously circulating all around' (6).

This perception of connectedness extends beyond the text itself, although it is the text that highlights (and in some sense creates) connections between readers. To give a famous example, Dickens told Angela Burdett Coutts in 1858 that 'It is very curious to see how many people in black come to Little Dombey. And when it is over they uniformly go away as if the child were really Dead – with a hush upon them' (23 August 1858. Pilgrim 8. 632–34). The word 'uniformly' is an odd one to use in the context of personal grief but subtly reinforces the central role played by Dickens himself as the key individual governing his audience's emotion. A few weeks later he wrote to Forster that 'I was brought very near to what I sometimes dream may be my Fame, when a lady whose face I had never seen stopped me yesterday in the street, and said to me, *Mr Dickens, will you let me touch the hand that has filled my house with many friends*' ([11 September 1858]. Pilgrim 8. 656–57). In this account Dickens both stimulates and superintends the imaginative responses of the reader he encounters.

The journalistic and fictional narrators are key to orchestrating and supervising this relationship; from the apparently diffident appeals of the early 'Boz' sketches to the trenchant moralising of *Nicholas Nickleby*, Dickens's development of a recognisable narrative voice – or more accurately, series of voices – is inseparable from the construction of an imagined reader. This assumed reader is depicted as both receptive and active in response to the text and as increasingly responsive to Dickens himself, as the writer of a particular body of work.

In 21st century celebrity-culture declarations of affection by the ultra-famous for their unknown fans have become commonplace, captured most problematically by the now-familiar image of the singer on a well-lit stage declaring 'I love you all' to an audience half hidden in the darkness of the auditorium. In a newly virtual world, the very idea of 'Facebook friends' similarly plays on this concept of a relationship that both does and does not exist. But this 'virtual' relationship is precisely the dynamic Dickens seeks to create. At different times and depending on the context in which they encounter his work, readers may suspend their disbelief in order to position themselves as the one privileged participant in the shared world Dickens creates; conversely they may seek mutual engagement based on their shared knowledge of his sketches and characters. Through his narrative personae, Dickens himself becomes both fictional and identifiable as the tangible writer who can actually be spotted in the locations he describes. Most obviously the conversational mode of the Boz narrator implies that he himself is personally accessible – always, so to speak, likely to be walking round the next corner.

From the start his writing incorporates direct address to the reader, and a sense of direct engagement is promoted through the tendency of Boz to materialise and direct the reader's gaze, remarking inconsequentially in 'The Boarding House' for instance, 'It is almost superfluous to say, that the lady whom we have just shown out at the street door (and whom the two female servants are now inspecting from the second floor windows) was exceedingly vulgar, ignorant, and selfish' (291). In one scene from *Pictures from Italy,* Dickens implicitly likens the transference of his own ideas to the imagination of the reader, to the use of shorthand as a quasi-miraculous transformation of spoken word into print, when he describes a meal as 'something with a vegetable or some rice in it, which is a sort of shorthand or arbitrary character for soup, and which tastes very well, when you have flavoured it with plenty of grated cheese, lots of salt, and abundance of pepper' (111–12).

In a mirror image of the 'creation' of ideal readers, the importance of constructing the writer himself increases with his fame. In one sense the actual writer may already be perceived as a known quantity, while the target reader remains invisible in the sense of being impossible to recognise on sight (although in a number of letters Dickens registers the presence of a fellow traveller reading one of his books or asking to have the writer pointed out). For the purposes of narrative interest, the reader is often assumed to be mysterious, and curiosity about their putative readers is ascribed to numerous Victorian narrators in fictional autobiographies, whose forms of address vary on a spectrum from the generic 'dear reader' to the more tentative 'if anyone reads this' – in each formulation this reader remains largely unindividualised. Importantly the image of the writer is carefully constructed for this supposedly unseen readership.

While Dickens in fact kept a steady eye on his readership, he as an author and public figure was constantly on display in ways that most of his readers were not, appearing as a speaker at literary dinners and a player in amateur theatricals open to the public, among other roles. As Marysa Demoor notes, 'Dickens's talent at selling himself and his books prefigured in many ways the more sophisticated marketing techniques of subsequent generations' (4). As an editor for the last 20 years of his life he also belonged to a known and visible work address. This in itself could be problematic – as Alexis Easley has shown, the very fascination with Dickens as an individual author created a threat to his personal identity, as 'On the one hand, this replication of images, as a form of hero worship, would seem to highlight Charles Dickens's individuality; however, this process of mass replication actually had the effect of effacing his identity, converting his image into mass-produced objects of exchange: *cartes de visite* and collectible photographs' (39).

This level of fame could certainly be inconvenient, and Dickens tells a marvellous story of going to see a villa he was thinking of buying, in 1851, when he unexpectedly ran in to the inmates, 'for it *has* inmates – as I found to my horror the other day, when a lady, with curls like tight sausages, rushed out of the dining room, card in hand, and enquired of the humble individual who now has the honour to address you, if he were the real original inimitable to whom she was indebted for so many hours of – &c &c' (to Henry Austin. 25 January 1851. Pilgrim 6. 267). Fictionalising the encounter Dickens nonetheless assumes that Austin will be able to complete what is implicitly presented as a familiar phrase in connection with his work.

While such tableaux themselves become part of the Dickens myth, the evidence of his private letters, as well as his professional correspondence with editors and other public figures, indicates that Dickens took the idea of personal 'affection' between himself and his public entirely seriously and that he actively sought to use it as a means of improving readers' condition. As Sarah Winter argues:

> Dickens's efforts to affect his readers *directly* through his writing – to teach them precisely how to read his novels ... deserve more detailed attention so that we may clarify how Dickens's fiction and celebrity author persona ended up playing such a salient role not only in shaping the nineteenth-century British literary field but also in providing a rationale for the emergent English literary canon. (4)

John Bowen stresses that 'The demand to be a collaborator of Dickens occurs throughout his fiction, most strikingly when his texts turn all their force to summon their readers to a responsibility beyond the text' ('Dickens and the Force of Writing' 267). Dickens's own participation encourages readers to remain tied to the books they have read, even in interacting with each other.

Clearly the relationship between author and reader shifted significantly over the course of Dickens's career. At the start of his career he was ready, in 'conversation' with readers, to admit the tension between the demands of writing and publication and the intermittent failure of the imagination. The narrator of 'The Parlour Orator' in *Sketches by Boz* remarks almost sarcastically that left alone in a pub parlour:

> If we had followed the established precedent in all such instances, we should have fallen into a fit of musing, without delay. The ancient appearance of the room – the old panelling of the wall – the chimney blackened with smoke and age – would have carried us back a hundred years at least, and we should have gone dreaming on, until the pewter pot on the table, or the little beer chiller on the fire, had started into life, and addressed to us a long story of days gone by. But, by some means or other, we were not in a romantic humour; and although we tried very hard to invest the furniture with vitality, it remained perfectly unmoved, obstinate, and sullen'. (234–35)

While 'tongue-in-cheek allusions to his narrative methods within the novels themselves are indeed far from infrequent' (Sadrin 1), such a candid avowal of the lack of inspiration within an actual text is not a hallmark of the later Dickens. It is Thackeray who brilliantly captures the idea that writers are finally unable to express their meaning, while readers are not in any case privy to their thoughts, in *Pendennis*, serialised between 1848 and 1850, where he observes that 'If the secret history of books could be written, and the author's private thoughts and meanings noted down alongside of his story, how many insipid volumes would become interesting, and dull tales excite the reader!' (432).

Dickens was always conscious of the gaps between his writing self, the literary circles to which he wanted to gain access, and the reader he was trying to draw into intimate relation to himself. He told Richard Bentley in 1836 that 'Since I have been a successful author, I have seen how much ill-will and jealousy there is afloat, and have acquired an excellent character as a quiet, modest fellow' ([5 December 1836]. 206–207. 207). But as his reputation increased, this 'modest' persona became increasingly untenable and he can be seen as a result constantly seeking to recalibrate or reaffirm his relations with readers. Ironically enough in light of his attacks on Byron, this strategic positioning includes an invocation of the Romantic imagination as an uncontrollable force.

By the time of writing *American Notes* Dickens was able to posit the imaginative vision as something both beyond his control and surpassing his powers of expression, as his inability to express what he sees becomes the mythical hallmark of the writer. Recalling the voyage by steamship, he writes of his impressions of a storm, 'Words cannot express it. Thoughts cannot convey it. Only a dream can call it up again, in all its fury, rage, and passion' (24).

At night:

> At first, too, and even when the hour, and all the objects it exalts, have come to be familiar, it is difficult, alone and thoughtful, to hold them to their proper shapes and forms. They change with the wandering fancy; assume the semblance of things left far away; put on the well-remembered aspect of favourite places dearly loved; and even people them with shadows. Streets, houses, rooms; figures so like their usual occupants, that they have startled me by their reality, which far exceeded, as it seemed to me, all power of mine to conjure up the absent; have, many and many a time, at such an hour, grown suddenly out of objects with whose real look, and use, and purpose, I was as well acquainted as with my own two hands. (19)

If one function of literature, as set out in Dickens's manifesto, is to infiltrate the lives of actual readers, then such accounts of the imperative dictates of his own imagination bolster his authority in entering the homes of readers and encouraging them to 'people them with shadows'. Notably in this formulation the assumed reader's imagination is once again subordinate to his own.

As Dickens's fame increased he clearly felt obliged to reassure readers that their praise was still of value to him. One correspondent is told that:

> I thank you, very earnestly indeed, for your unaffected assurance of interest and regard – which I so far deserve, that I can never feel indifferent to such a communication, and never fail to regard it as among the best honors that a writer can win. I have found such correspondents as you (I thank God) in every part of the world in which I have been; but the happiness of finding them is as new to me as ever. (To William Sawyer, 1 December 1848. Pilgrim 5. 452)

To his father in law George Hogarth he insists at around the same time that 'I am quite as sensitive to applause which I know to be sincere, as I was a dozen years ago – more so, I think' (To George Hogarth, 2 April 1848. Pilgrim 5. 271). In his last letters of the 1860s he responds in similar vein to correspondents who have written praising his books, but he is notably less defensive and more secure in his status. In 1868 one friend is told that 'You can not think what a pleasure it is to me to know that you have been reading my books while you have been confined to your room! I almost feel as if I had been your doctor and companion, I declare' (To Charles Eliot Norton, 23 November 1868. Pilgrim 12. 226), while to another he writes that 'very few things touch me so nearly as the knowledge that my fancies have become part of lives like yours' (To Arthur Helps, 30 November 1868. Pilgrim 12. 228–29. 228).

These letters encourage readers to mythologise their relationship with Dickens, but the books' fame has the potential to come off the page and attach itself to the writer in ways he had not intended. Paradoxically it was a potential barrier to informal networking on behalf of his children, as on the occasion when Dickens wished Charley's position at Barings to be secured by a word on his behalf, and 'I would have gone to Mr Bates myself in the course of tomorrow, but that I have the greatest delicacy in obtruding myself… what a private gentleman need not scruple to do, my consciousness of my own notoriety shrinks from' (To Miss Burdett Coutts, 6 September 1858. Pilgrim 8. 652–53. 652–53).

Notwithstanding such social complications, Dickens's public demeanour reflects a consciously literary image of the writer that in turn suggests the criteria by which he should be judged, an ostensibly straightforward model based on the acceptance of an author – book continuum. An important aspect of the Dickens myth, and a defining aspect of his authority, is the increasing insistence on the responsibility of the writer to inculcate lessons rather than simply entertain the leisure hours of the reading public. Writing to a journalist who had praised his books, he once claimed that:

> The view you take of the literary character in the abstract, or of what it might and ought to be, expresses what I have striven for, all through my literary life. I have never allowed it to be patronized, or tolerated, or treated like a good child or a bad child. In simply doing my plain duty by it, I am always animated by the hope of leaving it, a little better understood by the thoughtless than I found it'. (To James B. Manson, 25 September 1858. Pilgrim 8. 670–71. 671)

Within the novels themselves much the same idea is promoted, even at the risk of overwriting the literary culture on which they depend. The highly allusive *David Copperfield* creates an image of the writer as both created by circumstances and directed by an innate sense of his vocation. As Kathryn Chittick notes, 'Dickens's novel of literary apprenticeship contains no fond accounts of the Bohemia frequented by Arthur Pendennis' (8), whose chronicler is the first to admit that 'A literary man has often to work for his bread against time, or against his will, or in spite of his health, or of his indolence, or of his repugnance to the subject on which he is called to exert himself, just like any other daily toiler' (*Pendennis* 380). Rather 'David Copperfield approaches reporting with a blueprint for fame' (Chittick 8). Robert Douglas-Fairhust argues that while Dickens presented himself as having had no assistance at the start of his career, notably discoursing on his unaided early struggles in a speech of 1867, this was a largely inaccurate picture of his strategic planning in the 1830s. 'Not only had he started by following in the footsteps of his uncle, but he then energetically set about gathering every additional companion, introducer, and adviser he could' (*Becoming Dickens* 138).

The interplay of personality and availability of the text in different forms is crucial to the construction of the writer / reader dynamic as well. Winter locates the celebrity effect of Dickens as a symbol in the circulation of his 'Boz' image, 'We could view the pseudonym "Boz" as a precursor to the iconic image of the twentieth-century celebrity, since it seems to have functioned analogously as a kind of verbal token or souvenir that could be exchanged among readers as a sign of their participation in the young author's popularity' (Winter 112). In other words 'Dickens's celebrity became knowable, and nameable, when a certain multiplicity of early readers began to carry around his novels' words inside their heads, particularly his characters' idiosyncratic styles of speech, and to use those words in their own speech …' (Winter 86). Malcolm Andrews points out that 'Boz was out to create the taste by which he was to be enjoyed. Not to be in on Boz's jokes implied exclusion from the circle he was so successfully drawing around him – and risked the reputation perhaps of a slight lack of sophistication' (*Dickensian Laughter* 9).

8 *Introduction*

Importantly Robert Patten and more recently Sarah Winter have pointed out that Dickens's rise to fame was enabled in the first instance by the serialisation of his novels, a history that has been occluded by his subsequent marketing as a cultural phenomenon with a unique status independent of the strategies that made him famous in the first place. As Patten argues:

> Charles Dickens constructed himself over the decades as a separable and distinct, unique author. ... Dickens's biographers, following John Forster's lead, reinforced the notoriety and singularity of Charles Dickens, author, rather than 'Boz', the editor and collaborator. Severing Dickens's periodical fictions from their magazine contexts allowed them to be reinterpreted as self-referential biographical disclosures. ('Dickens as Serial Author', 143)

Serial publication may itself facilitate the celebrity effect: that the instalments keep coming stands as a reminder of the writer's living presence, which in turn allows the possibility of a relationship; further, readers may feel a greater investment in a story the ending of which is not yet finally determined.

As both Patten and Winter suggest, the context in which material is circulated is a key determiner of reader response and the status of the author. And as Kate Flint argues:

> Necessarily, authors are continually in dialogue with their readership, or projected readers: to understand this relationship means considering how books were encountered (in libraries – whether private, including the phenomenon of the circulating library, or public and as private possessions); where and how they were read (aloud within a family group; in solitude; greedily; dutifully; as part of formalized or self-directed education; passed from one person to another in a workplace); and exploring the concerns about reading that were publically expressed, whether such concerns involved the possibility that print would corrupt morals, or would inflame readers politically. (*The Cambridge History of Victorian Literature* 7–8)

To make an obvious point, the sheer length of the three-decker novel both prolongs the narrator's control over the reader's experience and increases the chances of the same reader losing concentration or allowing his or her own imagination to take off at a tangent (as repeatedly happens to David Copperfield and Dickens's other child readers, when they take characters from remembered stories and infuse them with new life). Nor was Dickens always able to control the context in which he was read, a point made most obviously in the reprinting of passages severed from their original instalments, in the periodical press.

In a discussion of periodical excerpting as a practice, Nicholas Dames argues that:

> what rests at the heart of the theory of reading offered by the long extract is not an issue of length (the space taken up by, or yielded to, the object of analysis) but an issue of time: the time it takes, while reading, to have a feeling. The unit of feeling implied by Victorian critical protocol is remarkably brief: a passage, a description, an authorial sentiment. These extracts are meant ideally to be monads, single – perhaps even foreshortened – examples of repeated affective prompts. ('On not close reading', 22)

This account resonates with the Victorian commonplace book and with the modern popularity of inspirational quotations, often removed from their original context to appeal to the broadest possible range of readers and seem applicable to any number of situations.

A desire to regain control of the reading experience is registered in a number of Dickens's letters, which themselves re-contextualise or highlight particular passages from the novels. In his letters to Angela Burdett Coutts about the Urania Cottage project, he shows an acute awareness of the context of reading, recommending books he felt could mediate between the material conditions of the inmates' lives and the ennobling vision he sought to instil. In one letter of 1848 he reports himself 'much dismayed by what I have heard about the books (I mean the reading books) at the Home, and imagine there is some mistake, but it makes me very unquiet ...' (To Miss Burdett Coutts, 7 January 1848. Pilgrim 5. 224–25. 225). Later that year he wrote again suggesting Wordsworth and Crabbe as suitable reading for the women, on the grounds that 'All people who have led hazardous and forbidden lives are, in a certain sense, imaginative; and if their imaginations are not filled with good things, they will choke them, for themselves, with bad ones' (To Miss Burdett Coutts, 15 November 1848. Pilgrim 5. 440–41. 440). A few months later he described *The Vicar of Wakefield* as 'a book of which I think it is not too much to say that it has perhaps done more good in the world, and instructed more kinds of people in virtue, than any other fiction ever written' (to Angela Burdett Coutts, 29 March 1849. Pilgrim 5. 517). In Dickens's own mind the ability to infuse the immediate vicinity with persuasive fantasy is not limited to his own readers or necessarily to habitual readers at all. His appeal is notably based on the need to direct a pre-existing imaginative faculty, which may otherwise be rendered unsafe. The women's imaginations are presented here as a vacuum that will be filled with 'good things' or bad.

Dickens's awareness of his readers' imaginative response in turn permeates the construction of his own literary texts, in which the key effects are achieved by the careful positioning of writer and reader in relation to one another through the controlling voice of the narrator. This study will therefore give sustained attention to the positioning of the writer and construction of the reader as mutually dependent activities, *within* the written text. Within his own books, readers are positioned in particular tableaux (a notable instance being Dickens's famous image of his books as guests around the Christmas fireside), and particular passages directly reference his awareness that the reader is actually holding a physical book. The materiality of the book mediates between the narrator and the reader: this literalises the sense in which Dickens's characters become 'real' entities who can take their place at the fireside and in the home; in *A Christmas Carol*, the narrator can stand 'at the elbow' of readers (drawing attention to the likely posture of a reader actually holding the book in which this line appears).

Leah Price points out that journals such as *Household Words* 'simplified a reality in which members of the same family might read different books side by side in the parlour, while the same newspapers that commuters used to carve out privacy were sold by the cries of newsboys, read aloud and passed around from hand to hand' ('Victorian Reading,' 45). But at one level, the very fact that they may *not* be reading in the contexts attributed to them fictionalises readers and draws them further in to the imaginative world controlled by the narrator.

A number of 19th-century authors deploy meta-textual strategies, even joining the reader on the margins of the text while they comment on realist conventions – 'all this time I am keeping myself waiting at my own halldoor while detailing my family's genealogy' remarks the narrator of Rhoda Broughton's 1867 *Cometh up as a Flower* (41). But Dickens's suggestions to the implied reader operate in both directions, playing with the idea of a narrative presence that infiltrates the reader's mind and home, as well as taking the reader to the scene of action. As the characters enter the home of the reader, so the narrator develops strategies to make the reader similarly 'knowable' – essentially by creating him or her. The reader has access to infinitely reproducible printed copy of both authorised and pirated versions of Dickens's text. This copy may literally become the property of a reader, who is at liberty to annotate it or turn down pages, to establish or draw out particular meanings. Under these conditions the narrator's aim is to persuade them to read in certain ways. It is no coincidence that the 'good' characters are often readers, capable of instructing their 'real life' counterparts in how, and even *what*, to read in order to help them respond appropriately to Dickens's text.

While the eponymous narrator of *David Copperfield* famously defends his reading of 18th-century novels on the ground that 'whatever harm was in some of them was not there for me' (53), other narrators are more alive to the quality of reading material consumed by different figures and how this can be used as an index to character. In *Nicholas Nickleby* the narrator energetically satirises the simulation of imaginative response; through the posturing of Mrs Wittiterly (who exhausts Kate by forcing her to read aloud from cheap library novels) and Miss Knagg, who believes her brother to be a literary genius because he is ostentatiously misanthropic, the narrator demands that readers engage in a more genuine relationship with 'better' literature.

Such policing of reading within the printed page itself is potentially problematic, as Price demonstrates in her discussion of the range of ways authors found to solve this very dilemma:

> Printed attacks on printed matter always risk self-referentiality... Conduct books remarked that trashy reading took time away from outdoor activity, but neglected to count the hours eaten up by their own perusal. Some genres circumvented this problem by distinguishing the readers discussed from the readers addressed: thus, men were instructed on how to control their daughters' reading, or middle-class philanthropists informed about the reading habits of mechanics. In obscenity trials, too, middle-class male jurors were asked to speculate about the effects of a book on their housemaid. ('Victorian Reading' 54)

This controlling of readers by other readers is of course open to abuse, as Dickens powerfully displays in his construction of Fagin as a manipulative 'false guardian' figure in *Oliver Twist* who both allows Oliver to be framed for the theft of Brownlow's books and forces the 'wrong' reading on him, and in Mrs Wittiterly's abuse of Kate in *Nicholas Nickleby*. For Mrs Wittiterly books, fashionable society and dancing are virtually interchangeable signifiers of status and serve little other purpose. But that Fagin should choose such a means of influencing the vulnerable Oliver is telling.

The ideal reader is constructed as having already formed a love of books during childhood, creating a link to the narrator (this is one of the few consistent and knowable characteristics Dickensian first-person narrators tend to have). The Dickensian narrator (and characters such as Tom Pinch) often focuses then on this memory of childhood, rather than adult reading, as practised by the assumed (or created) reader. Dickensian narrators set up a frame of reference through their numerous allusions to shared reading, often drawing on non-specified editions of iconic tales such as the Arabian Nights or well known fairy stories, as well as to culturally embedded works such as *Robinson Crusoe*. Wu Di suggests that 'the child reader in many ways represents the ideal reader for Dickens' (168) and certainly the Gradgrind children in *Hard Times* are damaged initially because they have no access to fairy tales, in contrast to Tom, Scrooge and David Copperfield, who all recall their childhood reading as important. This may suggest that for some of the characters, reading is something that has shaped them before the start of the story, rather than being something they do within the world of the novel itself (incidentally if the imagined community Dickens creates often has as much to do with the generic experience of childhood reading as with any particularised text, this raises the question of what his readers are supposed to be doing when they come to his work as adults).

But having once established the integrity of his own literary practice, Dickens deploys an authoritative narrative voice to highlight particular behaviour and demand that the reader reconsider it, through the act of reading. The early novels are instrumental in establishing a moral centre from which judgements can be made or by which readers should regulate their own behaviour. In order for this strategy to succeed, it is clearly important for Dickensian narrators to establish the sense of a shared identity, which will be accessible across class boundaries.

From the 1840s onwards he began reading parts of his work aloud to friends to test their response, anticipating one context in which the novels might be expected to be read after publication. In a much-quoted letter to Catherine Dickens, he describes the experience of reading *The Chimes* to an all-male audience, exulting in the visceral transference of imaginative response, 'If you had seen Macready last night – undisguisedly sobbing, and crying on the sofa, as I read – you would have felt (as I did) what a thing it is to have Power' (2 December 1844. Pilgrim 4. 234–35. 235). It is unclear from this comment whether Dickens is celebrating the power of his writing, the effectiveness of his reading style, or both. Perhaps surprisingly, Catherine is told that she herself would have *felt*, rather than simply witnessed, what it means 'to have Power'. This identification of the imagined witness with the author (in both senses) of the quasi mystical 'Power' seems literally to conflate writer /speaker and reader / listener in an imaginative bond. Such a total merging of identities is extreme even in Dickens's creative expression. Nonetheless it highlights the intensity of purpose underlying much of his early fiction, as he tests out theories of reader response on his characters within the imagined world of the text.

Unlike Thackeray or Trollope, Dickens's narrators tend to avoid referencing particular novels of recent date, in favour of a more loosely identified reading experience; Dickens's direction of the reader's inclination (which would be both perfected and parodied by the suggestive conversation of Inspector Bucket in *Bleak House*) is closely linked to the persuasive methods of rhetorical speech. Contextualising this technique through a comparison with earlier writers such as Goldsmith and Lamb, Valerie Purton suggests that where Dickens's precursors require their readers be constantly alert to shifts in narrative stance, 'Dickens's readers, in contrast, are in a tight authorial embrace, forced to read in only one way' (120). This style, Purton argues, is based on a deliberate engagement with the sentimental tradition, as:

> nineteenth-century sentimental writing, in writers as different as Dickens and George Eliot, developed into a rhetoric of intensification which functioned to disable thought and to build up an emotional climax in the audience reader. Thus a new sentimental paradox emerged in nineteenth-century literature: a highly stylised and thoughtful rhetoric was developed in order to disarm and disable thought. (159)

As Juliet John points out, this stylised presentation of character may appear unimpressive under the test of critical analysis, but it nonetheless remains effective, as 'during the experience of reading, Dickens's melodramatic presentation of violent passion is often surprisingly powerful' (*Dickens's Villains* 104).

In later novels the reader is encouraged to ask questions, as the narrators become less reliable. Shifts in tone in the early novels already suggest that, in John's words, 'If Dickens envisaged the perfect author-reader relationship as a marriage of equals, then perhaps the ideal reader, like the ideal author, would maintain the ability to immerse him- or herself in emotional experience and to detach him- or herself from the experience simultaneously' (*Dickens's Villains* 138). But in the early novels the narrators make little or no attempt to conceal their didactic agenda, whether in melodramatic or realist mode. This technique is also used in the non-fiction and is most apparent at moments where it fails, as in the rather clumsy denial of any attempt to indoctrinate the reader of *American Notes*:

> There are many passages in this book, where I have been at some pains to resist the temptation of troubling my readers with my own deductions and conclusions; preferring that they should judge for themselves, from such premises as I have laid before them. My only object in the outset, was, to carry them with me faithfully wheresoever I went, and that task I have discharged. (266)

By this stage in his career, Dickens clearly feels certain of his audience – while he politely terms the imposition of his own agenda (which by his own account he has supposedly resisted doing), 'troubling' the reader, he strongly implies that they will only be able to 'judge for themselves' in the absence of his clear direction on particular issues; even in this instance their judgement is constrained by the premises he has 'laid before them' (the suggestion of a metaphorical feast, or by extension, an engaging read, is suggestive here). He is apparently confident that he has 'carried them with him' in both senses on this metaphorical journey. There is a similar dynamic in *Pictures from Italy*, where he creates the reader through an act of imagination, 'I have only now, in passport wise, to sketch my reader's portrait, which I hope may thus be thus suppositiously traced for either sex', including 'Very cheerful' eyes' and other features of the ideal Dickensian reader (7).

In the later novels readers develop with Dickens in their ability to respond to complex ideas. In John's analysis of melodrama in Dickens's narratives, this means that:

> Transparent, idealized character types remain integral to Dickens's vision, but he attempts to resolve the "problem" of their unreality by highlighting their fictional status. The reader is thus given the choice of

> whether or not to believe in them and how to interpret them. Dickens employs melodrama, that is, with a self-consciousness that becomes more noticeable as his career nears its end. (*Dickens's Villains* 175)

The mythologising of author and reader is likewise recalibrated as part of this process. As the novels become more sophisticated, so Dickens continues to reconfigure the reader, aligning market demand with the moral and emotional demands made on the author as his very success creates a more discerning and demanding audience. In an allusion to his writing of *David Copperfield* in the spring of 1849, he told one correspondent that 'The world would not take another Pickwick from me, now; but we can be cheerful and merry I hope, notwithstanding, and with a little more purpose in us' (To Dudley Costello, 25 April 1849. Pilgrim 5. 527).

From their earliest engagement with Dickens's writing, readers are given a script to follow, one that includes cues for response and implied gaps where the reader's voice might come in. But interestingly the emphasis on readers' ability, or even moral obligation, to insert themselves into the gaps of writing informed Dickens's prose some time before he became a published author. In one particularly emotional letter to Maria Beadnell, he deploys what would become a sort of trademark literary move, in which the writer's skilful use of language draws the reader's attention to its own supposed inadequacy. Refusing to believe that he has wounded her as she claims, he tells her:

> Your own feelings will enable you to imagine far better than any attempt of mine to describe the painful struggle it has cost me to make up my mind to adopt the course which I now take… If (I can hardly believe it possible) I have said any thing which can have that effect I can only ask you to place myself for a moment in my situation and you will find a much better excuse than I can possibly devise. (18 March [1833]. Pilgrim 1. 16–17)

In other words, no amount of epistolary lashing can fully explain the impact of Maria's hurtful behaviour on her young lover, and she must therefore become the agent of her own conviction, while also devising an excuse (which he is constitutionally unable to do) for whatever she believes him to have done. By implication Maria, unlike Dickens, *does* know exactly how to devise ingenious excuses. More importantly in this context, Maria's feelings should enable her to imagine for herself what Dickens's words fall short in describing. This strategy resurfaces a quarter of a century later in *David Copperfield*, where the eponymous narrator famously galvanises the reader's empathetic emotion through the claim that no imaginative depiction can overstate or even do justice to the 'secret agony' he undergoes, and later comments of Rosa Dartle that 'No description I could give of her would do justice to my recollection of her' (459).

Any account of the writer / reader relationship as established and sustained through narrative needs to be complicated through an inclusion of Dickens's huge volume of correspondence, much of which is directly concerned with the establishing of literary hierarchies and modes of reading. In an early letter to Henry Belcombe, Dickens posits a reciprocal relationship between Lamb's work and the other books on his shelf, writing somewhat disingenuously, 'You will not (I hope) think the worse of Charles Lamb for coming off the shelves of Charles Dickens. He has grown somewhat dingy in that worthy's keeping, but the best minds rust in inferior company, and I confidently hope that your chaise may restore him' (To Dr Henry Belcombe, 8 February 1838. Appendix to Pilgrim 7. 789). Significantly *Household Words* contributor Percy Fitzgerald remembered him in 1912 as 'the most brilliant letter writer of his time' (25), and letters have an important status in the novels, as well as forming the basis for travel writing and even autographs. Readers may choose to correspond with the actual writer, whose response in turn affirms his or her sense of personal relationship. These actual readers are in turn fictionalised in further letters in which Dickens discusses them with friends such as Forster; conversely in his published work he often responds to imagined readers as if in conversation with them.

The terms of the 'shared imaginary' emphasised by Dickens himself in creating a myth of his relationship to readers he may never have met, is set out in a number of his letters. Read together, letters and fiction reveal a mutual dependency, a relationship that helps to explain why letters become such an important motif in the novels. The power of reading is readily understood even by characters, such as Krook in *Bleak House*, who are themselves unable to read. In *Martin Chuzzlewit*, Lewsome's written confession that he has supplied Jonas Chuzzlewit with the means of murdering his father, itself becomes an object of fascination, 'The landlord read it: the landlady looked over him. The chamber-maid, in the back-ground, made out as much of it as she could, and invented the rest; believing it all from that time forth as a positive piece of evidence' (352).

Ironically, one letter from Dickens to Edward Taggart warns against just such credulity, advising him to be suspicious of a begging letter as a polished piece of fiction that displays the familiar features of its genre, 'there was a narrative, in its general features sufficiently like this (to one, as I am, in the habit of constructing fictions and curiously watching them) to awaken great suspicion' (20 January 1857. Pilgrim 8. 267–68. 267). As this warning reminds us, Dickens's own letters often use literary techniques familiar from the novels, and 'Dickens the letter-writer commanded as broad a range of voices as did Dickens the novelist' (Bodenheimer. *Knowing Dickens* 23). David Paroissien agrees that 'we might consider the many modes of expression evident in the letters he sent to real people an extension of perhaps his most distinctive gift as a novelist – the skill with which he created so many individualized characters each with his or her voice, vocabulary, and mode of speech' ('Faithfully Yours, Charles Dickens', 36–37). Importantly, letter writing allowed a

16 *Introduction*

more flexible and individualised approach than serial fiction; as Paroissien also notes, 'The quality of Dickens's own letters rests on his mastery of two important skills: his exuberant spontaneity and linguistic inventiveness and the subtlety with which he fitted the content and style of his letters to different correspondents ('Faithfully Yours, Charles Dickens', 36).

Letters and novels often use parallel strategies, including teasing meta-textual commentary, where the narrator apparently parodies his own and readers' belief in the existence of the characters. Dickens's enjoyment of different styles, according to the context and the correspondent addressed, is brilliantly captured in a letter to Andrew Dalglish in 1848, in which he responds to a complaint from a theatrical manager during a series of amateur performances.

> My Dear Sir
>
> I beg to acknowledge the receipt of yours of the 19th, informing me of the terms on which you have engaged the Theatre. I subscribe to them very readily – having no choice – but am bound to say…
>
> -------------
>
> I write thus far, for you to read to the implacable Alexander the Little, if you think right; but I must break off here, to say that I laughed heartily on receipt of your letter this morning, and that the picture of the Manager and his greatest chum nearly coming to single combat, has been really too much for my gravity (which is far from imperturbable) ever since (21 June 1848. Pilgrim 4. 345–46. 345).

Letters such as the one cited above regularly fictionalise the figures they discuss. But to this day Dickens's fame rests largely on the mythology of his characters, and from an early stage his shared imaginary incorporates his own (and more rarely, other authors') characters across both private and public modes. The appearance of fictional characters in Dickens's letters provides an early signal of the way in which a shared knowledge of his books acts as a signifier of personal relationship, both with personal friends and with the reading public.

Allusions to his own characters proliferate in his letters from around 1842. Writing from his first American tour, he uses his characters' idiom as a form of shorthand in jokes to friends, as in his agreement to avoid the steamboat to Buffalo, 'Sich (as Miggs would say) is Mrs D desires; and as my wishes is to please her inclinations, it will be my endeavours to make myself conformable to her dispositions, though I *am* but a husband' (To David C. Colden, 4 April 1842. 183–85. 184). Writing to Cornelius Felton and to Forster he repeatedly invokes the speech or appearance of his characters, telling Felton that he wishes he could attend a dramatic performance, 'your spectacles gleaming not unlike those of my dear friend

Pickwick' (21 May 1842, 243–45. 243) or that he has treated seasick passengers with two companions 'habited as Ben Allen and Bob Sawyer' (31 July 1842. 291–93. 293). In letters to Forster he makes comments such as 'Wasn't it worthy of Crummles' (26 May [1842]. 245–48. 247) or 'as Mr Kenwigs woud say' ([16 September 1842]. 325–26. 325. All references to vol 3 of the Pilgrim edition).

By 1849 he has begun to reference characters currently being serialised, as where he says of himself that, 'I write, as my friend Mr Micawber says, "with a sickly mask of mirth"' (To John Leech, 5 October 1849. Pilgrim 5. 619–20. 621) or 'Mr F's Aunt sends her defiant respects' (To W. C. Macready, 22 March 1856. Pilgrim 8. 74–75). Some characters, such as Tiny Tim, became so popular that their identifying catch phrases could be invoked years later with an incomplete reference, such as 'Many Happy New Years! And so, as Tiny Tim observed, &c –' (To W. H. Wills, 1 January 1856. Pilgrim 2–32). The incomplete *Mystery of Edwin Drood*, which Dickens was writing in 1870, makes a passing allusion to the Circumlocution Office of *Little Dorrit* (*Edwin Drood* 91), while a letter from the same year makes an unattributed reference to Miggs in the phrase 'Sich was my intentions' (To Mr and Mrs J. T. Fields, 14 January 1870. Pilgrim 12. 464–66. 446). As Dickens surely anticipated, other writers continued to reference his characters throughout the century. As late as 1897 F. C. Burnand was able to update the Tuggses as precursors of the fin de siècle "'Arry", commenting in a comic tour guide illustrated by Phil May, 'henceforth to be known in Dickensian phraseology as "T'otherest" and "T'other Guvnor"' (2), that 'Nowadays, indeed, the Tuggses still come down to Ramsgate, as why should they not, being highly respectable people, with perhaps a light-'arted 'Arry or a coquettish "Charlotta" in the family party?' (34–35).

An equally important function of letters is to invoke the writer during the moment of reading, and so collapse the time passed between writing and reading. One means of achieving this is through constantly drawing attention to the physicality of the letter itself, as the paper and ink symbolically pass through Dickens's hand and subsequently impress themselves on the eyes of the reader. This imaginative substitution in Dickens's letters often takes the form of a more satisfactory letter for a brief one, as in 'This is a poor return (I look down and see the end of the paper) for your letter, but in its cordial spirit of reciprocal friendship it is not so bad a one if you could read it as I do' (To the Rev. Edward Taggart, 28 January 1847. Pilgrim 5. 19–20. 20). In return he occasionally offers a reciprocal act of imagination, telling an American friend in 1868, 'Don't write me a long letter, as an obligation on you. A bulletin will be quite enough. I will lengthen it out, in imagination' (To Mrs Charles Eliot Norton, 5 November 1868. 215–16. 216).

Poignantly one of his last letters, written to his son Alfred, was to just this effect. In the final lines Dickens suggestively replaces what he has actually said with an intimation of what he feels in thinking of his son on the other side of the world; in this formulation the implied feeling itself carries more weight than the language with which it is surrounded on the page, 'This is not a letter, so much as an assurance that I never think of you without hope and comfort' (To Alfred Dickens, 20 May 1870. Pilgrim 529–30. 530).

He is also adept at inserting himself in to the mind of the reader, through stressing the physical act of writing. In a letter to Samuel Ward in 1842, Dickens comically invokes the constraints of actual writing to suggest both the unreliability and the corporeality of the writer. Just as Fanny Squeers tells Ralph Nickleby that her father 'requests me to write to you, the doctors considering it doubtful whether he will ever recuvver the use of his legs which prevents his holding a pen', while she herself is 'screaming out loud all the time I write' (175), Dickens absurdly claims that 'I write this with my hands in a basin of water; being in the very act of trimming myself for going out' (13 February 1842. Pilgrim 3. 57–58). He tells his old teacher William Giles in 1848 that '… if I could make a bow in writing, I certainly should do it' (To the Rev. William Giles, 31 October 1848. 432–33. 432); in 1861 he composes a letter 'with the wind blowing so that I can hardly hear myself write' (To John Forster, [?24 November 1861]. Pilgrim 9. 518–19. 502); and in 1867 a shipboard letter to Georgina Hogarth comically invokes the discomfort of the voyage in the claim that 'I write with great difficulty, wedged up in a corner, and having my heels on the paper as often as the pen' (13–17 November 1867. Pilgrim 11. 477–79).

The hazards of this immense correspondence become apparent in numerous letters Dickens was forced to write, apologising for apparent rudeness when missives were left unanswered because he had been abroad – as he told one old friend ruefully in 1868 on his return from America, 'I am wallowing in half a year's arrears of Papers, but hope soon to see Land and you' (To B. W. Procter, 11 May 1868. 105); more embarrassingly yet, in 1855 a letter from William Giles was twice refused at the door. In slightly querulous mode, Dickens explained that where the writer could not be safely identified, his servant had orders to refuse all letters with insufficient postage, rather than pay the additional cost. His reason was that 'Hundreds of letters from every conceivable kind of person of whom I have no sort of knowledge, on every possible and impossible subject with which I have nothing to do, are addressed to me every week of my life' (To the Rev. William Giles, 16 September 1855. Pilgrim 7. 702).

Despite such inconvenience Dickens clearly used his daily correspondence to affirm his literary status, and also as a genuine form of creative expression and engagement with readers. As Paroissien rightly stresses, 'Behind Dickens's varied epistolary voice lurks another: that of "The Inimitable"' ('Faithfully Yours, Charles Dickens', 43). Equally, Dickens is responsive to letters he receives, lamenting to Forster from his American trip of 1842, over a missing steamer, 'I think of your letters so full of heart and friendship, with perhaps a little scrawl of Charley's or Mamey's, lying at the bottom of the deep sea; and am as full of sorrow as if they had once been living creatures' (To John Forster, 28 February 1842. Pilgrim 3. 95–96. 96).

If letters are 'living creatures', the imaginative boundaries between reading, writing and public authorship are always permeable. In a plaintive letter to Angela Burdett Coutts in 1843, Dickens begins by discussing Lockhart's article on the writer Theodor Hook, who died in debt; inevitably compares this to his own situation as a writer; and finally reminds her of his own divided role as a writer of both letters and novels, '... few have known such suffering and bitterness at one time or other, as those who have been bound to Pens. A pleasant thought for one who has been using this very quill all day!' (2 June 1843. Pilgrim 3. 499–500. 500). In this analysis, Dickens is both present in a very human sense (the concrete reality of 'this very quill' can be inferred from the ink it has arranged on the page), and shadowy (to the readers who will only receive his printed text, and by whom he will remain unseen and potentially unappreciated). It also of course implies the complimentary assurance that the writer of publicly renowned literature, who has been working hard all day, now uses the same pen to address a more personal form of writing to this particular reader.

In a number of letters apologising for not having been in touch more regularly, Dickens is even able to proffer a non-existent series of letters as imaginative vehicles for real ones. In 1849 he assured one such correspondent that:

> You did not mean to give me a reproachful shock in the sight of your pretty handwriting, but you did. My conscience, so awakened, is very hard with me for that I have not written to you before. If you knew what an enormous number of letters, chiefly about nothing, I am obliged to write to all sorts and conditions of men (and women), and how regularly I correspond with you in intention, you would quite forgive me, and regard me as the best of correspondents. (To Mrs Olliffe, 20 November 1849. Pilgrim 5. 655)

A letter of 1865 insists that 'As usual, I have been always writing to you (though you have never known it) from the hour in which I received your annual Xmas letter' (To W. W. F. de Cerjat, 16 March 1862. 52–55. 52).

Those who fail to accept these terms are sternly reproved, in letters that deliberately position the writer as a dedicated author rather than simply a private correspondent. When Maria Winter (neé Beadnell) complained in 1855 that Dickens was apparently avoiding her society, she was reminded:

> I hold my inventive capacity on the stern condition that it must master my whole life, often have complete possession of me, make its own demands upon me, and sometimes for months together, put everything else away from me. If I had not known long ago that my place could never be held, unless I were at any moment ready to devote myself to it entirely, I should have dropped out of it very soon. All this I can hardly expect you to understand – or the restlessness and waywardness of an author's mind.

Maria at this point is aligned with others of Dickens's acquaintance, who fail to realise that 'it is impossible to command one's self sometimes to any stipulated and set disposal of five minutes – or that the mere consciousness of an engagement will sometimes worry a whole day. These are the penalties paid for writing books' (To Mrs Winter, 3 April 1855. Pilgrim 7. 583–84). In a less hostile letter to his brother in law, Dickens had explained a few years earlier that any emotional distraction was inimical to the process of literary composition. Explaining why he could not attend a meeting of the Metropolitan Sanitary Association, he wrote that 'If I get fierce and antagonistic about burials, I can't go back to Copperfield for hours and hours. This is really the sort of condition on which I hold my inventive powers; and I can't get rid of it' (To Henry Austin, 12 May 1850. Pilgrim 6. 98–99. 99).

But notwithstanding his cultivation of and insistence on his own status, Dickens successfully deploys the offer of reciprocity in drawing in readers, using paratexts, letters and speeches to depict himself as being likewise an adult reader. If he too is a reader, this in itself implies a writer or series of writers, and it is important to remember that Dickens was reading and responding to letters from readers, discussing their experience of his work to date, during the actual construction of the novels. During the writing of *The Old Curiosity Shop* he told Chapman and Hall that, 'I am inundated with imploring letters recommending poor little Nell to mercy. – Six yesterday, and four today (it's not 12 o'Clock yet) already!' (24 November 1840. Pilgrim 2. 153). The ms letters further the relationship with individual readers, by offering a tangible 'proof' of their involvement – where Dickens responds in writing to readers' suggestions for the plot, they must be reminded by definition that the story has not yet been 'finalised' as print – there is still time to save Paul Dombey or Little Em'ly. This correspondence suggests a level of collaboration in the writing of fiction (this becomes literally true in certain cases, for instance the dramatic volte face in the presentation of Miss Mowcher in response to complaints from the original of this character and again in the alteration to the ending of *Great Expectations* at the instigation of Bulwer Lytton).

In addition to corresponding with individuals, Dickens duly signals his sense of this reciprocal relationship with readers in general, through incorporating their imagined responses into his printed texts. In its most extreme form, this reciprocity can even suggest that Dickens himself is in some sense a conduit for readers' own imaginations, as in his famous claim in the preface to *Pictures from Italy* that 'This book is a series of faint reflections – mere shadows in the water – of places to which the imaginations of most people are attracted in a greater or lesser degree, on which mine had dwelt for years, and which have some interest for all' (5–6). Meanwhile prefaces to later editions of *Oliver Twist, Nicholas Nickleby* and *Martin Chuzzlewit* partially 'rewrite' the texts in light of reader response. In his preface to the third edition of *Oliver Twist*, Dickens stakes his claim to artistic expression through a quotation from Fielding, before invoking some positive reader response to the original publication, from 'those who sympathised with me and divined my purpose at the time, and who, perhaps, will not be sorry to have their impressions confirmed under my own hand' (liii). Notably Dickens enlists his unnamed readers as allies but also potential correspondents, as the printed preface becomes a form of personal letter written 'under my own hand' (of course it is actually printed) and dated in letter style, 'Devonshire Terrace, April, 1841' (lvii).

It is clearly important for Dickens to present himself as a reader, as well as a writer, given his focus on reading practices; interestingly he never loses sight of the relative status of himself and his correspondents. In a moment of humility he once wrote to Thomas Carlyle that 'I am always reading you faithfully, and trying to go your way' (To Thomas Carlyle, 13 April 1863. Pilgrim 10. 233), and soliciting work by Edward Bulwer Lytton for *All the Year Round* in 1861 he wrote hyperbolically, 'I can honestly assure you that I have never been so pleased at heart in all my Literary life, as I am in the proud thought of standing side by side with you before this great audience' (To Sir Edward Bulwer Lytton, 23 January 1861. 374).

An early letter to the Rev. G. R. Gleig suggests that Dickens was quite capable of strategically positioning himself as both reader and writer simultaneously, using his knowledge of an author's works in the place of a letter of introduction, 'I venture to address you as an old friend; for your writings – I believe – have had no more constant and admiring acquaintance than myself even among *their* large circle of friends'. (22 October 1838. Pilgrim 1. 443). Writing to Thomas Hood in 1841, he addresses him as 'My dear Hood – for though I have only shaken hands with you once in the body, we have had so many pleasant meetings in the Spirit, that I cannot hold you at arm's length and call you "Sir"' (17 February 1841. Appendix to Pilgrim 7. 824–25. 824).

A rather more effusive letter to Washington Irving in the same year repeats the trope of a friendship that already exists through literary exchange, although in this case the reader persona implies Dickens's better-known function as an author:

> I have been so accustomed to associate you with all my pleasantest and happiest thoughts, and with my leisure hours, that I rush at once into full confidence with you, and fall – as it were naturally, and by the very laws of gravity – into your open arms. Questions come thronging to my pen as to the lips of people who meet after long hoping to do so. I don't know what to say first, or what to leave unsaid, and am constantly disposed to break off and tell you again how glad I am this moment has arrived. (21 April 1841. Pilgrim 2. 267–69. 268)

Stressing the reciprocity of his response to Irving, he places himself and his correspondent on an equal footing, imagining them as 'people who meet after long hoping to do so'. While the 'meeting' is at this stage a purely imaginary one, the literary basis of each writer's idea of the other effects a kind of mutual possession, in which pens substitute for lips, and the writer is tempted to interrupt himself in his pleasure that 'this moment has arrived'. Unlike his own readers, who associate him with their 'pleasantest and happiest thoughts' only through the mediating narrator, Dickens is confident that Irving's arms are 'open' to receive him. In a subsequent letter to Lady Holland, Dickens again insists on the physicality of his writing, when he assumes that 'you would like to hear from my own lips that I am well'. He goes on to explain, in notably less emotional terms than in his letter to Irving, 'You will have smiled, before getting so far, at my using the word "lips"; - but my pen has so long supplied the place of a voice, that the expression comes quite naturally to me' (22 March 1842. Pilgrim 3. 150–52. 150). No wonder then that he posits a barrier to communication in depriving himself of speech while writing, stressing eating rather than having to hold a knife and fork in one letter, when 'I am dining early, before reading, and write literally with my mouth full' (To John Forster, [28 January 1859]. Pilgrim 9. 18).

Dickens claims a similarly visceral experience of the physical act of writing fiction, responding to a curious correspondent in 1856 with the memorable disclaimer, 'In reply to your second question whether I dictate, I answer with a smile that I can as soon imagine a painter dictating his pictures' (To Frau Alberti, 30 April 1856. Pilgrim 8. 104–105. 104). This use of the page as a vehicle for intimacy can even imply the negation of time itself, as when Dickens tells Forster that he will write his thoughts from Italy as if he were able to converse with him, 'You will have lots of hasty notes from me while I am at work: but you know your man; and whatever strikes me, I shall let off upon you as if I were in Devonshire-terrace' (To John Forster, [8 October 1844]. Pilgrim 4. 199–200. 200).

As many of his letters explain, keeping up with his daily correspondence was a daunting task in itself. But through the mass production of fiction Dickens is able to respond to readers collectively, allowing each of them to respond individually to his authorial persona as he or she 'meets' him in his books. The extension of this intimacy to the wider public depends on Dickens's assumption that they too 'know their man', and enter willingly into a reciprocal relationship with him. In return for providing quality reading he insists that in turn they should read the right books.

This model of mutual affection between writer and reader effectively bypasses the role of critics in determining what should be read, but this exchange becomes more complicated in light of Dickens's developing relationship with other writers during the 1850s, notably through his editorship of *Household Words* for most of this decade. As a successful author, Dickens himself was frequently approached by literary aspirants for assessment of their work. He clearly took this often overwhelming responsibility seriously, writing detailed critiques and where necessary warning the correspondents against mistaking their vocation. Typical advice includes, 'If you cannot grace truth in the narration, and have not the faculty of telling it in writing, you should either leave it untold, or leave it to the chance of being told by someone else' (To W. P. Snow, 6 September 1847. Pilgrim 5. 159–60. 160). One aspiring poet was told to, 'think of the vast crowd of young men who can write verse, and of the handful who can write poetry; and rely upon it that the worst you may ever have heard or read of the misery inseparable from a mistaken ambition, in Letters, is nothing to the dread reality' (To Samuel Newton, 1 April 1848. Pilgrim 5. 270–71. 271). Given the frequency of such requests for advice or assistance, he sometimes felt the need to assure correspondents that 'Although your letter is one of hundreds that are constantly addressed to me, and that vary very little in their general purport, I believe I have considered it as if its contents were quite new to me' (To Richard Lee, 1 February 1859. Pilgrim 9. 24).

Encouraging the working class poet John Overs in his dedicated efforts to publish in the intervals of his work as a cabinet maker, Dickens positions himself as a critic and patron. By this stage his own readers are acolytes rather than judges or patrons, as they had been in *Sketches by Boz*. But a writer like Overs was in a very different position; as David Vincent shows, working class writers struggled to find a readership among themselves and:

> The local gentry or, increasingly, the urban middle-class, who took up a poor but promising versifier, exacted a price. ... Constantly reminded of his dependency on those who assisted him, the struggling poet found it impossible to develop a clear sense of either his own identity or that of his audience. Even when his book was published, it would not yield sufficient financial return to emancipate the author from his employment or his patron, and he was left with a future precariously balanced between the uncertainties of the labour market and the whims of prosperous literati who had scant sympathy for any signs of social or ideological deviancy on the part of their humble muses. (Vincent 215)

Dickens himself implies that the disadvantages of class can be overcome by genius, although it is unclear whether he is congratulating himself on his own rise or occluding it, as he had done in distancing himself from the working class Overs. Commenting on the work of a gardener with literary aspirations, he told one intermediary that:

> It seems to me to be no better and no worse than a vast cloud of verse, that is always rising from all sorts of quarters. I see something every day, of the misery and bitterness consequent on mistaken rushings into print. I would on no account encourage a tendency to authorship in this writer. It would be to do him no kindness. He cannot too clearly understand that the difficulties under which he writes, are no reason for his writing; and that the men who have laid down the spade or hammer for the pen, and become famous, have been among the most

24 *Introduction*

> extraordinary men the world has ever produced. (To Mrs M'Ian, 8 July 1850. Pilgrim 6. 127)

The very success that gives Dickens such authority in pronouncing on ms work (notably he feels able to pronounce on the merits of amateur verses although he was not himself a poet), can be seen as a barrier to his commenting on other published writers of a comparable social standing, as he explains in a letter to G. H. Lewes in November 1847, 'I ought to have written to you long ago about Ranthorpe, but I have a most accursed diffidence about writing to men concerning their own books, as if I were setting myself up for a kind of literary special-pleader, and sending out my opinions with grave importance' (7 November 1847. Pilgrim 5. 190–91. 190). Despite this anxiety Dickens continued to comment on published and unpublished work by other writers, according to their status. Something of the tension inherent in this position comes across in a letter written to Douglas Jerrold a year earlier, in which Dickens confides that 'there is no such good way of testing the worth of a literary friendship as by comparing its influence on one's mind, with any that literary animosity can produce' (24 October 1846. Pilgrim 4, 642–45. 642).

From the inception of the weekly *Household Words* in 1850, this critical role was formalised, albeit sometimes delegated to the sub-editor Wills. Dickens's rejection letters were firm but constructive and polite. Privately he could be blunter, telling the long suffering W. H. Wills that one writer's efforts 'are washy in the last degree. There is really nothing whatever in them. ... I would as soon dine off an old glove, as read such pale literary boiled veal' (27 April 1856. Pilgrim 8. 99). As the editor of *All the Year Round* from 1859, he would later explain to the author of *The Autobiography of a Working Man* why he was rejecting her friend's series of letters, 'Why, you suggest more, in the least eventful page of our friend Bill, than this gentleman can in all these words! Compare his letters with the letters of the private soldiers in the Crimea!' (To the Hon. Eleanor Eden, 11 March 1862. 49). Again he was more direct in his dealings with his sub-editor, dismissing one regular contributor's efforts with the comment 'Fitzgerald writes so loosely, that he really seems sometimes to write in his sleep' (To W. H. Wills, 26 August 1866. 237–38. 237).

This authority as writer and critic was sustained in the face of a degree of opposition, when 'the critics discovered that Dickens was popular because he was irrelevant and unserious – a bit of light reading for the light-headed. ... There is a sense in which Dickens's entire professional course after 1850 was his enormous wager against that proposition' (Grass 110). As Bodenheimer argues:

> The Victorian habit of judging writers by comparisons with others also contributed to the negative turn in contemporary reviews of his work. When Thackeray appeared on the scene in 1847, the originality and humor that had amazed Dickens's early readers was set up

against Thackeray's more restrained social worldliness; when George Eliot emerged in the late 1850s, Dickens's treatment of character was measured against her intellectual habits of moral analysis.

(*Knowing Dickens* 3–4)

In *The Warden*, published in 1855, Anthony Trollope pointedly wrote:

> In former times great objects were attained by great work. When evils were to be reformed, reformers set about their heavy task with grave decorum and laborious argument. An age was occupied in proving a grievance, and philosophical researches were printed in folio pages, which it took a life to write, and an eternity to read. We get on now with a lighter step, and quicker: ridicule is found to be more convincing than argument, imaginary agonies touch more than true sorrows, and monthly novels convince, when learned quartos fail to do so. If the world is to be set right, the work will be done by shilling numbers'. (124)

Despite this criticism, Trollope's narrator goes on to admit that if the Dickensian hero and heroine 'walk upon stilts' it is because 'heroes and heroines, I fear, ever must' while 'their attendant satellites are as natural as though one met them in the street'. Significantly they 'will live till the names of their callings shall be forgotten in their own, and Bucket and Mrs Gamp will be the only words left to us to signify a detective police officer or a monthly nurse' (124).

But the attitude against which Dickens was contending resurfaces in the parodic treatment of 'light' literature in Trollope's *The Three Clerks*, first published in 1857. Actually starting at the beginning of a story, one character in discussing a first novel called *Crinoline and Macassar*, is:

> A devilish bore, you know, for a fellow who takes up a novel because he's dull. Of course he wants his fun at once. If you begin with a long history of who's who and all that, why he won't read three pages; but if you touch him up with a startling incident or two at the first go off, then give him a chapter of horrors, then another of fun, then a little love or a little slang, or something of that sort, why, you know, about the end of the first volume, you may describe as much as you like, and tell everything about everybody's father and mother for just as many pages as you want to fill. At least that's what the editor says. (211)

In a final ironic touch, it transpires that the heroine of the story has her dresses made 'at the distinguished establishment of Madame Manalini, in Hanover Square' (246), while on the safe delivery of his child 'Macassar in his joy got hold of Mrs Gamp, and kissed her heartily, forgetful of the fumes of gin' (267). Such meta-fictional allusions suggest that the critical reception of Dickens's mid-career novels is at odds with the assumptions made by younger writers as well as being sometimes misaligned with the response of the reading public. Nonetheless the second half of his career is increasingly preoccupied with the contingent status of writing and the possible interpretations and misinterpretations of readers. The increasingly complicated investment in the authority of writers and the instability of reader response will be a guiding feature of the second half of this study.

This introduction has argued that Dickens sets out the terms of his relationship with readers within the written text, while his actual readers are fictionalised in their turn, not least through letters commenting on his interactions with members of the public. Notably Dickens himself superintends the imaginative act, most visibly where his characters are presented as infiltrating the actual lives of readers, allowing the figure of the author to break down boundaries between different types of writing as cultural exchange.

Chapter one further considers the accessibility of the writer in his imagined conversation with readers and what it means to be specifically a reader of Dickens. It is centrally concerned with his sense of himself as a 'serious' as well as a comic writer and how this self-representation is aligned with his growing authority within the written text. Chapter two focuses on biographical and autobiographical representations as a means of further mythologising the figure of the writer, while chapter three destabilises the proffered intimacy of the author / reader relationship through a comparison of the editorial voice deployed in *Household Words* and *All the Year Round* with the strategic modes of address adopted by unreliable first person narrators in fiction of the 1850s and '60s. Chapter four charts Dickens's growing mistrust of the written word, which is increasingly presented as inauthentic or manipulative. Finally chapter five explores the ways in which Dickens himself became the fictionalised subject of literary biography.

1 Reciprocal Readers and the 1830s–40s

Perhaps surprisingly the impact of Dickens's writing on the sense of personal relationship felt by many readers is not dependent on the possibility of his presence. The afterlife of the Dickensian text is deeply felt in later books such as Robert Allbut's *Rambles in Dickens Land*, first published in 1886 and updated in 1899, in which he moves the novelist's imagined scenes into the material world through the responsive mind of the reader, 'It is one of the magic legacies left by the great romancers, that the scenes and characters which they described should possess for most of us an air of reality, so convincing as sometimes to put staid history to the blush. The *novelist's ideals become actual to the popular mind*' (ix introduction. Emphasis added), in a formulation according to which readers themselves assume the novelistic faculty, 'He that found out this rare world has made it fully ours. Let us visit our inheritance, or revisit it, if that be the better word. Let us make real the scenes we have read of and dreamt of – peopling them with the folk of Dickens, so that familiar faces shall look upon us from familiar windows, familiar voices greet us as we pass' (xxi–xxii introduction).

Readers might be expected to respond to the literary text in different ways, as Gissing implies in his study of Dickens written nearly 30 years after his death, making the rather odd assumption that 'on the whole it was for men that Dickens wrote. To-day the women must be very few who by deliberate choice open a volume of his works' (*Charles Dickens: A Critical Study* 111). Price has shown that men were expected to read more actively, while women were encouraged to copy out extracts in commonplace books, precisely to combat a tendency to passive 'skimming' ('Victorian Reading' 38). But Dickens's writing makes it very clear that both male and female readers are expected to participate in actively finding meaning in the scenes he relates and adapting his precepts to their everyday lives. Notably he was delighted that in his public readings the response of his auditors was to express personal affection for him as a writer, but also to share in creating the theatrical effect, 'The audience do everything but embrace me, and take as much pains with the readings as I do' (To John Forster, [?18 December 1868]. Pilgrim 12. 250–51. 251). Nonetheless this pains taking is directed and affirmed by the author himself.

His trademark style depends for its effect on the creation of a 'limited intimacy' with the reader, and this dynamic is effected through the assumption of mutual regard and even shared experience of particular scenes, whether these are read internally or shared through the practice of reading aloud (as Dickens himself ultimately shared his own writing with a live audience). While there is no sure means of enabling the 'correct' reading, Dickens himself encouraged his readers to adopt his characters as tokens of cultural exchange beyond the parameters of the text, and Rachel Ablow confirms that 'nearly all of Dickens's eulogists, in one form or another, traced readers' attachment to the writer to the nature of his characters' (*The Marriage of Minds* 17).

But for such early readers in particular, Dickens was initially associated with humour rather than serious moral purpose or emotion, and the early work therefore marked him as a popular entertainer rather than a moral guide. Leigh Hunt admitted as much in his praise of *Nicholas Nickleby* in 1838:

> You have made me laugh heartily in the midst of trouble, & shed painful yet hopeful tears. Your genius for the serious, & even the terrible, as well as the lively, surprised me, for I had known you hitherto only through the medium of extracts in other works, and one solitary number of Nickleby. (From Leigh Hunt to CD, July [1838]. Pilgrim 1. 685–86. 686)

Critical commentary, as well as the quality of the writing itself, was key to changing this perception; stressing the importance of Forster's championship, Douglas-Fairhurst argues that Dickens attained a more secure role through the mediation of a credible authority beyond his own:

> Of particular relevance to Dickens was Forster's stress on the idea that good writing and popular writing should not be thought of as mutually exclusive categories. ... It took a writer like Dickens to prove that the same novel could please servants and cabmen as well as readers of *Paradise Lost*, but it took a tireless campaigner like Forster to persuade them that reading about Oliver Twist or Little Nell might be more than a guilty private pleasure'. (234)

Intervention by possibly partisan reviewers was a familiar dimension of Victorian literary culture, and as late as the 1850s Thackeray's fictional author Pendennis found it necessary to proffer an explicit denial that writers were bound by patronage in the same way as practitioners of medicine and the law, claiming independence if not financial reward for authors, 'The prizes are great, to be sure, in the law, but what a prodigious sum the lottery ticket costs! If a man of letters cannot win, neither does he risk so much. Let us speak of our trade as we find it, and not be too eager in calling out for public compassion' (938). Even artists, claims Pendennis, are more hampered than writers in having to put up with the condescension of ignorant amateurs,

'And, seeing how severely these gentlemen were taxed in their profession, I have been grateful for my own more fortunate one, which necessitates cringing to no patron; which calls for no keeping up of appearances; and which requires no stock-in-trade save the workman's industry; his best ability; and a dozen sheets of paper' (938).

At just this time Dickens was answering numerous letters from literary aspirants seeking his support or intercession with publishers, which he explained to them in almost every case would be both impractical and wholly ineffectual. In this model proposed by writers at the start of their careers, publishers and editors rather than readers are seen by the uninitiated as potential patrons, and a more successful writer becomes a chosen intermediary rather than necessarily a professional hero. While Dickens may have resented this attitude, he makes it clear in his responses that he himself does not want to be accorded the role of literary patron. While he was often sent volumes dedicated to him, and responded favourably to a number of requests from writers asking if they could so dedicate particular work, he refused on at least one occasion, telling his correspondent that 'I do not appreciate such proposals the less, because I often decline them' (To unknown correspondent, 27 January 1864. Pilgrim 10. 350).

As Dickens was always aware, his own status as a writer was contingent on both his place in the literary hierarchy and in the literal sense on being read (and therefore financially sustainable) at all. His own novels are carefully directed through the marketing of different editions, but in each case Sambudha Sen argues that 'the Dickensian novel was addressed to a respectable, predominantly middle-class audience, and it achieved its political effects gradually and indirectly in some corner of the mind of the reader who read Dickens in her leisure time for pleasure rather than for political education' (9). This perception can be set against Forster's insistence that Dickens's preoccupation with ordinary life was the source of his appeal to all classes:

> Thousands were attracted to him, because he placed them in the midst of scenes and characters with which they were already themselves acquainted; and thousands were reading him with no less avidity because he introduced them to passages of nature and life of which they before knew nothing. ... Only to genius are so revealed the affinities and sympathies of high and low, in regard to the customs and usages of life; and only a writer of the first rank can bear the application of such a test. ... It would equally startle both high and low to be conscious of the whole that is implied in this close approximation; but for the common enjoyment of which I speak such consciousness is not required. (vol 1. 83)

The readers' engagement with this intimate communication of imaginary events is intensified by the inclusion of prefaces, either written with the volume publication of a serial in mind, or revised to accompany a new edition.

Typically these prefaces tell readers what Dickens felt in writing the work and by extension what they ought to feel in reading it. Readers are asked to enter relations with the author in which, in Ian Duncan's words, they become 'friends, host and guest, fellow-travellers' (195). In the process they create an imaginative loop, in which the reader's first encounter with the volume edition is a reminder of authorial monitoring – as the reader starts on the text, it is with the reminder that Dickens is already waiting at the end. Precisely this way of reading is endorsed by the current practice of suggesting that readers turn to the critical introduction after reading the novel itself. On occasion Dickens will literally position his readers in particular attitudes, reading by their own firesides at Christmas, to cite the most recognisable instance.

Despite his disclaimers, Dickens's books are designed to induce readers to imagine characters' experiences for themselves with the guidance of the narrator, based on the moral values he has instilled. Most blatantly, the 'reader's passport' included in *American Notes* both incorporates a range of readers and insists that they are all essentially the same, using a form designed to identify individuals and self-consciously eliding all such distinguishing features (even down to gender):

> I have only now, in passport wise, to sketch my reader's portrait, which I hope may thus be thus suppositiously traced for either sex:
>
> | | |
> |---|---|
> | Complexion | Fair. |
> | Eyes | Very cheerful. |
> | Nose | Not supercilious. |
> | Mouth | Smiling. |
> | Visage | Beaming. |
> | General Expression | Extremely agreeable (7). |

But the status of reading for either sex is both contested and contingent in Victorian culture, as 'The question of what exactly counted as "reading" made visible tensions between a rhetoric of moral, economic, or intellectual self-improvement and a reality in which literacy was put to more mundane uses' (Price. 'Victorian Reading' 41). Most obviously, letters stand somewhere between the high status literary text and the account books or bills that presumably constituted a high percentage of domestic reading. Another sensitive reader, Guy Morville in Charlotte Yonge's *The Heir of Redclyffe* (1853), finds that his imagination is stimulated by the sight of letter paper itself during his enforced separation from Amy, 'As long as Charles wrote, he fancied her sitting by, perhaps sealing the letter, and he could even tell by the kind of paper and envelope, whether they were sitting in the dressing-room or down-stairs' (274).

For Dickens himself readers' participation in the shared imaginary his books create crucially enables new relations beyond the fictional text, including those conducted through letter writing. In an extreme example, in one letter Dickens declares love for a woman he has never met, on the basis of their shared response to *David Copperfield*, 'For the earnestness of your feeling towards me, I can never feel sufficiently proud or sufficiently grateful; and for the love you bear to my favorite book (for your sympathy has truly divined that it *is* my favorite), I must love *you* – if I may – in return' (To [Frau Alberti], 31 January 1856. Pilgrim 8. 40–41. 40). In his declaration of affection for this sympathetic stranger, Dickens implicitly conflates book and author; more importantly, Frau Alberti has no way of knowing that he is the character as well as the story, David as well as *David Copperfield*.

This process of creating and educating readers takes place not only in the pages of Dickens's novels, but also in his personal correspondence – it is surely no coincidence that he advised another writer in 1866, 'Suppose yourself telling that affecting incident in a letter to a friend' (To Mrs Brookfield, 20 February 1866. Pilgrim 11. 160–61. 161). Occasionally even the earlier letters reveal Dickens constructing a relationship with his reading public, readers who are not privy to this private correspondence. Writing to Thomas Mitton shortly after the publication of *A Christmas Carol* in 1843, he told him, 'I am extremely glad you *feel* the Carol. For I knew I meant a good thing. And when I see the effect of such a little *whole* as that, on those for whom I care, I have a strong sense of the immense effect I could produce with an entire book. I am quite certain of that' (To Thomas Mitton, [6 December 1843]. Pilgrim 3. 605–606). Dickens does not specify on whom this 'immense effect' will be produced, but the obvious inference is that he means the wider public rather than simply his intimate friends. The positioning of 'those for whom I care' in a subordinate clause suggests at one level that these readers may themselves be exceptional in their response to the book (Dickens is pleased by the effect on them in particular); read another way, the commas emphasise the possible redundancy of this test case audience, serving much the same function as brackets between 'when I see the effect of such a little *whole* as that' and 'I have a strong sense of the immense effect I could produce'. By the end of the sentence, in other words, the public who will avidly read *A Christmas Carol* have themselves become 'those for whom I care'.

Elsewhere Dickens shows an awareness of his dual role as an educator of readers and also a strategist. He claimed in a preface to the third edition of *Oliver Twist* in 1841, that he had no faith in over-delicate readers, and that '… I will not, for these readers, abate one hole in the Dodger's coat, or one scrap of curl-paper in the girl's dishevelled hair. I have no faith in the delicacy which cannot bear to look upon them' (lv). But his anxiety to avoid offence is nowhere better summed up than in a much-quoted letter of 1857, in which he complains to an imagined censor:

> O my smooth friend, what a shining impostor you must think yourself and what an ass you must think me, when you suppose that by putting a brazen face upon it you can blot out of my knowledge the fact that

this same unnatural young gentleman (if to be decent is to be necessarily unnatural), whom you meet in those other books and in mine, *must be* presented to you in that unnatural aspect by reason of your morality. ... (To John Forster, [15 August 1856]. Pilgrim 8. 178–79. 178)

In essence Dickens is imaginatively siphoning off a particular reader and explaining what he would write if he felt able to defy the cultural censorship impeding his work. Indeed a number of his letters discuss conversations with critics and friends about the course of particular novels. Tellingly he was wary of over-exposure, arguing in a letter of 1843 that by physically removing to Normandy or Brittany and writing nothing for a year, he could 'strengthen my position with my readers, instead of weakening it, drop by drop, as I otherwise must' (to John Forster [1 November 1843]. Pilgrim 3. 587–88. 588).

Even in this context letters, to which no threat of over-exposure was attached, could provide a means of imaginative communication with readers. Ultimately the persistent association of power with the written word assumes a transference of the author's imagination, or even presence, to the mind of the reader, and significantly, a number of Dickens's letters in the Pilgrim collection draw attention to the physical act of writing: he jokes that he has his hands in water as he writes; complains that those bound to the pen are likely to endure suffering, and he has been using a quill all day; writing can take the place of speaking, while thoughts come ready made to the point of the pen. This habit is a hallmark of his early correspondence and continues up until the time of his death – in one thank you letter, he tells the donor of a box of cigars that 'I will inaugurate the first chapter of the next book (whenever it comes into life; it is in the land of shadows now, unknown to me, and waiting to be born) by fumigating it in MS with a Cigar reserved from this very box' (To Captain E. E. Morgan, 24 September 1857. Pilgrim 8. 453), while in 1868 he wrote to his American publisher J. T. Fields on his voyage back to England that 'you may find this legible, but I rather doubt it; for there is motion enough on the ship to render writing – to a landsman, however accustomed to pen and ink – rather a difficult achievement. Besides which, I slide away gracefully from the paper, whenever I want to be particularly expressive' ([26] and 30 April 1868. Pilgrim 12. 98–100. 100).

Dickens clearly realised the effectiveness of this essentially literary strategy from an early stage of his career, telling two different correspondents in 1837 and 1838 that 'I have just looked at the date of this letter. If blushes could be forwarded by the General Post this sheet of paper would be rose-coloured when it reached you' (To the Rev. E. S. Dixon, 2 December 1837. Pilgrim 12. Appendix A 559) and 'If I could send a blush by the general post this sheet of paper would be rose-coloured by the time it reaches you' (To Edward Wood, 12 December 1838. 562–63. Pilgrim 12. Appendix A 562).

If this collapsing of the distance between writer and posted letter allows the imaginative substitution of one for the other, there is a similar inflection in the novels, which remind the reader of a narrator physically taking up a pen to write or reluctantly dismissing himself from the scenes he has described. The early journalism develops the apparently spontaneous but contrived voice of Boz in 'conversation' with readers, and in setting up this relationship the periodical pieces both enable and anticipate strategies that later became crucial to the mythologising of author / reader relations in the novels.

'My Hand Shakes to Such an Extent': *Sketches by Boz* and the Early Journalism

The voice of Boz works with Dickens's own literary persona to elide the gap in the midst of story, lived experience and public debate, and it does this through the crafting of literary address. Notably the Boz narrator develops relations with the reader but also suggests the limits of this relationship. Despite the focus on the presence of the writing narrator and for all their inclusive construction of an assumed readership, and joyous satire of figures outside it, the *Sketches* display a less private and intimate response to readers than Dickens's later work tried to convey. Notably the journalistic narrator brings the reader towards the site of the imagined or recorded action, rather than taking characters in to the scene of 'the domestic hearth', as Dickens the novelist would be famous for doing. Reading the sketches in their collected form highlights Dickens's developing sense of a relationship with readers, as the first-person narrator takes on the role of confidential gossip, tour guide, and social commentator. The Boz persona developed in these early sketches and is self-consciously associated with the London streets, later identified by Dickens himself as a key source of his imaginative power.

Writers of a later generation would often focus on the impact of Dickens's writing on their own imaginative lives or on the imaginative act as transference, that itself led to social change. In his memoir of working with Dickens as a contributor to *Household Words* and *All the Year Round*, G. A. Sala cites Dickens's fiction as an influence on topical journalism, which in turn he presents as a lever for effecting social reform. According to Sala, the nefarious Yorkshire schools were 'knocked on the head' as the imagined world of Dotheboys moved across the pages of the novel and into the realm of non-fiction, 'His novels acted upon journalism; journalism reacted upon public opinion; public opinion became at last a pressure; and that pressure was ultimately adequate to change or to abrogate old laws or to enact new ones' (42).

Again prefiguring the novels, Dickens's early journalism seeks to create a readership and then manage those readers through apparently individualised direct address. One of his key techniques for doing this is the dissolution of boundaries between readers themselves and between modes of narrative address. John Drew describes the importance of paratextual conditioning to

Dickens's relationship with his target audience in terms of startlingly modern technique:

> the central emphases we may detect in Dickens's paratextual guidance, on immediacy of address, rapidity and extensiveness of circulation, on fluidity of form, on accessibility to the widest range of readers both socially and geographically, justifies (with minimum reliance on poetic licence) the borrowing of the exclusively modern term 'e-text' to indicate certain properties of his periodical writings that lent them a surprising currency and adaptability. (67)

Reader engagement is key to Dickens's ideal of reciprocal imaginative encounters, but the challenge for the writer is informing readers that imagination is the password to this new literary club, a dilemma that is resolved by inviting them to see themselves moving through the text. Of the surviving letters collected in the first volume of the Pilgrim edition, a number of the earliest relate to writing or the imagination.

With the publication of Dickens's first sketch comes a renewed awareness that writing and reading are mutually dependent activities – specifically he must write *well* in order to be read at all. Ten years before writing to Mitton about *A Christmas Carol*, Dickens's frame of reference can already be seen slipping between private and public as he shares his excitement at the appearance of his first sketch. Writing to his friend Henry Kolle in December 1833, to tell him that 'A dinner at Poplar Walk' was in the current issue of the *Monthly Magazine*, he tells him in a ps that 'I am so dreadfully nervous, that my hand shakes to such an extent as to prevent my writing a word legibly' ([3 December 1833]. 32). In this instance of course Dickens refers to his handwriting being supposedly illegible to a single, known reader. Nonetheless his difficulty in 'writing a word' stands as a reminder that the printed text of 'A dinner at Poplar Walk' is based on the same controlling intelligence. The writer of the letter is now an author.

As the authority of the writer increases, the role of the reader subtly alters. *Sketches by Boz* initiates the possibly parodic appeal to readers' patronage in the preface to the first edition of the first series. Likening his first edition of collected sketches to a 'pilot balloon', he invokes both his own aspirations and his publisher's requirement that the book make a reasonable profit, 'devoutly and earnestly hoping it may *go off well* – a sentiment in which his Publisher cordially concurs', to persuade readers to vindicate his having made 'so perilous a voyage in so frail a machine'. This assumption of reckless adventuring is carefully set off against the known quantity of his illustrator Cruikshank, whose readiness to join the enterprise – 'The application was readily heard, and at once acceded to' – coupled with Boz's own success in periodical publication, suggests that despite the author's protestations, no 'further excuse be wanted for adding this book to the hundreds which every season produces' (*Sketches by Boz and Other Early Papers* unpaginated). In this appeal to readers, Dickens overtly positions himself as an applicant for the readers' consideration, whose function (beyond the obvious one of buying the volume) is not clear in the preface itself.

In his preface to the second edition, however, Boz starts creating a sense of relationship, in which both he and his readers are mindful of the immediate success of his work, 'He has only in one single sentence to acknowledge, with feelings of the deepest gratitude, the kindness and indulgence with which these volumes have been universally received, and the unlooked-for success with which his efforts have been crowned' (xl). Fourteen years later this rung on the ladder could be safely kicked away, and in the preface to the first cheap edition in 1850, a more assured and authoritative Dickens invokes an image of himself as a young author in the mould of Copperfield (the hero of his eponymous novel published in volume form in the same year), 'The whole of these Sketches were written and published, one by one, when I was a very young man. They were collected and re-published while I was still a very young man' (xli).

As Slater perceptively argues, this Cheap Edition was appearing in weekly facsimiles and monthly parts at the same time as the last numbers of *David Copperfield* and 'His primary concern, apparently, was to soften down what might now seem crude and unworthy of the author of *Copperfield* in the language of his first book, and to update some of the social comment' (*Charles Dickens* 313). The deprecating tone of Dickens's own retrospective appraisal of course also allows him to remind readers (not once but twice) of just how young he was when he first found literary fame. Nonetheless he clearly had ambivalent feelings about this early work, writing to an anthologist in 1866 that 'I would rather not have Mr Sparkins or any of his immediate family quoted, because they are juvenile and hasty productions' (To Antonin Roche, 8 October 1866. 254).

Despite their careful revision for volume publication, the collected sketches do retain a number of self-deprecating allusions to Boz's dependence on sustaining his readers' interest, which had been a feature of their initial publication in *The Monthly Magazine, The Morning Chronicle, The Evening Chronicle* and *Bell's Life* between 1833 and 1836. Even at the time Boz impressed readers with his ability to capture contemporary London. But Jeremy Tambling argues that memory of the past is also a significant feature of this early work, in that *Sketches by Boz* has a sense of achievement in evoking what has disappeared, as though Dickensian London was gone before it started in Dickens' (38)

If the streets are in a constant state of flux, the *Sketches* also reveal the elusive nature of the narrative voice itself. Robert Douglas-Fairhurst sees this voice as both connective and protean:

> What reconciles London's two-faced potential for sociability and loneliness in Dickens's early sketches is his narrator. In many ways Boz is easy to mistake for Dickens himself, from his pinhole-sharp vision to his unpredictable sharp turns between humor and pathos; but as he developed in the years 1834–1836, Boz started to take on

the independent life of a fictional creation. In fact, he became as hard to pin down as London itself, less a human being than the city's conscience given legs and a voice (*Becoming Dickens*, 153)

Importantly, as Douglas-Fairhurst notes, the narrator is a companion for both reader and character, as 'his writing repeatedly zooms in on isolated individuals and keeps them company on the page' (153).

In one sense the stance of this companionable narrator is staunchly anti-individualist, notwithstanding the assertion of his own unique personality. Determined as he was to promote imagination as the province of both writer and reader, it is hardly surprising to find Dickens deriding the mythos of the Romantic personality. The satirical attacks on literary pretension find their most frequent target in what he saw as the solipsism of Romantic literature, culminating in the devastating portrait of Leigh Hunt as the posturing Skimpole in Dickens's mid-career novel *Bleak House*. Critiquing Skimpole as a product of his false education, Jarndyce himself is forced to admit that 'he is all sentiment, and – and susceptibility, and – and imagination. And these qualities are not regulated in him, somehow. I suppose the people who admired him for them in his youth, attached too much importance to them, and too little to any training that would have balanced and adjusted them, and so he became what he is' (619–20).

At the start of the writer's career, *Sketches by Boz* defines Dickens's urban narrator against Byron in particular. The pretensions of the eponymous Horatio Sparkins (who is specifically compared to Byron) are met with good humoured rebuttal by his auditors – '"He talks very loud and nicely," timidly observed Tom, "but I don't exactly understand what he means"' – before he finally turns out to be a shop assistant; a character in 'The Boarding House' wears 'a black ribbon round his neck instead of a neckerchief' and insists on dragging quotations from *Don Juan* in to his conversation (276), while 'The Tuggses at Ramsgate' features a young man whose Romantic leanings are closely linked to the class pretensions of his family. Seizing the opportunity of the parents' inheriting a small fortune, he promptly changes his name from Simon to Cymon, but even before this transformation:

> There was that elongation in his thoughtful face, and that tendency to weakness in his interesting legs, which tell so forcibly of a great mind and romantic disposition. The slightest traits of character in such a being, possess no mean interest to speculative minds. He usually appeared in public, in capacious shoes with black cotton stockings; and was observed to be particularly attached to a black glazed stock, without a tie or ornament of any description. (327)

The reader of these sketches by contrast is aligned with a group identity, being invited to stand next to Boz himself, the better to enjoy this individualistic posturing.

A number of the *Sketches* are meta-textual, allowing the narrator to play with ideas of time and limited intimacy. At one point he jokes, 'We pause for a reply; – and, having no chance of getting one, begin a fresh paragraph' ('Hackney Coach Stands,' 85). Daniel Hack has identified this conflation of text and the material world as characteristic of Dickens's style, arguing that 'No Victorian writer devotes more attention to the physicality of material writing and signs than does Charles Dickens' as 'again and again his novels explore the potential significance of writing's physical materiality' (37). The constant references to picking up the pen as a thought occurs, or the space to be allowed for the article as it is being written, both give the narrator a sense of immediacy and unexpectedly distance him from readers – the pen is not visible in the manuscript, which has itself been typeset sometime after the moment of recorded 'thought'.

But through the bird's eye view enjoyed by Boz, the narrator is able to begin to construct a relationship with readers who are themselves positioned within a class and moral hierarchy, through what Forster later called an 'unusually truthful observation of a sort of life between the middle class and the low, which, having few attractions for bookish observers, was quite unhackneyed ground' (vol 1. 61). Chittick notes that the figures who populate the early *Sketches by Boz* are slightly higher up the social scale than Dickens himself (45–46). In the later vignettes however, the characters are predominantly shabby genteel or lower middle class, with the reader (and so implicitly, the narrator himself) being grouped somewhere vaguely above them. While this strategy accords increased authority to both Boz and the reader as constructed here, Sen suggests that nonetheless 'Dickens's attempt discursively to separate himself and his readers from his low-life characters is always in danger of becoming undermined by the central activity of the book: walking' (91).

As class differences are threatened or elided through this positioning, the narrator reveals and gently mocks social aspiration in characters such as Cymon né Simon in 'The Tuggses at Ramsgate', who abhor 'anything "low"'. At the same time he overtly appeals to just such a middle-class readership on behalf of the urban poor. This assumed readership is constructed as potentially overly fastidious and in need of reminding of social responsibilities towards a working class that in all likelihood at least some of them had just left or were in danger of joining. Arguably the narrator asserts authority over the reader by a subtle reminder of his having penetrated this particular foible. In 'Gin Shops' the readers are taken to task for their putative reaction to a description that has in fact never been given:

> We have sketched this subject very slightly, not only because our limits compel us to do so, but because, if were pursued farther, it would be painful and repulsive. Well disposed gentlemen, and charitable ladies, would alike turn with coldness and disgust from a description of the drunken besotted men, and wretched broken down miserable women,

who form no inconsiderable portion of the frequenters of these haunts; forgetting, in the pleasant consciousness of their own rectitude, the poverty of the one, and the temptation of the other'. (184–85)

The ideal reader is willing to accompany Dickens and observe with him. In 'London Recreations' (1835) the controlling voice proffers the invitation, 'let us beg our readers to imagine themselves stationed by our side in some well known rural "Tea gardens"'(97), while in 'A Parliamentary Sketch' the reader is inched into the sketch itself by slow degrees as the narrator confides, 'You see this ferocious-looking gentleman' … 'we have contrived to make our way to the Lobby, and you can just manage to catch an occasional glimpse of the House …' (154), before assuming, 'You are curious to know who that young man in the rough greatcoat is, who has accosted every Member who has entered the House since we have been standing here' (155). More disturbingly, 'A Visit to Newgate' threatens to collapse the boundary between material and textual as it comments, '… if we noticed every gate that was unlocked for us to pass through, and locked again as we had passed, we should require a gate at every comma …' (201).

The narrator of the pieces collected in the Dent edition as *The Amusements of the People and Other Papers: Reports, Essays and Reviews 1834–1851* becomes increasingly conscious of creating and addressing a known audience. The form of address varies according to the context as the narrator declaims in 'Pet Prisoners', 'we put it to our readers' and 'We submit to our readers' or makes way for a half apologetic first-person narrator in 'The Ghost of Art', who nonetheless assumes a shared knowledge of literary conventions as a sufficient form of introduction:

> I am a bachelor… I need scarcely add, perhaps, that I am in love, and that the father of my charming Julia objects to our union. … I mention these little particulars as I might deliver a letter of introduction. The reader is now acquainted with me, and perhaps will condescend to listen to my narrative. (259)

In fact even this apparently diffident narrator is subtly guiding readers to the knowledge they may conceivably not possess through their previous reading, in this case that romance narratives depend for their effect on the formulaic plot of Julia and her forbidding father.

Dickens's astute appraisal of the market is incorporated into his reviewing; at his most inclusive he enables readers to notice for themselves the populist mode that he is recommending to other writers. A review by Dickens of Robert Hunt's *The Poetry of Science, or Studies of the Physical Phemonena of Nature* significantly notes that the author 'by rendering the general subject popular, and awakening an interest and spirit of inquiry in many minds, where these had previously lain dormant, has created a reading public' (131).

The inaugural *Household Words* manifesto published in March 1850 reminds readers that they are a supposedly unified audience. 'A Detective Police Party' (1) is reminiscent of de Quincey's invitation to the reader of *Confessions of an English Opium Eater* (1821) to imagine a room for themselves, in its use of what a later generation would call 'interactive' strategies:

> Paint me, then, a room seventeen feet by twelve, and not more than seven and a half feet high. This, reader, is somewhat ambitiously styled, in my family, the drawing room: but, being contrived "a double debt to pay", it is also, and more justly, termed the library; for it happens that books are the only article of property in which I am richer than my neighbours. (261)

By this stage of Dickens's journalistic career, roles have shifted and the reader is no longer a patron but a privileged observer 'behind the scenes':

> The reader will have the goodness to imagine the Sanctum Sanctorum of Household Words. Anything that best suits the reader's fancy, will best represent that magnificent chamber. We merely stipulate for a round table in the middle, with some glasses and cigars arranged upon it; and the editorial sofa elegantly hemmed in between that stately piece of furniture and the wall'. (267)

Notably readers are allowed to visualise the room as 'best suits their fancy', becoming actively involved in the creation of the imagined (albeit in this case, real) environment of the *Household Words* office. This imaginative capacity in readers is invoked in a different context in a letter of 1863, where Dickens mediates between Macready and Forster after an estrangement of some duration; telling Macready that Forster is keen to apologise, he configures the speakers as literary characters and reader respectively, 'If you will fill this up, in your mind, with a picture of the dining room in Montagu Square, and he and I sitting opposite each other at the table, you will have a perfect knowledge of the circumstances' (To W. C. Macready, 7 September 1863. Pilgrim 10. 285). In addressing the readers of a journal and mediating between friends, Dickens draws on precisely the same literary technique, urging his readers to imagine freely for themselves. In both cases however he has himself already decided what they will see.

'Ready Made to the Point of the Pen': *Oliver Twist*

The subtext of author / reader relations is made visible in the central scenes of *Oliver Twist*, a novel that itself incorporates Dickens's growing sense of himself as a successful author negotiating a particular professional status, while trammelled by the unfavourable terms of his publishing contract; in the novel he asserts his narrative authority through the familiar right of criticism, in the play on relative status among different figures including writers, book sellers, beadles and readers. In a letter to G. H. Lewes Dickens can be seen both disavowing and intensifying the myth of his own imaginative power, accounting for characters and incidents as apparently outside the creative mind of the individual. In answer to a question, presumably about how he had come up with a particular idea, he claimed that 'It came like all my other ideas, such as they are, ready made to the point of the pen – and down it went' ([?9 June 1838] 402–403. 403). Arguably the novel itself is as much about reading as it is about the more obvious themes of poverty and criminality. As Patrick Brantlinger observes:

> books and reading are a central feature of the story, as is more obviously the question of Oliver's education. Will his ultimate teachers be Brownlow and the Maylies, or Fagin and Sikes? It is while Brownlow examines a bookseller's wares that the Dodger and Charlie Bates pick his pocket. It is while returning books to that same bookseller that Oliver is recaptured by the thieves, who make great fun of his apparent bookishness. (70)

This meta-textual focus raises questions about what kind of fiction we are being asked to read, especially given the origin of the book as a series of papers in *Bentley's Miscellany*, an ephemeral journal. A subtly different dynamic is set up for the reader who can hold the book and see that there will be an ending. This assurance is important if 'We do not read *Oliver Twist* as a detective story, with the simple aim of finding out what happens at the end: we read it to the end to verify our guesses and to have the satisfaction of seeing in black and white that what, from time immemorial, was intended to happen has come to pass in actual fact' (Sadrin 34).

Oliver's apparently passive acceptance of events and circumstances is ruptured only at points where he is called on to condone or enact disloyal or immoral behaviour (one of his few outbreaks occurs when Noah Claypole insults his dead mother, and this provides the catalyst for his decision to abscond to London). Sadrin is at least partially justified in claiming that 'A fairy-tale hero never interferes with his fate. He does not choose, he waits. He does not act, he endures. Oliver is such a hero. ... Major decisions concerning his lot are even taken when he is not there' (35).

The reader however must expect to play a more active role in *Oliver Twist* than does the eponymous hero. Importantly this role includes empathy with uneducated working class figures, albeit mediated through the innocuous responses of the somewhat nebulous Oliver to an apparently grotesque world of adult villainy (it is easily forgotten that Oliver himself is unable to determine the ages of the criminal children such as Charley Bates and the Dodger). As Sen points out with reference to Dickens's wider fiction, 'Dickens self-consciously defamiliarized the language of power, representing it not as it really was but as it appeared to those excluded from its processes' (26).

In the text the writer is constructed as a biographer whose task it is to record actual events, a myth that depends on the collusion of a 'knowing' reader, who is half-jokingly encouraged to accept this role. Despite his insistence to readers that Oliver was intended to represent 'the principle of Good surviving through every adverse circumstance, and triumphing at last' (Author's Preface to the third edition liii), the letters in which he figures are far more redolent of middle-class concerns about the veracity and general trustworthiness of the urban poor. A letter written while he was writing the early scenes suggests that Dickens had initially planned a more detached role for the narrator, jokingly asking Bentley 'Have you seen Oliver Twist yet? I have taken a great fancy to him – hope he deserves it' [?20 January 1837. Pilgrim 1. 225]. As late as 1843 he was writing to Angela Burdett Coutts about a Ragged School in Saffron Hill, and telling her, 'I blush to quote Oliver Twist for an authority, but it stands on that ground, and it precisely such a place as the Jew lived in' (16 September 1843. Pilgrim 3. 562–64. 562). What both letters also suggest is a residual diffidence about the status of the writing itself, in terms of its 'authority' and how far it 'deserves' to be popular with readers.

Crucially, Dickens's developing aesthetic literary endeavour must be informed by moral intent if it is to succeed as authentic art. This status is often signalled, particularly in the early work such as *Oliver Twist*, through contrast with false claims to a literary vocation made by various characters. In a parodic scene near the beginning of the story, the beadle Mr Bumble confides, to the admiration of Mrs Mann (who is presumably illiterate), that he names the workhouse children in alphabetical order:

> 'Why, you're quite a literary character, sir!' said Mrs Mann.
> 'Well, well,' said the beadle, evidently gratified with the compliment; 'perhaps I may be. Perhaps I may be, Mrs Mann'. (7)

The reader on the contrary is positioned as both a connoisseur of particular types of fiction and someone with experience of life outside the text. For instance when the histrionics of Mrs Sowerberry persuade her husband to beat the hapless Oliver, the reader is assumed to be expecting just such an outcome; this expectation is implicitly based on both the reader's own marital experience and his understanding of the kind of humour Dickens deploys, in this case the 'scolding wife' motif:

> If he had hesitated for one instant to punish Oliver most severely, it must be quite clear to every experienced reader that he would have been, according to all precedents in disputes of matrimony established,

a brute, an unnatural husband, an insulting creature, a base imitation of a man: and various other agreeable characters too numerous for recital within the limits of this chapter. (52)

A letter to John Forster during the initial serialisation of the story in monthly parts serves as a reminder that the reader in Dickens's fiction stands both within and outside the text, 'Believe me that it affords me great pleasure to hear that you continue to read my writings, and far greater gratification than I can well describe to *you* to hear from your own lips that poor Oliver "affects" you – which I take to be the highest of all praise' ([?26 May 1837]. 262), although Forster would inaccurately claim that his advice had started with Pickwick (Forster vol 1. 71).

At various other points in the novel the boundaries among writing, reading and the imaginative and actual worlds break down. Within the text 'real time' collides with the act of writing in the suspended time of the narrative, when Oliver's fainting is described as:

A weakness on his part, which affords the narrative an opportunity of relieving the reader from suspense, in behalf of the two young pupils of the Merry Old Gentleman; and of recording
   That when the Dodger... (91)

The indented space and capital 'T' visually emphasise to the reader that this shift is contrived, while the phrase 'relieving the reader from suspense' registers that such shifts in focus between characters are a traditional strategy for maintaining interest. This playfully meta-fictional interruption affords readers a moment of relief, through distancing them from the characters. Humorously invoking the idea that a character must not be abandoned as long as he requires the writer's offices, the narrator suggests that while he is supposed to be omniscient, in fact he must physically leave Oliver in Brownlow's house and cross London to Fagin's den, in order to record events there. This highly self-conscious allusion to the role of the narrator carefully inserts him in to the story itself.

It is slightly later in the novel that the acute Fagin imposes a regime of psychological torture on the young Oliver, leaving him alone for long periods before finally bestowing on him a book of sensational crimes (presumably the *Newgate Calender*) as a substitute for human company. As Brantlinger points out, this book is sufficiently well-thumbed to suggest that it has been used for a similar purpose in the instruction of previous boys in the criminal sub-culture, and its efficacy is not necessarily disproved by its failure in this instance, 'That Oliver is repelled instead of won over by Fagin's book doesn't gainsay the possibility of such a conversion' (72). Indeed 'in *Oliver Twist*, Dickens appears to reject the equation between ignorance and crime by making his criminals readers and by pointing to the existence of a criminal literary subculture' (73). This reading helps to explain why the novel was accused of participating in rather than rejecting the infamous 'Newgate novel' as a dangerous form of cheap literature associated with the idealisation of criminals and crime.

Thackeray directly attacks *Oliver Twist* as an example of the genre, in his satirical *Catherine* (1840), insisting that:

> The public will hear of nothing but rogues; and the only way in which poor authors, who must live, can act honestly by the public and themselves, is to paint such thieves as they are: not dandy, poetical, rosewater thieves; but real downright scoundrels, leading scoundrelly lives, drunken, profligate, dissolute, low; as scoundrels will be. They don't quite Plato, like Eugene Aram… or die whitewashed saints, like poor "Biss Dadsy" in "Oliver Twist". No, my dear madam, you have no right to admire and sympathise with any such persons, fictitious or real: you ought to be made cordially to detest, scorn, loathe, abhor, and abominate all people of this kidney. (34)

A more tolerant view was later taken by Anthony Trollope in *The Three Clerks* (1858) the narrator admitting at one point that:

> Poor Bill! I have a sort of love for him, as he walks about wretched with that dog of his, though I know that it is necessary to hang him. Yes, Bill; I, your friend, cannot gainsay that, must acknowledge that. Hard as the case may be, you must be hung; hung out of the way of further mischief; my spoons, my wife's throat, my children's brains, demand that. (517)

Trollope alludes to Sykes as a recognisable type of the literary villain, in the context of a particular social dilemma with which his readers would be conversant: how best to protect the respectable middle class against urban criminality. Notably he does not specify how the class predicament of the uneducated Sykes has contributed to his position as a criminal in constant danger of the gallows, nor does he explicitly categorise him as a product of the Newgate School of fiction. It is simply assumed that readers are conversant with *Oliver Twist* and will reach similar conclusions about the necessity of hanging him.

While Dickens strenuously denied that he belonged to the Newgate School, Juliet John argues that '*Oliver Twist* is alone among the Newgate novels in analysing the role of the storyteller, entertainer, or purveyor of fictions in the power dynamics of 1830s Britain. For *Oliver Twist* offers a sustained self-reflexive exploration of both Newgate fiction and the function of the entertainer in social structures of oppression. … Fagin is central to this critique …' (*Dickens's Villains* 129) in presenting the book to Oliver.

While Fagin assumes that his young victim will take the hint and ask to be integrated into the actual gang represented by (and in) such books, the terrified Oliver reacts very differently in thrusting the book from him, falling to his knees and praying for deliverance (157). In doing so he reminds the reader of what is expected when they are presented with the 'wrong' type of crime fiction, reinforcing the point that the scandalous events relayed by Dickens himself are supposed to be morally bracing rather than titillating.

In this scene the physical book is threatening in its sensational rendering of stories of crime, intuitively related by Oliver to Fagin's gang. When the book itself is pushed away and Oliver prays directly to God, he implicitly signals a distrust of the written word with its potential for persuasion and treachery. However the Bible itself is a missing object in this scene, as Oliver's prayer for deliverance suggests that he has at some point somehow internalised its message. The reader of *Oliver Twist* presumably remains absorbed in this textual account of the dangers of reading, insulated by the narrator's silence from the material Oliver has been invited to read, a depiction of criminal life that lies just below the surface of the main narrative. Dickens's reader too is being asked to internalise the written text through reading and crucially imagining the power of what the narrative leaves unrecorded. Once again, words are used to gesture to their own inadequacy but also to stimulate the imaginative faculty.

But like Oliver, the reader is also expected to absorb particular messages from the text, possibly even at the expense of what is actually there. In a revelatory exploration of failed marriages in Dickens's fiction, Kelly Hager demands that we reconsider what we think we know about these novels. In revisiting the prehistory of *Oliver Twist*, we are reminded for instance that Oliver's father became engaged to and seduced his mother, knowing that he was legally unable to marry her. In stressing the positioning of this inset story, Hager uncovers one way in which Dickens is able to keep faith with readers, while diverting their attention from what they have just been conscientiously told:

> while it seems hard to believe that any reader could overlook it or its ramifications for the plot of *Oliver Twist*, the fact that it is told in two pages, 40 pages from the end of the novel, and at a point in the novel where the reader is more interested in the fate of Sikes (who has just killed Nancy) and Fagin (who is in jail awaiting trial) than in a story about two characters she does not even know virtually guarantees that the reader will read it quickly, impatiently, and carelessly. (58)

But the danger remains in what readers may absorb or how they are likely to interpret particular incidents. In this respect the Newgate novel anticipates the debate over New Woman fiction in the 1890s, a genre that was similarly attacked from the inside by its own proponents. Thackeray's *Catherine* includes a barbed moonlight scene between Catherine and her former lover, in which the narrator satirically demands praise from the reader:

> Without bragging at all, let us just point out the chief claims of the above pleasing piece of composition. In the first place, it is perfectly

stilted and unnatural; the dialogue and the sentiments being artfully arranged, so as to be as strong and majestic as possible. Our dear Cat is but a poor illiterate country wench, who has come from cutting her husband's throat; and yet, see! she talks and looks like a tragedy princess, who is suffering in the most virtuous blank verse. This is the proper end of fiction, and one of the greatest triumphs that a novelist can achieve; for to make people sympathise with virtue is a vulgar trick that any common fellow can do; but it is not everybody who can take a scoundrel, and cause us to weep and whimper over him as though he were a very saint. (129)

As for Dickens in *Oliver Twist*, Thackeray's dilemma is that it is virtually impossible to satirise the genre without promulgating it in the act of writing scenes like this.

Inevitably the passage of time makes a difference to the perception of *Oliver Twist* as a dangerous example of Newgate fiction, as perhaps does the accumulation of a respectable Dickens canon, governed by his carefully crafted prefaces. By the time Thackeray came to write *The Newcomes*, serialised between 1853 and 1855, he had allowed his narrator (revealed as none other than the eponymous Pendennis of the earlier novel) to satirise one character for her ascetic religious principles in the matter of reading, when 'a profane work called *Oliver Twist* having appeared about this time… it is a fact that Lady Walham became so interested in the parish boy's progress that she took his history into her bedroom (where it was discovered, under Blatherwick's *Voice from Mesopotamia*, by her ladyship's maid) and that Kew laughed so immensely at Bumble the Beadle, as to endanger the reopening of his wound' (496). In a further allusion to Oliver's adventures, two women oppose each other, and the interest their combat has for them is measured by the relative lack of interest the book is able to secure; Pendennis notes satirically that 'George Barnes got *Oliver Twist* out, and began to read therein. Miss Nancy and Fanny [sic] again were summoned before this little company to frighten and delight them. I dare say even Fagin failed with the widow, so absorbed was she with the thoughts of the victory which she had just won' (502). Thackeray's characters confirm that while the writer may feel regret at parting with his characters, readers need have no such qualms; in one of the bestselling novels of 1899, Mary Cholmondeley continues to assume readers' acceptance of the afterlife of the text, allowing her morally ambivalent hero Hugh Scarlett to tell his lover of his desire through an allusion to the novel. In a conversation about the time that must elapse before their marriage, destined never to take place, '"Are these such evil days, Hugh?" "I am like Oliver Twist," he said, "I want more"' (*Red Pottage* 196).

Hager suggests that Dickens was not unique in his own expressed reluctance to part from his fictional creations, '… it is not uncommon for Victorian novels and novel-readers to have a hard time letting go of their characters; readers and writers often seem to want to follow them into the future, to learn what happened next, and even to suggest that while the novel itself is ended, its characters' lives will continue beyond its pages' (183). Thackeray tends to be remembered for describing his *Vanity Fair* characters as 'puppets', but the ending of *The Newcomes* shows just such a reluctance to finish what must be one of the longest novels of the period:

> As I write the last line with a rather sad heart, Pendennis and Laura, and Ethel and Clive fade away into fable-land. I hardly know whether they are not true: whether they do not live near us somewhere. They were alive, and I heard their voices,; but five minutes since was touched by their grief. And have we parted with them here on a sudden, and without so much as a shake of the hand? Is yonder line (---------) which I drew with my own pen, a barrier between me and Hades as it were, across which I can see those figures retreating and only dimly glimmering? (1007)

Refusing to provide a prescriptive ending, in this case whether or not Ethel and Clive will have children, he advises the reader that 'You may settle your fable-land in your own fashion. Anything you like happens in fable-land. … Friendly reader! may you and the author meet there on some future day' (1009).

Dickens achieves a slightly different effect with the ending to *Oliver Twist*, in which the characters are both rendered fictional and given a life outside the text, in a final conflation of the time of writing with the narrative time this creates. The narrator indirectly reminds readers that while the writer is mortal, the characters are presumably 'of all time', as he comments. 'And now, the hand that traces these words, falters, as it approaches the conclusion of its task: and would weave, for a little longer space, the thread of these adventures'. In the following line, he apparently suggests that by depicting a fictional joy, the writer is able to participate in it as a character, 'I would fain linger yet with a few of those among whom I have so long moved, and share their happiness by endeavouring to depict it' (439). Dickens would often claim, as he did in his letter to Lewes, that his characters were independent of his creative will and that he simply saw what was presented to him, a position he implies in these closing lines.

The writer must detach himself from the fictional world he has created, but the characters themselves are now fixed and permanent; by implication their happiness is not dependent on being depicted, although the writer's participation is contingent. In other words, what is being recorded will exist in the imaginative world regardless of whether it is ever portrayed in fiction. By extension, this means that by the end of the novel (as it became) Dickens's characters have gained a version of literary immortality, in which their existence is no longer determined by being written – or even read.

Dickens's confidence in his success and concomitant readiness to take on a new role in relation to his readers is nowhere more apparent than in his letter to Richard Bentley requesting him to substitute 'Charles Dickens' for 'Boz' as the author of *Oliver Twist* ([12 November 1838]. 453).

'Charity Must Have its Romance': *Nicholas Nickleby*

Kathryn Chittick describes the preface to *Nicholas Nickleby*, in which Dickens configures the monthly numbers of the novel as 'the correspondence of one who wished their happiness' (li), as being 'in some ways more remarkable than the novel itself. ... The fact that Dickens was now no longer advertised as Boz but actually had his portrait as the frontispiece to the volume publication of *Nickleby* gives some idea of how far the cult of a Dickensian personality or sensibility had gone' (137). At this point the focus of Dickens's attention demonstrably shifts from the insistence on the status of the writer (which can now be safely assumed) to strategies for testing the integrity of the reader. The preface itself both invites personal response and puts limits on it, while the early chapters of the novel instruct the reader in how to read both the text itself and the codified status of characters within it in different ways. But the narrator also makes it quite clear that readers will be judged on their response to what they read.

The dedication to Macready 'as a slight token of admiration and regard, by his friend, the author' signals the life of the author beyond the published text in which it appears. Asking him to accept this dedication, Dickens wrote, 'let me tell the world by this frail record that I was a friend of yours and interested to no ordinary extent in your proceedings at that interesting time when you shewed them such noble truths in such noble forms – and give me a new interest in, and association with, the labour of so many months' (21 September 1839. Pilgrim 1. 582–83). At a dinner to celebrate the completion of the novel, Macready made a speech in reply to which Dickens 'stated that the *Nickleby* had been to him a diary of the last two years: the various papers preserving to him the recollection of the events and feelings connected with their production' (Macready, 'Dear Dickens is a Most Extraordinary Man!' 29). A diary is almost by definition a private form of writing, and in this avowal of the monthly numbers of *Nickleby* as the coded publication of personal history or inner feeling, Dickens anticipates a key trope of his later fiction. By implication the dedication to Macready both publicises the feeling of one friend for another and gestures towards a more private history communicable to the reader only in part. It is in a further close-circuit communication, a private letter, that the author explains how 'this frail record' will nonetheless 'tell the world' about Dickens's friendship for Macready, an artist who (presumably like Dickens himself) can show 'noble truths in noble forms'.

The incorporation of guidance on active reading practices in *Nicholas Nickleby* says much, not just about Dickens but about the moral attitude he wants readers to adopt beyond this particular novel. In essence Dickens tells his reader how to approach the text and even how this might conflict with what a reader of popular novels might typically expect to encounter. Dickens's awareness of literary convention and the plotlines likely to be provided for readers' consumption are referenced in *Oliver Twist*, but in places the reader of *Nicholas Nickleby* must read for plots that are partially submerged beneath narrative rhetoric. Hager suggests one such thread in arguing that 'It is only our conditioned mode of reading... which blinds us to the way in which Nicholas Nickleby's plot is initiated by, and revolves around, the failure of marriage' (64). The reader is called on to be alert, as Daniel Tyler shows in an astute analysis of the description of a Newgate hanging where the dying prisoner sees a crowd of faces but 'not one – not one – that bore the impress of pity or compassion' (30). In this affective scene 'The wry choice to repeat the words "not one" ... calls attention to the verbal artistry, and since it might require a reader to draw back from the immediate concern of the passage to notice it, the sentimental prose tests the reader's own response to the pathetic scene' (Tyler, introduction. 16).

Specifically the reader's attention is directed to authentic and inauthentic language, as speech is used to comment on the written word and vice versa. Self-mythologising quickly emerges as a theme in the novel, through such comic episodes as the woman travelling to Yorkshire by coach who insists that she will soon be overtaken by her own carriage. The credibility of the landlady at a coaching inn where the party stops to change horses is implicitly set against the discernment of the well-primed reader, who has been entertained with the narrator's account of these proceedings for some miles previously. When the woman asks the landlord to set a boy at the door to keep watch:

> The people of the house were evidently overcome by this request, and when the lady charged the boy to remember, as a means of identifying the expected green chariot, that it would have a coachman with a gold-laced hat on the box, and a footman, most probably in silk stockings, behind, the attentions of the good woman of the inn were redoubled. (55)

In this formulation (as in the scene where Sowerberry is forced to beat Oliver Twist) the reader is constructed as more knowing than the landlady, but the incident is humorous largely because of the narrator's written comments, presented as interjections – the immediacy of clauses such as 'when the lady charged the boy' and 'the attentions of the good woman... were redoubled', suggest verbal communication rather than a written rendition of the story.

At other points the narrator gives direct guidance, while still maintaining a gap between what the reader is assumed to understand and what the characters themselves fail to notice. Notably Ralph Nickleby's real nature is revealed to the reader even before his first meeting with his brother's family. In a strategy suggestive of a gossiping conversation, the narrator first hints at the evil nature portended by Ralph's appearance and then disclaims any intention of drawing attention to it at this early stage:

> He wore a sprinkling of powder upon his head, as if to make himself look benevolent; but if that were his purpose, he would perhaps have done better to powder his countenance also, for there was something

Reciprocal Readers and the 1830s–40s 49

in its very wrinkles, and in his cold restless eye, which seemed to tell of cunning that would announce itself in spite of him. However this might be, there he was; and as he was all alone, neither the powder, nor the wrinkles, nor the eyes, had the smallest effect, good or bad, upon anybody just then, and are consequently no business of ours just now. (7)

While the novel clearly builds in elements of melodrama, a level of complexity is first introduced in the unlikely context of the parodically named United Metropolitan Improved Hot Muffin and Crumpet Baking and Punctual Delivery Company. The speeches at the inaugural meeting deploy rhetorical devices to persuade the audience to invest, citing the conditions in which the boys worked, 'nightly turned out into the wet streets at the most inclement periods of the year, to wander about in darkness and rain – or it might be hail or snow – for hours together, without shelter, food, or warmth' (15). There is nothing inherently risible in this description, until the orator overdoes it by reminding his listeners that the muffins have blankets and the boys do not, before finally delivering a bathetic account of a muffin boy who 'having been exposed to this inhuman and barbarous system for no less than five years, at length fell victim to a cold in the head, beneath which he gradually sank until he fell into a perspiration and recovered'. An alert reader should be discomfited by the narrator's linking of this anecdote to the second example, of the boy who was run over by a hackney carriage and had his leg amputated, as he comments derisively that 'This was the department of the subject that took the meeting, and this was the style of speaking to enlist their sympathies. The men shouted; the ladies wept into their pocket-handkerchiefs till they were moist, and waved them till they were dry; the excitement was tremendous' (15).

The first encounter between Ralph and Nicholas further complicates the status of sympathy itself – reminding the reader that death is both poignantly personal and a universal 'commonplace', this scene manoeuvres the reader into a particular relationship with the central characters:

> 'Mine was no common loss!' said Mrs Nickleby, applying her handkerchief to her eyes.
> 'It was no *un*common loss, ma'am,' returned Ralph, as he coolly unbuttoned his spencer. 'Husbands die every day, ma'am, and wives too' (23).

Taking aim at Mrs Nickleby's conventional language, Ralph wrongly believes that he can strip it of meaning by replacing it with his own callous logic. As Purton suggests, the villain is doubly ruthless in violating the family's language of emotion, 'Just as Fagin manifests himself in the most sentimental space of all, Oliver's bedroom at Mr Brownlow's, so the sentimental Nickleby family are flung into the world of Ralph Nickleby and usury and have their vocabulary of sentiment shredded in the encounter' (98).

The reader must in turn be careful to avoid falling into the trap set by the worldly Ralph, who leads Mrs Nickleby to expose the least attractive side of her nature as she lugubriously complains of her husband's supposed fault in making bad investment of his funds (in fact at her insistence):

> In examining different aspects of sentimental rhetoric, Dickens shows himself to be keenly aware of the effects he creates. The shedding of tears is first ruthlessly ironised – through Mrs Nickleby's weeping at the thought of the lost thousand pounds – but later in the scene shown as *genuine* evidence of the family's sentimental credentials (Purton, 2012 100).

As the initial exchange between Ralph and his brother's family makes clear, while the status of the characters is dependent ostensibly on the patronage of Madame Mantalini, Mrs Wititterly and the other employers or social commentators of the novel, it must ultimately be determined purely by the reader's 'interest' in them as the heroes of the story, and the reader must in turn learn to suspend judgement at particular points. Where *Oliver Twist* took as its aim, if only in retrospect, the resistance of innate good to the dictates of a deprived environment and corrupt associates, the agenda of *Nicholas Nickleby* could be seen as the rehabilitation of the ordinary. When Mrs Nickleby says that her husband died 'of a broken heart', Ralph callously but accurately deconstructs this description as 'the cant of the day'. Guided by the narrator, however, the reader interprets the loss of a character who has never appeared in the text, as significant, only pages after deprecating the false sentiment accorded to the spurious muffin boys.

Such self-mythologising alerts the reader to the dangers of indulging in fantasy, but the novel also suggests the dangers of less obviously deceptive language, as used most persuasively in written advertisements. At the start of the novel Nicholas himself is taken in by the falsely persuasive advertisement for Dotheboys Hall, his worry at not having an MA causing him to ignore the sinister phrase 'no vacations' in the prospectus. Later in the novel he will be similarly persuaded by the false promise of the employment bureau:

> It was a shop-front, fitted up with a gauze blind and an inner door; and in the window hung a long and tempting array of written placards, announcing vacant places of every grade, from a secretary's to a foot-boy's. Nicholas halted, instinctively, before this temple of promise, and ran his eye over the capital-text openings in life which were so profusely displayed. (186)

Here 'capital-text' correlates directly to lived experience in the mind of the character reader, suggesting that the larger the type, the more positive the outcome it offers.

This naïve optimism is in obvious contrast to the false piety of characters such as Squeers and Snawley, who approach each other under cover of appropriate platitudes. Their first meeting demonstrates Squeers's verbal tic of obsessively reciting his own spurious claims for the school:

> Affecting not to see him, Mr Squeers feigned to be intent on mending a pen, and offering benevolent advice to his youthful pupil.
> "My dear child," said Mr Squeers, "all people have their trials. This early trial of yours that is fit to make your little heart burst, and your very eyes come out of your head with crying, what is it? Nothing. Less than nothing. You are leaving your friends, but you will have a father in me, my dear, and a mother in Mrs Squeers. At the delightful village of Dotheboys, near Greta Bridge in Yorkshire, where youth are boarded, clothed, booked, washed, furnished with pocket-money, provided with all necessaries –"
> "It *is* the gentleman," observed the stranger, stopping the schoolmaster in the rehearsal of his advertisement. (32)

Significantly Squeers is literally 'rehearsing' his written advertisement as he sizes up Snawley. It is this translation of written language into sententious speech that alerts the reader to the preposterous mendacity of the speaker. Over the next few minutes the two gradually reveal their motives to each other:

> 'They have come to the right shop for morals, sir.'
> 'You are a moral man yourself,' said Mr Snawley.
> 'I rather believe I am, sir,' replied Squeers.
> 'I have the satisfaction to know you are, sir,' said Mr Snawley. 'I asked one of your references, and he said you were pious'. (33)

Squeers's ambiguous phrase 'the right shop for morals' is both a colloquialism, echoing the Dodger's lament that 'This ain't the shop for justice' in *Oliver Twist*, and a veiled admission that his own morals are for sale. Through their successive exchanges, the two characters establish a tacit understanding of the way in which language can be made to substitute for reality – creating a hall of mirrors effect, Snawley claims to 'know' that Squeers is moral because a referee chosen by himself 'said' that he was pious. By the time Ralph and Nicholas enter the room, this transferred 'knowledge' allows Snawley himself to serve as referee, with the authority to endorse Squeers as a moral man. It is Ralph who checks this display of unmerited approbation:

> 'I feel bound to assure you, sir, and I am proud to have this opportunity *of* assuring you, that I consider Mr Squeers a gentleman highly virtuous, exemplary, well-conducted, and –'
> 'I make no doubt of it, sir,' interrupted Ralph, checking the torrent of recommendation; 'no doubt of it at all. Suppose we come to business?' (37)

The understanding between the first two characters anticipates a later conversation between Squeers and Ralph, in which Smike is discussed and Ralph translates a basic metaphor into material terms:

> 'nobody at home you know, if you knocked ever so often.'
> 'And you did knock pretty often, I dare say?' muttered Ralph.
> 'Pretty well,' returned Squeers with a grin. (439)

Like the earlier interplay of written and verbal communication, as speech frames particular lines from a written advertisement, such jokes can be used to make visible the ways in which reader response is governed not by what happens, but by how it is expressed. As Andrews points out, one of the narrator's most extraordinary achievements is to derive humour from the brutal scene in which Squeers knocks a small boy off his trunk and then knocks him back on, while he talks to Snawley. Andrews suggests that readers feel able to laugh because 'The brutality, wretched though it is, is temporary only. We sense this about Squeers's villainy because of the very different way in which the novel's other principal villain, Ralph, is presented with no humour and with sinisterly obscure motives for his cruelties. ... Ralph's is a melodramatic villainy, whereas Squeers's is a pantomimic villainy' (*Dickensian Laughter* 48).

Despite his evident enjoyment of his own hypocrisy, shown in his first conversation with Snawley, the narrator will make it clear that Squeers also attempts to deceive himself with the fiction that he is a paternalistic and benevolent figure, 'Squeers covered his rascality, even at home, with a spice of his habitual deceit; as if he really had a notion of some day or other being able to take himself in, and persuade his own mind that he was a very good fellow' (87). This comment links Squeers to both the vanity of his daughter Fanny, who looking in the mirror, 'like most of us ... saw – not herself, but the reflection of some pleasant image in her own brain' (135) and more crucially Bray who, as Ralph observes, first agrees to sell his daughter and then 'is trying to deceive himself, even before our eyes, already. He is making believe that he thinks of her good, and not his own' (624). Notably the reader derives this insight into Bray's behaviour not from the moral narrator, but from the knowing villain of the novel. The moral epicentre of the novel therefore becomes skewed at this point, as the reader starts to take cues from the very figure towards whom their moral indignation is directed.

The status of the reader has already been complicated through the novel's satirical conflation of 'great' and 'fashionable' literature as indulged in by various characters. The hardworking Miss La Creevy's miniatures are gently dismissed by an amused narrator, who registers 'one of a literary character with a high forehead, a pen and ink, six books, and a curtain. There was, moreover, a touching representation of a young lady reading a manuscript in an unfathomable forest' (19). Elsewhere a professed love of literature is linked to affectation, through characters such as Miss Knag's Byronically inclined brother, who 'did find so much in the books he read, applicable to his own misfortunes, and did find himself in every respect so much like the heroes... that he took to scorning everything, and became a genius; and I am quite sure that he is, at this very present moment, writing another book' (223). Worse still is the jealous and heartless Mrs Wittiterly, who forces Kate to read her long passages from insipid 'society' novels and fails the test of responding appropriately to Shakespeare's birthplace, gushing to Mrs Nickleby, 'I don't know how it is, but after you've seen the place and written your name in the little book, somehow or other you seem to be inspired; it kindles up quite a fire within one' (352).

The reader of Dicken's implicitly superior novel is not allowed to be complacent, however. By this stage the narrator has already condemned putative readers for whom Kate's sufferings have to be made titillating or excised altogether, in a passage reminiscent of Boz's supercilious reader who will 'turn with coldness and disgust' from too much detail:

> There are many lives of much pain, hardship, and suffering, which, having no stirring interest for any but those who lead them, are disregarded by persons who do not want thought or feeling, but who pamper their compassion and need high stimulants to rouse it.
>
> There are not a few among the disciples of charity who require, in their vocation, scarcely less excitement than the votaries of pleasure in theirs... In short, charity must have its romance, as the novelist or playwright must have his.

For this reason the details of her employment at Mme Mantalini's have been only roughly sketched in:

> The life to which poor Kate Nickleby was devoted... was a hard one; but lest the very dulness, unhealthy confinement, and bodily fatigue, which made up its sum and substance, should deprive it of any interest with the mass of the charitable and sympathetic, I would rather keep Miss Nickleby herself in view just now, than chill them, in the outset, by a minute and lengthened description of the establishment presided over by Madame Mantalini' (215).

The implication is that the narrator is confined to attractively presented fiction rather than social commentary, and by implication then the reader is forced into something like an uneasy identification with Mrs Wittiterly, as well as being allowed to share the narrator's satire of her superficial posturing. Through this positioning the reader's need for imaginative stimulation is apparently distanced from the narrator's corresponding need to provide imaginative figures. But despite the accusatory tone of this passage, Dickens seems to have retained a very real sense of his relationship to readers as both paternalistic and market based. In a letter to the writer Mrs S. C. Hall, he denied that he had exaggerated the state of the Yorkshire schools, incidentally proffering a complex model of the writer's role, 'Depend upon it that the rascalities of those Yorkshire schoolmasters *cannot* easily be exaggerated, and that I have kept down the strong truth and thrown as much comicality over it as I could, rather than disgust and weary the reader with its fouler aspects' (29 December 1838. Pilgrim 1. 481–83. 481).

As a writer of fiction, Dickens's imaginative power lies precisely in the ability to transform or exaggerate what he sees; as a social commentator he both denies any distortion of what he has observed and at the same time claims to have disguised 'the strong truth' with his own talent for comedy. The aim of his semi-humorous presentation of the schools is to avoid causing 'weariness' or 'disgust' to the reader, who must be persuaded to enjoy the story in order to respond to the social critique. What remains unstated, although presumably obvious to another writer, is that Dickens himself makes his living from fiction and is therefore obliged to study the market even as he attempts to influence it.

Just as Dickens himself would soon begin to write in the style of particular characters, or allude to them in the context of later events, readers continued to ask questions about the story of *Nicholas Nickleby*, testifying to the continued appeal of the novel long after its original publication. In answer to a letter in 1845, Dickens wrote good humouredly, 'Mr Charles Dickens sends his compliments to Mr McKean, and begs to say, in reply to his letter, that the Proprietress of the Mangle is certainly *not* the original Mrs Mantalini, or (lawfully speaking) any Mrs Mantalini at all' (to Andrew McKean, 27 October 1845. Pilgrim 4. 416).

The text itself encourages the reader to engage in the vicarious rewriting of fictional history. At one point Ralph projects alternative histories for himself:

> He thought of what his home might be if Kate were there; he placed her in the empty chair, looked upon her, heard her speak; he felt again upon his arm the gentle pressure of the trembling hand; he strewed his costly rooms with the hundred silent tokens of feminine presence and occupation; he came back again to the cold fireside and the silent dreary splendour; and in that one glimpse of a better nature, born as it was in selfish thoughts, the rich man felt himself friendless, childless, and alone. (400–401)

This one imaginative act prefigures the final revelation that he is Smike's father and has had the choice of a different life (significantly it is his unchristian rejection of his convicted associate Brooker that precludes his learning of this relationship in time; rather than try to prolong Smike's life, he hunts him to his death). But this final revelation towards the very end of the novel carries the suggestion that such powerful imaginative re-envisioning is available to the reader at least through an engagement with Dickens's fiction. This is just what characters in the later novels are able to do, often basing their imaginative acts of restitution and punishment on what they have read. In an extreme instance, in *Our Mutual Friend* Boffin is inspired to teach Bella through showing her parallels with her own behaviour in the biographies of misers. Learning how to read and respond to texts is a key element of the eponymous hero's development in both *A Christmas Carol* and *Martin Chuzzlewit*.

'It Will Bring You Home for an Hour or Two': *A Christmas Carol*

In Dickens's account we literally are what we read. Childhood engagement with fairy tale is vital, but (as he would signal with the reawakening of Louisa's imagination in *Hard Times*, published in 1854) it is never too late to learn. The function of the Christmas books, as Dickens came to see it, was nothing less than to revitalise his contemporaries' moral responses by associating his fiction with what is almost the most jubilant day in the Christian calendar, in a sort of salvation by reading. The first and most successful, *A Christmas Carol* (1843), stands as the ultimate conversion narrative for both Scrooge and the reader and literally begins Scrooge's redemption with an embodied engagement with his childhood reading. In his introduction to the OUP edition, Robert Douglas-Fairhurst asks, 'What does Scrooge learn about himself? Precisely what Dickens's readers are expected to learn about themselves, which is that even activities with the potential to isolate people from one another, including the act of reading, can be transformed into models of reciprocity and trust' (xiv).

In the course of Scrooge's reawakening, the reader is required to exercise a level of imagination, joining the dots between the scenes of his life, as revisited with the spirits. As usual this is done under the guidance of a controlling narrator, who reinforces or expands the commentary of the several ghosts. Parker comments that:

> The voice we hear speaking to us in the *Carol* is at once capricious and authentic. Dickens's third-person narrators are normally protean. The narrator of the *Carol* is that and more. He seamlessly blends the sensational, the comic, the heartbreaking and the wonderful ... We are confronted with an amalgamating sensibility, a narrative intelligence which, without restraint, probes the facts of his story for different kinds of significance. Sometimes we are invited to suppose we are witnessing a game, played to arbitrary rules. Sometimes the demand is that we look unflinchingly beyond the story, at distressing social realities. Sometimes we are caught in a web of imagination, and made to rejoice or suffer with the characters. (206)

This positioning of the reader, as 'We find ourselves repeatedly called upon to adjust the way we are responding' (Parker 207), involves a degree of trust in a narrator who tells this 'fireside' story in a spirit of affectionate intimacy (he is by implication an invited guest in the homes where he envisages the story being read), but one who also insists that its message should be absorbed by the domestic reader.

A characteristic blurring of boundaries between narrator and reader, imaginary text and lived experience, is suggested in the depiction of Scrooge's nephew as the type of man both are able to encounter, 'If you should happen, by an unlikely chance, to know a man more blest in a laugh than Scrooge's nephew, all I can say is, I should like to know him too. Introduce him to me, and I'll cultivate his acquaintance' (56). Dickens's offer of a relationship beyond the text is of course illusory, based on the idea that a fictional narrator can move between the world of the story and the everyday world of the reader. But underlying this figure of speech is the reminder of both the earlier Boz persona and at one remove an actual author who could be encountered in London, where the story itself is set and where a number of his readers are likely to live.

Importantly the ethos of the story was presented as essentially transferable to other writers when in his first plans for what would become *Household Words*, Dickens could confidently describe its scope and ethos in terms of '*Carol* philosophy, cheerful views, sharp anatomization of humbug, jolly good temper' (to John Forster [? Early July 1845] Pilgrim 4. 327–28. 328). Through the avoidance of explicit detail of just what this philosophy might mean, Dickens both places the onus on readers to work out their own moral redemption and apparently gives them considerable scope for adapting his message to their own circumstances. In Parker's account of how this works, 'He would achieve wholeness in texts he wrote about Christmas, by compelling the changeless and the changing to vitalize each other. Against the rhythm of the annual festival, transcending the vicissitudes of life, he would set contingent narratives of life and death, love and grief, joy and sorrow, success and failure, preserved in the memory of merrymakers' (128–29).

Through shared reading, Dickens's considerable audience can all benefit from the regenerative function of memory. But this overt use of the past as a vehicle for redemption involves a more demanding involvement from the reader than a simple acknowledgement of the power of memory. Crucially Scrooge is present in both time zones at the same time, and readers are invited to set one against the other. This narrative interplay reminds readers that the young Scrooge is himself an imagined figure (the reader watches him as he himself watches Ali Baba and the other figures from his own childhood reading); the figure of the aged Scrooge inserted into the scene against his will may even serve as a stand-in for the reader of the *Carol* itself, who must also learn how to respond correctly to the messages of fictional texts.

In his communications with friends, Dickens invested the book with a semi-magical power, sufficient even to collapse physical distance during the act of reading. He told Macready, who was in America when the book appeared, 'It pleases me to think that it will bring you Home for an hour or two. And I long to hear you have read it, on some quiet morning' (3 January

1844. Pilgrim 4. 9–13. 12). While he knows that he will receive a response by letter, Dickens imagines himself hearing rather than reading that Macready has enjoyed the story, in a phrase that comes suspiciously close to 'hear you read it'. In a discussion of the Christmas stories including the *Carol*, Tyler notes that they 'repeatedly draw attention to their own process of narration by way of an exaggeratedly meticulous narrative voice. In this, they are indebted partly to an oral tradition of retelling ghostly tales, where the tales become performative acts in their own right' ('Spectres of Style' 97).

The significance of its being a Christmas book lies in the reconfiguration of relations between narrator and reader, who have apparently come together for a purpose just as the various characters are gathered for communal acts of seasonal celebration. The reader immediately registers that the narrative voice is using an oral rather than a written register in the opening sentences 'Marley was dead, to begin with. There is no doubt whatever about that' (9). Indeed he aligns himself with the garrulous story teller round the Christmas fire as:

> He elaborates a fussy self-consciousness about his task as a story-teller and teasingly spins out what amounts to a shaggy-dog story (about the importance of knowing that Marley *was dead*). ... In these opening paragraphs he very strongly projects not only his own presence as story-teller... but also the co-presence of the reader / listener whom he is button-holing energetically. (Andrews, *Dickensian Laughter* 54)

In this first page, 'Through the erratic pacing, the narrative swerves and the switches of register Dickens tactically disorients his reader (who was sitting comfortably initially and waiting for the *story* to begin) so as to induce a dependency on his narrator self' (Andrews, *Dickensian Laughter* 55–56). But if the reader is invited to identify with the narrator, it quickly becomes apparent that anyone engaging fully with the story is not expected to be a passive spectator of the ghostly scenes that follow.

In recalling Scrooge's childhood, Dickens equips him with the creative faculty later attributed to a young David Copperfield, as he watches characters from books processing past the windows of the school where he has been abandoned at Christmas, 'a lonely boy was reading near a feeble fire; and Scrooge sat down upon a form, and wept to see his poor forgotten self as he used to be' (31). It is possible to see this scene as simply an instance of Scrooge's self-indulgence (a few years later Dickens's autobiographical fragment would include a similar pity for his child self). However it mirrors the earlier passage in which 'The air was filled with phantoms, wandering hither and thither in restless haste', one of whom 'cried piteously at being unable to assist a wretched woman with an infant, whom it saw below, on a doorstep. The misery with them all was, clearly, that they sought to interfere, for good, in human matters, and had lost the power for ever' (26). The scene in which Scrooge observes his earlier self is based on the premise that both narrator and reader are in turn standing silently behind him and must learn as he does from the experience.

In this scene the narrator both invokes the experience of readers and provides them with an imaginary world they may have missed as children or been unable to create for themselves. At the same time, he provides the readers of his own novels with a template of how to process and configure characters such as Scrooge himself, implicitly suggesting that they allow characters to move from the page and in to the immediate surroundings where the book is being read. The narrator joins the reader in this act of reading, insisting that:

> The curtains of his bed were drawn aside, I tell you, by a hand. Not the curtains at his feet, not the curtains at his back, but those to which his face was addressed. The curtains of his bed were drawn aside; and Scrooge, starting up into a half-recumbent attitude, found himself face to face with the unearthly visitor who drew them: as close to it as I am now to you, and I am standing in the spirit at your elbow. (28)

As Tyler points out:

> As a way of describing one's own narrative presence in a ghost story, this is remarkably stark and full of self-conscious irony. It continues the glimpsed recognitions, set in train by the opening sentence, that the ghost story itself seems frequently to offer a submerged commentary on the nature of fiction and how we read it' ('Spectres of Style' 97).

Leaving aside the dubious spirit pun, the narrator has taken charge of the reader as a matter of course in the slightly argumentative 'I tell you', before confirming his position 'at your elbow', albeit he is only present 'in the spirit'. The sleight of hand works largely because Dickens's actual existence allows readers to accept the false logic, according to which the 'spirit' presence of the narrator can be taken as an endorsement of Marley's ghost. This positioning itself allows the narrator to read his own words with the reader, aligning himself as both educator and participant in the experience of reading Scrooge's story. Narrator and reader can watch together as the characters take on new life and parade before them.

Dickens's letters show that he was particularly taken with the idea of his Christmas book as a physical presence in the homes of readers. Thanking Laman Blanchard for a review in *Ainsworth's Magazine*, Dickens told him, 'When I think it likely that I may meet you... I shall slip a Carol into my pocket, and ask you to put it among your books for my sake. You will never like it the less for having made it the means of so much happiness to me' (4 January 1844. Pilgrim 4. 13). In a letter to Cornelius Felton he says that he is enclosing a copy:

> Being a Ghost Story of Christmas by Charles Dickens. Over which Christmas Carol, Charles Dickens wept, and laughed, and wept again,

and excited himself in a most extraordinary manner, in the composition. ... And by every post, all manner of strangers write all manner of letters to him about their homes and hearths, and how this same Carol is read aloud there, and kept on a very little shelf by itself. (2 January 1844. Pilgrim 4. 2–5. 2)

Given the improbability of a shelf constructed of such dimensions that it would hold only one book, Dickens is either implying that no other book is considered by these readers worthy of being put next to the *Carol* – or someone in the chain of correspondence is quite simply making this up. But it is only fair to add that in Forster's *Life of Dickens* he does confirm:

There poured upon its author daily, all through that Christmas time, letters from complete strangers to him which I remember reading with a wonder of pleasure; not literary at all, but of the simplest domestic kind; of which the general burden was to tell him, amid many confidences, about their homes, how the *Carol* had come to be read aloud there, and was to be kept upon a little shelf by itself, and was to do them no end of good. (Forster vol 1. 300)

In 1847, when he was in the middle of *Dombey* and debating whether or not he could write a Christmas Book and still meet his other commitments, Dickens wrote to Forster setting out the considerations for and against. Setting the moral responsibility over the financial loss if he failed to write a volume in time, he describes the proposed book as if it were literally a substitution for himself as an invited guest, '... I am very loath to lose the money. And still more so to leave any gap at Christmas firesides which I ought to fill' ([12 September 1847]. Pilgrim 5. 165). In this elision across the two letters between the 'very little shelf' where the *Carol* is kept and the chair by the fire reserved for an honoured guest, Dickens becomes both author and book, a characteristic conflation in his writing that is always in danger of becoming fractured.

Despite Dickens's emphasis on the power of the reader to move characters out of and beyond the text in which they first appear, his own imagined relationship with individual readers depended on his provision of material with which to fuel these visions. When a cheap periodical pirated the *Carol*, Dickens was understandably furious, not least about the loss of control over his own work. He wrote to Thomas Mitton that 'my book is made to appear a wretched, meagre, miserable thing; and is still hawked about with my title and my name – with my characters, my incidents, and whole design' (7 January 1844. Pilgrim 4. 16–17. 17).

Over the coming decades the afterlife of the *Carol* would become a familiar aspect of national culture, informing a number of other novels and stories. Another old man in William Morris's *News from Nowhere* (1890) hopes that the first-person narrator will return to the past and change the future, just as the book itself is intended to change contemporary attitudes.

It is not difficult to see the influence of Dickens in this trope of a character whose knowledge of the future can miraculously change the past, and a further reference to *A Christmas Carol* is reinforced in the narrator's comment on the teasing of characters who refuse to join in the haymaking, 'much as if in Dickens's time some young people were so wrapped up in their work that they wouldn't keep Christmas' (149). The boatman Dick is so inspired by this old man that he records of him, 'somehow he makes us think of all kind of things; and already I feel as if I could understand Dickens the better for having talked with him' (*News from Nowhere* 116–17).

Thackeray famously called the *Carol* a 'national benefit', and *The Newcomes* includes an affectionate parody of the type of reading effected by the young Scrooge, in a scene where the ingenuous Colonel Newcome holds forth on literature to Pendennis, not realising in time that Pendennis's clerk has entered the room. Discussing what he would say to Fielding's Tom Jones if he came in at that moment, he assures his listener, 'I would say, "How dare you, you hireling ruffian, to sully with your presence an apartment where my young friend and I are conversing together? where two gentlemen, I say, are taking their wine after dinner? How dare you, you degraded villain!" I don't mean you, sir. I – I – I beg your pardon' (51).

In a commemorative issue of *Cassell's Magazine* in 1912, the centenary of Dickens's birth, Owen Oliver published a short story called 'A Christmas Bonus' with the subtitle "How a business man who hated "Christmas customs" came to wish that there were two Christmases in one year'. The narrator begins with a mock diatribe against Christmas boxes:

> Merry season indeed! Indigestible pudding and interruption of business, and snow in your shoes and a cold in your head; Christmas cards from poor relations – sprats to catch mackerels! – and howling waits, and armies of cadgers who've annoyed you all the year touching their caps and smirking and wishing you a merry Christmas! (339)

In a humorous twist on the relationship between Scrooge and Cratchit, the businessman narrator is presented as a fair if comically grumbling employer, who brings together his assistant and his former lover from whom he parted eight years earlier, before ultimately proposing marriage to his female clerk.

A Christmas Carol remains one of Dickens's best-loved works and led to a series of Christmas books, as well as stories written either alone or collaboratively with journal contributors between 1850 and 1867. Dickens himself came to feel in the end that the success of his Christmas stories for *Household Words* and *All the Year Round* had become an annual burden, complaining to his actor friend Charles Fechter in 1868 (it is not clear whether the allusion to haunting is intentionally meta-textual) that 'I feel as if I had murdered a Christmas number years ago (perhaps I did!) and its ghost perpetually haunted me' (8 March 1868. Pilgrim 12. 67).

'A crowd of phantoms waited on his pleasure': *Martin Chuzzlewit*

A sustained engagement with reader response across different modes of writing has proved to be a key feature of Dickens's narrative method from the start of his career. In *Martin Chuzzlewit* (1844) he both draws attention to the material basis of the imagination and shares his implicit mistrust of the written word, rendering this novel one of his most conflicted in its account of the imaginative process as practised by both the narrator and the assumed reader.

The highly visible inter-dependence of letters, non-fiction and fiction is an important feature of Dickens's writing about America. Readers of *Martin Chuzzlewit* might be expected also to have read *American Notes* (1842), and successive editions of each text were prefaced by authorial commentary, implicitly linking the two. In what would become a familiar device, *American Notes* included new prefatory matter in 1850 and 1868 (Forster's *Life* subsequently made available Dickens's original, unpublished preface to the first edition), while *Martin Chuzzlewit* included new prefaces in editions of 1850 and 1867, with an additional postscript in 1868. This use of letter-style prefaces in some senses levels the playing field, increasing the sense of intimacy between author and readers, who are invited to position themselves as privileged correspondents. The connection between readers of the published works and readers of private letters is made explicit in a letter from Dickens to the wife of David Colden, in which he tells her that he has no time to pursue his own inclination for writing, 'And even now, in this Preface or Prologue to our future correspondence (in which I mean to shine very much) I have only time to be dull, and inclination to be bright' (To Mrs David C. Colden, 15 July 1842. Pilgrim 3. 271–72. 271).

Habitual readers of Dickens would be likely to expect an authorial injunction to act on what they read, but once again in *Martin Chuzzlewit* the act of reading in itself becomes a moral choice. Each new generation of readers coming to the novel through the 'Notes' had already been exposed to potential satire through the figure of the boat passenger on the return trip to England, who is unaware of the novelist's close proximity (they are in adjacent cabins) and confides to his wife '"that Boz will be writing a book bye and bye, and putting all our names in it!" at which imaginary consequence of being on board a boat with Boz, he groaned and became silent' (*American Notes* 219). In his playful communication of this overheard complaint, Dickens reminds readers once again that writers and 'ordinary people' are watching each other both in and beyond the text in which their main encounters take place.

The self-consciousness created by the sudden awareness of Dickens's observation is well caught by his holiday acquaintance Eleanor Christian, in her description of the embarrassment she and her companions felt in being caught 'talking nonsense' in his presence. He would sometimes appear to be concentrating on other things entirely and:

> Many times were we duped by this false appearance of abstraction and were deluded into talking nonsense, arguing illogically, and making silly jokes under the impression that he was miles away in a land of his own peopling, surrounded by characters of his own creation. Then suddenly up would go the curtain from his veiled vision, and he would break forth into most amusing but merciless criticisms of all our conversation. ('Dickens on Holiday (1840) and Afterwards' 34)

Christian's discomfort is caused less by the fact that she herself has become aware of talking nonsense than by the sudden realisation that she has become a character adapted to mimicking reproduction by the famous author.

In writing *Martin Chuzzlewit* Dickens plays with just such anxieties (or possibly aspirations), but this depiction of character becomes a two-way process, as newspaper accounts follow Martin throughout his progress round the States, and the narrator in turn comments on these free-floating and ungovernable misrepresentations of his central character. In a further layer of representation, this mirrors what happens to Martin and Mark Tapley in the novel, as the serial form of the story allows the writer to incorporate responses as he goes. In a letter to W. H. Prescott on 10 November 1843 he complained jokingly that Cornelius Felton had answered a four-page letter with one of as many lines and warned that 'I am not quite certain whether he won't find himself in Chuzzlewit before long' (Pilgrim 3. 596–97. 597).

Particularly interesting given the permeable boundaries between print and speech elsewhere in the novels (most obviously in Squeers's obsessive repetition of his own advertisement), Michael Slater identifies the sense of immediacy that is such a feature of *Martin Chuzzlewit* as a representation of verbal communication, established through the idiosyncratic use of colons and semi-colons, 'This punctuation is rhetorical rather than grammatical in nature, as though Dickens were telling rather than writing his story, and contributes towards a further strengthening of that peculiarly personal intimacy with his readers already established as the hallmark of the writer Charles Dickens' (*Charles Dickens* 211). But the serialisation of the novel, while it potentially strengthened the relationship between author and readers (who waited for each instalment much in the way that they might wait expectantly for a letter from abroad), also brought its own problems. The ability to read the work in parts, seemingly as it was being written, also meant that readers could anticipate the ending without actually having it in their hands. The frustration this caused is clearly evident in a letter Dickens wrote to Lady Holland, assuring her that 'I am delighted to find that Chuzzlewit has risen so highly in your estimation. ... It is the great misery of such a form of publication that conclusions are necessarily arrived at, in reference to the design of the story, before the design becomes apparent or complete' (10 June 1844. Pilgrim 4. 144–45. 145).

From the outset the narrator draws on literary traditions and easily recognisable tropes (as he had done in *Oliver Twist* and *Nicholas Nickleby*) in order to challenge the authenticity of various characters, but also warns readers that in the course of the novel the Chuzzlewits will be shown to 'have still many counterparts and prototypes in the Great World about us' (5). Pecksniff himself is the natural successor to Squeers, and Dickens draws on his readers' assumed knowledge of the type (presumably including Squeers himself) in the satirical opening descriptions of the Pecksniff family circle, governed by the father's manipulative agency and foregrounding the designing Mercy, who 'sat upon a stool, because of her simplicity and innocence, which were very great: very great. Miss Pecksniff sat upon a stool, because she was all girlishness, and playfulness, and wildness, and kittenish buoyancy' (10). In repeating this phrase 'sat upon a stool' as a frame for her parodic 'kittenish buoyancy', the narrator notably increases the humour but also raises the stakes for the reader, who is implicitly warned not to try this at home.

While Dickens's preface highlights the theme of selfishness, the novel could just as easily be read as a treatment of hypocrisy – significantly, 'Pecksniffian' became shorthand for sanctimonious or pompous hypocrisy in Dickens's own informal register, while despite the title there is no corresponding word 'Chuzzlewitian' on record. In a further indirect warning to readers themselves, Mrs Todgers's boarders include 'a gentleman of a literary turn, who wrote squibs upon the rest, and *knew the weak side of everybody's character but his own*' (126. Emphasis added). Like *Nicholas Nickleby*, *Martin Chuzzlewit* traces the development of a central protagonist through his ejection from the domestic world in which he grew up and his subsequent travels through an alien landscape. But the title itself renders character status more ambiguous than it is made in the earlier novel, in that the eponymous hero might be either the elder or the younger Martin Chuzzlewit.

By the end of the novel Martin Chuzzlewit Senior has come to address an implied reader directly. Notwithstanding the clumsiness of his exhortation, the narrator apparently assumes that the reader is prepared for just such a personal application, which is introduced with no additional explanation:

> Oh you whose wealth, like mine, has been a source of continual unhappiness, leading you to distrust the nearest and dearest, and to dig yourself a living grave of suspicion and reserve; take heed that, casting off all whom you might have bound to you, and tenderly, you do not become in your decay an instrument of such a man as this. ... (691)

As in *A Christmas Carol*, a sense of the past is integral to the theme of redemption. Martin Senior vicariously lives his life for a second time as he watches his grandson's progress from selfish young man to morally responsible member of the community. Like the ghosts at the start of the earlier tale, he is unable to intervene in the vicissitudes of Martin and Mary (in this case, as it turns out, because to do so would both hamper Martin's moral awakening and warn Pecksniff that his mercenary plans were doomed to failure).

Like Martin Senior, the reader must learn which voices to trust and which to ignore. From the start this reader has, like the Chuzzlewits, been subjected to the narrator's ironic scrutiny, in the famous mock formal introduction of the characters, 'As no lady or gentleman, with any claims to polite breeding, can possibly sympathise with the Chuzzlewit Family without being first assured of the extreme antiquity of the race, it is a great satisfaction to know that it undoubtedly descended in a direct line from Adam and Eve ...' (1). In *American Notes* the narrator reprimands an imagined reader, whose anticipated response to the benevolent arrangements made for workers in Lowell factories (including the provision of pianos in boarding houses) is to decry the inappropriate aspirations of the working class, 'The large class of readers, startled by these facts, will exclaim, with one voice, "How very preposterous!" On my deferentially inquiring why, they will answer, "These things are above their station"' (78). The narrator of course never explicates whom this 'large class of readers' is, whose reaction must be forestalled. Rather he enforces acquiescence as the price of the reader's indemnity from such satire, declaring that:

> This history, having, to its own perfect satisfaction, (*and, consequently, to the full contentment of all its readers,*) proved the Chuzzlewits to have had an origin, and to have been at one time or other of an importance which cannot fail to render them highly improving and acceptable acquaintance to all right-minded individuals, may now proceed in earnest with its task. (5. Emphasis added)

The second chapter heading gives the reader a renewed invitation to become further acquainted with the Chuzzlewit family and a corresponding opportunity to decline, 'Wherein certain persons are presented to the reader, with whom he may, if he please, become better acquainted' (6). That the reader's agreement is a forgone conclusion is obvious from the previous invocation of 'the full contentment of all its readers'. The reader is manoeuvred into responding to the narrator as a consistently reliable voice, not least as a discerning reader of the gap between fiction and reality, highlighted by the satirical uncovering of inauthentic representations of class and moral status. At various points the narrator tells the reader both how to interpret imaginative projections and how to read selectively.

In return readers are understood to have certain expectations of the author. Dickens repeatedly positions himself as resisting attempts to lionise him, instead stressing his role as a form of moral guardianship through the publication of fiction. Dickens's letters to readers insist on the seriousness with which he took the writer / reader contract, and their grounds for trusting his good faith, both in and beyond the fictional world. Refusing to send a lock of his hair to some female readers during the American tour, he once again stresses the authenticity of his dealings with the public, 'You see how very candidly I deal with you. If I had been of a deceitful nature, nothing would have been easier for me to do, than to have got a lock of hair from one of the waiters, and forwarded it to you by post' (To unknown ladies of Plymouth, Massachusetts, 2 February 1842. Pilgrim 3. 47).

In *American Notes* Dickens good humouredly mocked his own appearance as an English celebrity, in his meeting with a Scottish doctor:

> Doctor Crocus and I shake hands; and Doctor Crocus looks as if I didn't by any means realize his expectations, which, in a linen blouse, and a great straw hat with a green ribbon, and no gloves, and my face and nose profusely ornamented with the stings of mosquitoes and the bites of bugs, it is very likely I did not. (200)

In both American books, the construction of myth is practised by, and has a significant impact on, a range of figures, a reach that allows it to signal danger or delusion, as well as the imagination. In the initial voyage of *American Notes*, the inadequate state-room fails utterly to live up to its own written advertisement, but is made more luxurious through a sense of camaraderie and by Dickens's willingness to make the best of things. In a triumph of the imagination over reality, the words of the false advertisement are good humouredly allowed to be valid after all. As the stewardess impresses him by her friendly behaviour, so the cabin 'expanded into something quite bulky, and almost boasted a bay-window to see the sea from' (13). This quality of readiness to be pleased finds its way into the presentation of Pinch, perhaps the most positive of Dickens's self-deceivers.

Deception in the novel may be either sinister or generally benign. Obvious frauds include the pretence indulged by Sweedlepipes that young Bailey, formerly of Mrs Todgers's boarding house, needs shaving; but also the reversible name of Montague Tigg / Tigg Montague, for whom Bailey now works. In an early American scene Martin is briefly distracted from his pure love for Mary Graham by the false charms of the Norris daughters, with their silk stockings and tantalising flashes of ankle. The reader has presumably been more suspicious than the credulous Martin of the family's ostentatious acquaintance with members of the English aristocracy and therefore is less surprised when they cut him despite his gentlemanly manners on learning that he was a steerage passenger on the way out.

But if the social chorus is implicitly unreliable, even writers can prove false as well as being close observers. Throughout the novel, the written word is misused for the creation of mythic identities tendentiously devised by unscrupulous characters (the most famous example being the ironically named Eden, where Martin and Mark almost die of fever). Many of these myths centre on literary tropes or metaphor. The narrator's authority is further sustained by repeated attacks on such 'false' literary claims, held out by a number of minor characters. In an early English scene, the grotesquely named Slyme ungraciously tells Tom Pinch and Martin:

> I am the wretchedest creature on record. Society is in a conspiracy against me. I'm the most literary man alive. I'm full of scholarship; I'm full of genius; I'm full of information; I'm full of novel views on every subject; yet look at my condition! I'm at this moment obliged to two strangers for a tavern bill! (96)

During his trans-Atlantic travels Martin Chuzzlewit receives a begging letter claiming:

> I am young, and ardent. For there is a poetry in wilderness, and every alligator basking in the slime is in himself an Epic, self-contained. I aspire for Fame. It is my yearning and my thirst.
>
> Are you, sir, aware of any member of Congress in England, who would undertake to pay my expenses to that country, and for six months after my arrival? (314)

The American writer Miss Toppit furnishes occasion for some of the narrator's most obvious enjoyment:

> 'Mind and matter,' said the lady in the wig, 'glide swiftly into the vortex of immensity. Howls the sublime, and softly sleeps the calm Ideal, in the whispering chambers of Imagination. To hear it, sweet it is. But then, outlaughs the stern philosopher, and saith to the Grotesque, "What ho! arrest for me that Agency. Go bring it here!" and so the vision fadeth'. (467)

Dickens had used meta-textual strategies from the *Sketches by Boz* onwards, but here his very awareness of the power of literature once again suggests a certain wariness of its possible effects, particularly where it exceeds the level of a Miss Toppit. Among other admonitions, the reader is told not to posture as a literary 'type', most directly through Tom Pinch's rejection of a despairing romantic role in relation to Mary Graham:

> 'You think of me, Ruth,' said Tom, 'and it is very natural that you should, as if I were a character in a book; and you make it a sort of poetic justice that I should, by some impossible means or other, come, at last, to marry the person I love. But there is a much higher justice than poetical justice, my dear, and it does not order events upon the same principle. Accordingly, people who read about heroes in books, and choose to make heroes of themselves out of books, consider it a very fine thing to be discontented and gloomy, and misanthropical, and perhaps a little blasphemous, because they cannot have everything

ordered for their own individual accommodations. Would you like me to become one of that sort of people?' (655–56).

Notwithstanding the attacks on literary poseurs and readers who insist on projecting themselves into inappropriately romantic roles taken from the novels they have read, *Martin Chuzzlewit* is consistent with Dickens's other writing in its celebration of the life-transforming potential of literature and the imagination. As he claimed to Forster, 'As to the way in which these characters have opened out, that is, to me, one of the most surprising processes of the mind in this sort of invention. Given what one knows, what one does not know springs up; and I am as absolutely certain of its being true, as I am of the law of gravitation – if such a thing be possible, more so' (To John Forster, [? Mid-February 1843]. 441). In this analysis of the creative imagination, the process of literary creation is first invoked as a quasi-science (obliquely suggested in the phrase 'this sort of invention') and then elided, as the suspension of disbelief in what 'springs up' is predicated on what one already 'knows'. The pronoun 'one' might by this point stand equally for writer, reader or both. In a rather haphazard mixed metaphor, the 'invention' of characters has developed a more organic capacity to 'spring up', a process more believable than the scientific law of gravitation. The imaginative function of literature, in other words, has taken on a standing equal to that of science, and its laws are more convincing in proportion as the story is not devised by the writer but happens semi-autonomously.

Notwithstanding the narrator's exposure of false or inauthentic writing practices (including Pecksniff's advertisements with their links to the swampy 'Eden' by which Martin is also deceived), the central myth governing the moral economy of *Martin Chuzzlewit* is predicated on an essentially literary understanding of the world. Despite his final resistance to the willed imposition of an inappropriate plot on his life story by the purblind Martin or the more calculating Pecksniff, Tom Pinch himself is the character most associated with books and reading, moving between the imaginary realm of childhood reading and the material object itself. It transpires that Tom's imagination is based on his childhood reading of *Robinson Crusoe* and *Philip Quarll*, and it is through this imaginative faculty that he persistently views Pecksniff (rather than himself) as an idealised hero.

In a more sophisticated novel, when David Copperfield makes this mistake with Steerforth, the reader is implicated in succumbing to the fascinations of this false friend, rather than enjoying a sense of greater insight. In the earlier novel it is the narrator rather than Tom who presents the world of books as an escape from what the reader at least can recognise as Pecksniff's tyranny, through an invocation of the *Arabian Nights* during the visit to a children's bookshop, 'Which matchless wonders, coming fast on Mr Pinch's mind, did so rub up and chafe that wonderful lamp within him, that when he turned his face towards the busy street, a crowd of phantoms waited on his pleasure, and he lived again, with new delight, the happy days before the Pecksniff era' (65).

Notwithstanding his naïve responses and the assumption by other characters that he is incapable of taking care of himself, at two key points in the novel Tom's relationship with books themselves is used to signal his essentially practical nature. The imaginative and the material are linked both in the visions of the characters and through the uses to which books are put. When Martin leaves Pecksniff's house, he is selfishly exasperated with Tom for having pressed a stray volume of – of all things – a French translation of *The Bachelor of Salamanca*' on him at parting, with one page carefully folded down. Assuming that the page is intended by way of gratuitous inspiration or advice, he is surprised to find that it actually contains a bank note. This suggestion of money and books as reversible or interchangeable is a reminder of the status of books as objects of exchange – Forster's *Life of Charles Dickens* reinforces the importance of book pawning to Dickens's imagination when he recalls how the young Dickens was sent out to raise money on his father's library, 'the account of the sales, as they actually occurred and were told to me long before David was born, was reproduced word for word in his imaginary narrative' (vol 1. 17). In the fragment as cited in Forster's biography Dickens literally substitutes bread, a potent literary symbol of threatened starvation throughout the century, for an imagined and presumably unattainable book, 'Once, I remember tucking my own bread (which I had brought from home in the morning) under my arm, wrapped up in a piece of paper like a book' (vol 1. 23).

Later in the novel Tom will be offered congenial work cataloguing books, just as his financial position becomes untenable. This work allows him to indulge his literary inclinations as well as demonstrating his organisational skill; having spent a certain number of hours a day on his paid employment, he feels at liberty to take the volumes home and read them before returning them the following day. In a number of novels of the period, a widely held knowledge of the status of books leads to the false currency of the pretence that a character is reading an ennobling passage, as a deceptive index to their moral nature. Notably Tom reads in private as a reward to himself for a day's work well done.

Again signalling the difference between authentic and false responses to the world, in Tom's imagination a moral crisis can alter the material world with which it is associated. Having once realised that he has been mistaken in his estimate of Pecksniff's character, he finds that his surroundings have apparently changed:

> Oh! What a different town Salisbury was in Tom Pinch's eyes to be sure, when the substantial Pecksniff of his heart melted away into an idle dream! He possessed the same faith in the wonderful shops, the same intensified appreciation of the mystery and wickedness of the place; made the same exalted estimate of its wealth, population and resources; and yet it was not the old city or anything like it. (477)

The balance can only be restored in sleep, when he 'dreamed about him as he Never Was' (436) and so brings the town back in to alignment with the character he had created for his former employer.

Elsewhere in the novel dream states are imbued with an uncontrollable agency, once more suggesting the power of literature to alter the material world; when Martin and Mark are safely asleep in the boarding house, they 'mingle in their sleep the shadows of objects afar off, as they take fantastic shapes upon the wall in the dim light of thought without control', leaving the novel itself, 'a dream within a dream', free 'as rapidly to change the scene, and cross the ocean to the English shore' (254). In this passage the characters' dreaming is not subject to corporeal constraints, but is made imaginatively visible to the reader as a series of projected images – the shadows of objects thrown against the wall. By a process of rapid association, the reader is then incorporated into the dream, imaginatively able to change the scene and cross the ocean. As in the presentation of the terrain in *Oliver Twist*, the readers are bound to align themselves with the narrator, while the narrator is in theory bound by the movements of the characters, but is nonetheless able to move great distances in a moment.

American Notes offers a heightened awareness of the way in which material objects can function as imaginative prompts; in one memorable passage the traveller's half-asleep response to objects is mediated by an earlier reading of books, which are themselves registered as both images and physical artefacts. As Dickens watches the stumps of trees strewing the road ahead, in the dark:

> They were often as entertaining to me as so many glasses in a magic lantern, and never took their shapes at my bidding, but seemed to force themselves upon me, whether I would or no; and strange to say, I sometimes recognised in them, counterparts of figures once familiar to me in pictures attached to childish books, forgotten long ago'. (215)

The process whereby familiar objects half seen through the darkness adopt shapes regardless of, even contrary to, the will of the individual, is a familiar image suggestive of childhood imagination. In a circular movement Dickens aligns the impression made on him by the tree stumps with his youthful response to literature, suggesting that an early immersion in books has created the imaginative faculty that now enables him to recall them. The phrase 'pictures attached to childish books' is suggestive both of textual illustrations and of the power to visualise the characters he reads about.

In a letter to Maclise the material world is invested with quasi-material life, presumably derived from an absorption in books of travel:

> The railroads go through the low grounds and swamps, and it is all one eternal forest, with fallen trees mouldering away in stagnant water and decayed vegetable matter – and heaps of timber in every aspect of decay and utter ruin. I dress up imaginary tribes of Indians, as we rattle

on, and scatter them among the trees as they used to be – sleeping in their blankets, cleaning their arms, nursing brown children, and so forth. ([?22 March 1842]. Pilgrim 3. 152–55. 154)

Interestingly it is not just literary sources that are important to characters. The Dickensian narrator may politely assume that his readers have a long-standing relationship with fiction, fairy tale and romance, from which they derive their imaginative faculties. But as the letter to Maclise suggests, the novels are in fact steeped in non-fiction manuscript and print sources, an aspect of reading that would become key to the plot of *Edwin Drood* in 1870. Like Dickens on board ship, as he almost manages to conjure up a state room out of his own good humour, Martin is able to appreciate basic food after his departure from Pecksniff's:

> the mind so soon accommodates itself to the necessities of the body, that this poor waggoners' house-of-call, which he would have despised yesterday, became now quite a choice hotel; while his dish of eggs and bacon, and his mug of beer, were not by any means the coarse fare he had supposed, but fully bore out the inscription on the window-shutter, which proclaimed those viands to be "Good entertainment for Travellers". (185)

The sense in which this repast becomes 'good entertainment' is entirely dependent in other words on the spirit in which it is received. This lesson will be reprised in 'Eden', with the placard announcing Martin and Mark as architects. Mark's superior status is apparent in his display of this advertisement, which he knows to be hopeless:

> lastly, he brought forth a great placard (which Martin in the exultation of his heart had prepared with his own hands at the National Hotel), bearing the inscription, CHUZZLEWIT & Co., ARCHITECTS AND SURVEYORS, which he displayed upon the most conspicuous part of the premises, with as much gravity as if the thriving city of Eden had had a real existence, and they expected to be overwhelmed with business. (329)

While the central characters are morally very different, their education is effected in very similar ways, through an increasingly complex understanding of the value and function of words.

By the end of the novel Tom has adopted a more mature view of Pecksniff, benevolently giving him money in response to the false claims set out in a series of begging letters. Pecksniff by this point has become associated with characters such as Slyme, who also make false use of words – having abused the writer / reader contract from the start through this false advertising (linked to the Eden scenes in America); he is now permanently excluded from the world of the imagination.

But outside the world of the novel Dickens's inability to control the way he was read or presented to the public was nowhere more obvious (or more intensely felt) than in the hijacking of his work in America. Complaining to Lord Brougham about the lack of a copyright law, he inevitably cites the failure of overseas publishers to pay authors; however he is also incensed by the threat to authors' standing, as they have no power of veto over the context in which they are presented to new readers:

> The system, as it stands, is most iniquitous and disgraceful. A writer not only gets nothing for his labours, though they are diffused all over this enormous Continent, but cannot even choose his company. Any wretched halfpenny newspaper can print him at its pleasure – place him side by side with productions which disgust his common sense – and by means of the companionship in which it constantly shews him, engenders a feeling of association in the minds of a large class of readers, from which he would revolt, and to avoid which he would pay almost any price. (22 March 1842. Pilgrim 3. 144–45. 145)

He repeatedly refused to correct (or he claimed, even to read) false accounts of his comments on the Americans and even spurious letters he had supposedly written, which appeared in American newspapers over the next few years. But whether this was a consolation or not, Dickens was at least able to contextualise his own work through such letters as these.

In keeping with his other letters from the early 1840s onwards, he also uses jokes based on particular characters to add a further dimension to his communication with a particular or chosen reader. Where his letters from America had relied exclusively on allusions to previous work (including references to Pickwick and voiceovers of Miggs from the rather less popular *Barnaby Rudge*), during the serialisation of *Martin Chuzzlewit* he began to merge the boundaries between reader and character in new ways, through detailing the process of writing itself. In one such letter he tells Angela Burdett Coutts that 'Your note finds me in Mr Pinch's society. He seems comfortable and in good spirits: having a holiday'. (16 January 1843. Pilgrim 3. 424)

Perhaps significantly, he continues to draw elsewhere on the sense of an existing readership, for instance reviving his earlier Boz persona in order to present himself as a semi-fictional character for the amusement of Cornelius Felton. In a letter from Broadstairs he positions himself as if for the opening of a novel, 'In a bay-window in a one pair, sits from nine o'Clock to one, a gentleman with rather long hair and no neck-cloth who writes and grins as if he thought he were very funny indeed. His name is Boz' (1 September 1843. Pilgrim 3. 547–51. 548).

Two months later he was confiding to Forster that he planned to leave England for a year,[1] and a second letter on the same subject reveals frustration with his seeming inability to mould the reader's response. Specifically he finds himself unable to control how, or even if, he is read by large numbers of the public. In this formulation he is in competition with both rival authors and the reviewers who usurp his authority over readers:

> You know, as well as I, that I think *Chuzzlewit* in a hundred points immeasurably the best of my stories. That I feel my power now, more than I ever did. That I have a greater confidence in myself than I ever had. That I *know*, if I have health, I could sustain my place in the minds of thinking men, though fifty writers started up tomorrow. But how many readers do *not* think! How many take it upon trust from knaves and idiots, that one writes too fast, or runs a thing to death! How coldly did this very book go on for months, until it forced itself up in people's opinion, without forcing itself up in sale! If I wrote for forty thousand Forsters, or for forty thousand people who know I write because I can't help it, I should have no need to leave the scene. (To John Forster, [2 November 1843]. Pilgrim 3. 590–91)

Gissing has a point in characterising the denouement of *Martin Chuzzlewit* as the triumph of feeling over probability, as 'He involves himself in complications which necessitate leaps and bounds of perverse ingenuity. And at last, his story frankly hopeless, he cuts through knots, throws difficulties into oblivion, and plays up his characters to a final rally; so sure of his touch upon the readers' emotions that he can disregard their bewilderment' (*Charles Dickens: A Critical Study* 49). In Dicken's own formulation the novel is a comparative failure because readers have not accepted the author's guidance on how to read it or his assurance that his (notably Romantic) status as a writer is a sufficient guarantee of its quality.

Another popular and prolific writer half a century later would in turn satirise just this conflicted attitude to the reading public on the part of authors. In Marie Corelli's *The Sorrows of Satan* (1895) the aspiring author Geoffrey Tempest denigrates the public's lack of discernment even as he focuses his desires on achieving high book sales. Significantly in praising Tennyson's poetry to Forster in 1859, Dickens seems to assume that only a fellow writer (although interestingly he himself was not a poet) is capable of appreciating the quality of the writing, 'How fine "The Idylls" are! Lord! what a blessed thing it is to a man who can write! I thought nothing could be grander than the first poem till I came to the third; but when I had read the last, it seemed to be absolutely unapproached and unapproachable' (To John Forster, 25 August 1859. 111–13. 112).

In a spirit of renewed confidence, in a letter of 1845 he reverts to the importance of writing as an influence for good, telling Forster that 'I have written to little purpose, if I cannot *write myself right* in people's minds' ([?1 or 2 November 1845]. Pilgrim 4. 423). Whatever his professed ambivalence about the manipulative power of the written word, Dickens himself has no apparent reservation about steering his readers in a particular direction.

'The truest book as a man can write' *Dombey and Son*

The status of the written word and its relation to print are prominent features of Dickens's writing of the 1840s, but his writing from this period also registers the difficulty of controlling reader response beyond the page itself. In *Dombey and Son* private conversations are surreptitiously written down, interviews are given the false authority of print (a theme that would resurface in the cheap press reports of Krook's death in *Bleak House*), and culturally significant printed texts are misquoted in conversation. Elsewhere in the novel books are used in a range of ways identified by Price as characteristic of Victorian fiction more generally: they may be status indicators, barriers to unwanted conversation or (in the fantasies of Susan Nipper) even weapons.

Ablow claims that it is in the preface to the 1848 *Dombey and Son* that 'Dickens makes his first claim to have an emotional attachment to his characters that is akin to that of his readers' (*The Feeling of Reading* 20). In fact a version of this strategy would already be familiar to readers from the ending of *Oliver Twist*, in which the voice of the narrator merges with the sentiments of Dickens himself as he draws attention to the act of writing, 'I would fain linger' with the characters in order to 'share their happiness', mimicking the reader's presumed reluctance to close the book. Nonetheless this new use of prefaces to indicate and increase the sense of intimacy between author and reader is crucial in its assumption of a known relationship – implicit in Ablow's argument is the sense that readers of *Dombey and Son* are now expected to come to the novel already equipped with a feeling of sympathy for the author and his (as yet unknown) characters.

Arguably the writer can set up an assumed relationship with readers, 'touching' their emotions in this way, only by transgressing accepted social codes. Affective scenes are used as a stimulus for emotional response, which implicitly betray the author's own emotion in the most public way. This mode of narration is potentially problematic for both writer and reader – as the *fin de siècle* writer Mary Cholmondeley memorably put it, 'I wonder how I <u>could</u> write so plainly how I <u>could</u> say so many personal things, telling the passer in the street, and the people who dont like me what in real life I hardly tell to my intimate friends' (ms diary 9 October 1899). The status of this shared emotion is affirmed by the narrative voiceovers directing the reader's response.

Even to a mid-century reader Dickens's affective scenes might be considered damagingly feminine, although Charlotte Yonge's *The Heir of Redclyffe* ironically deconstructs such assumptions as part of the complacent Philip Morville's moral education. In a discussion of *Dombey and Son*, he advises his well-born but badly educated cousin Guy against such light reading, which by implication may be acceptable for his female cousins and their disabled brother Charles. Charles satirically exposes his sister Laura's lack of sensibility by relating how 'I made her read me the part of Dombey that hurts women's feelings most, just to see if she would go on – the part about little Paul – and I declare, I shall think the worse of her for ever

74 *Reciprocal Readers and the 1830s–40s*

after – she was so stony hearted, that to this day she does not know whether he is dead or alive' (30). Amy meanwhile is ultimately shown to be more feeling, although Laura teases her here with her excessive emotion, '"I can't quite say I don't know whether he lived or died," said Laura, "for I found Amy in a state that alarmed me, crying in the green-house, and I was very glad to find it was nothing worse than little Paul"' (30). Philip's humourless response is to tell Guy, 'it would be a pity to begin with Dickens when there is so much of a higher grade equally new to you. I suppose you do not understand Italian?' (31). By the end of the novel Philip will have learned to value the emotional responses he began by mistrusting, while Amy's responsive reading equips her to endure the death of her husband within a few months of their marriage.

Like *Martin Chuzzlewit*, *Dombey and Son* explores the status and impact of various types of writing, as well as the ways in which they are circulated. But its account of the ways in which writer and reader are positioned in relation to the text is considerably more complex. Some readers are more privileged than others in their ability to discern meaning, while Dickens's own relations with particular readers allow him to create a privileged 'inner circle'. Writing to Angela Burdett Coutts in January 1847 he merges the time of writing with the as yet unpublished revelation of Paul's death, 'Between ourselves – Paul is dead. He died on Friday night about 10 o'clock; and as I had no hope of getting to sleep afterwards, I went out, and walked about Paris until breakfast-time next morning' (18 January 1847. Pilgrim 5. 9). In several letters from these years he asks friends to consider his novels as coded communications, writing to William Haldimand during the writing of *Dombey and Son*, 'I wish you would regard my Christmas Books, and Dombeys, and so forth, as letters to you: and when you find anything you particularly like, would take it as your own exclusive property. Then I should be entitled to an answer, and should always be an active and punctual correspondent' (27 November 1846. Pilgrim 5. 664–66. 665). Clearly this exclusive right to the 'property' of Dickens's books is severely compromised by the addressing of such letters to different correspondents, but in this letter he seems to suggest a theory of appropriation by order of which individual readers can assume 'rights' in passages not necessarily intended for them personally.

Dombey and Son itself offers numerous examples of a hierarchy of reading, most obviously in the opposition between newspaper reporting and fairy tale. Paul clearly has the right idea when he translates character in to literary terms, 'studying Mrs Pipchin, and the cat, and the fire, night after night, as if they were a book of necromancy, in three volumes' (113) or in his way of showing respect for Feeder's knowledge of London (despite its being his own home town), 'Paul regarded him as if he were the hero of some book of travels or wild adventure, and was almost afraid of such a slashing person' (199). This vicarious adventuring implicitly links him to the more robust Walter, who finally voyages to the countries he has read about.

Unlikely as it seems, even Cornelia Blimber can benefit from a momentary indulgence in 'fancy'. When she appears in false plaits for the end-of-term evening party, it becomes clear that she has at least some tangenital contact with the theatre, in that she 'seemed to have her own little curls in paper underneath, and in a playbill too: for Paul read "Theatre Royal" over one of her sparking spectacles, and "Brighton" over the other' (208).

Early in the novel the death of the first Mrs Dombey uses generic allusions to newspaper print culture in order to invoke a particular reader response. The use of ephemeral newspaper sheets as furniture covers apparently sets universal death against the transient interests of life. Significantly however the narrator remarks on the inclusion of sensational murders among the items of news, 'Bell-handles, window-blinds, and looking-glasses, being papered up in journals, daily and weekly, obtruded fragmentary accounts of deaths and dreadful murders' (24). This casual use of accounts of death and murder subtly suggests that the symbolic exhaustion of Mrs Dombey's resistance (or as Mrs Chick would have it, her failure to 'make an effort') is a form of domestic murder, albeit one that is regarded as insignificant by her callous husband.

Later in the novel, such sensational stories are further complicated when Perch the messenger is interviewed by journalists and gives outrageously exaggerated accounts of the events surrounding Dombey's bankruptcy, purely in order to see his remarks in print. Unlike the transformative power of literary fiction, the newspaper is insufficient to explain or alleviate disaster, as shown when Rob the Grinder deserts Captain Cuttle and while he tries to read the news, 'never a word did Captain Cuttle understand, though he read a vast number, for Rob the Grinder was scampering up one column and down another all through the newspaper' (580). Elsewhere characters comment directly on the status and efficacy of the written word, which can be variously used to enlighten or mislead. Paul's alienation at Dr Blimber's is conveyed through his distress at his school 'analysis' or report and involves a sense of powerlessness to counteract the written word, '... Paul was an object of general interest; a fragile little plaything that they all liked, and that no one would have thought of treating roughly. But he could not change his nature, or re-write the analysis; and so they all agreed that Dombey was old-fashioned' (198). The seriousness with which Paul takes this dismissal is not the less poignant because no one – including the writer of the analysis – seems to know what is meant by the expression 'old fashioned'.

When Walter sets sail for Barbados on the *Son and Heir*, Toots reads a newspaper account to Captain Cuttle, according to which 'There can be no doubt that all surmises as to the fate of the missing vessel, the Son and Heir, port of London, bound for Barbados, are now set at rest for ever; that she broke up in the last hurricane; and that every soul on board perished' (490). The alert reader is prepared to distrust newspaper accounts, but as a retired sailor Cuttle explains that 'They don't romance, you see, on such pints. It's entered on the ship's log, and that's the truest book as a man can write' (492). The weight given to this professional assessment aligns Cuttle with Sol Gills's warnings against tales of adventure at sea, 'that's well enough in fiction, Wally, but it won't do in fact; it won't do at all' (43), despite the narrator's subsequent comment that 'the Captain implicitly believed that all books were true' (575). But in a triumphant restitution of the imaginative world, Walter's miraculous escape subverts any such insistence on the division between fiction and reality, when it turns out that the 'factual' ship's log is itself unreliable. The point here is not that Cuttle was wrong after all, rather that Walter's escape defies the odds as presented in the known accuracy of the ship's log.

With a flourish of fortuitous coincidences and miraculous interventions, in other words, Dickens steps in at the end to make the point once again that only the narrator is always right. If readers are encouraged to sustain their trust in the narrator, they are directed throughout the novel to make connections between the world of their daily experience and their participation in the imaginary community set up by Dickens as author. Like Scrooge, the abandoned Florence is a voracious reader. Less specific than the remembered reading included in the *Carol*, though, the fairy tale trope of the forsaken Florence in her 'enchanted' London house after Paul's death rests less on any particular source than on a generalised invocation of stories readers are likely to have absorbed as children. When the narrator asserts that 'No magic dwelling-place in magic story, shut up in the heart of a thick wood, was ever more solitary and deserted to the fancy, than was her father's mansion in its grim reality, as it stood lowering upon the street' (337), the reader is directed to exercise 'fancy' rather than recognition of a particular literary reference. But the same reader is constantly reminded that these ideas are presented in a Dickens-authored novel, through such meta-fictional commentary as 'It is half-past five o'clock, and an autumn afternoon, when the reader and Solomon Gills become acquainted' (38) or 'It was on the very same day whose evening set upon the last chapter …' (781). The committed serial reader who has followed the novel in its monthly parts towards its conclusion is rewarded by imaginatively sharing in the narrative judgement of Dombey towards the end, as the narrator urges, 'Let us be just to him' (683).

Florence herself provides a textual model of how the movement between fiction and human relations is expected to work, as when she questions Polly about her dead mother, "Come and sit down by me," said Richards, "and I'll tell you a story"' (26). Later she uses her reading to negotiate her new relations with Edith, 'Florence was, one day, sitting in her room, and thinking of the lady and her promised visit soon – for her book turned on a kindred subject – when, raising her eyes, she saw her standing in the doorway' (447). While Captain Cuttle in the Midshipman's parlour, toasts the deserted house, 'Florence bloomed there, like the king's fair daughter in the story' (339). Her association with books is such that it can be inferred by a close reader even when it is not specified. On the night of Walter's unexpected return, Florence has been described in the text as having spent the day with her needlework; there is no indication as to what she is doing at that moment, but the illustration shows her reading a book. Dickens was usually meticulous in checking illustrations, but his extant correspondence makes no comment at all on this act of artistic licence.

But books themselves are not an infallible indicator of a character's status; as in the numerous examples of newspaper reporting, books may be misused, ignored, or quite literally filled with the wrong words. In Brighton Florence patiently makes her way through piles of the tomes prescribed by Blimber, in order to help Paul, and Susan comments significantly, 'If it was to fling at Mrs Pipchin's head, I'd buy a cart-load' (177). Questioning what it is that offends him in Carker's house, the narrator notes the 'voluptuous' pictures and asks, 'Is it that the books have all their gold outside, and that the titles of the greater part qualify them to be companions of the prints and pictures?' (499) Dombey's house is little better, 'Ugh! They were black, cold rooms; and seemed to be in mourning, like the inmates of the house. The books precisely matched as to size, and drawn up in line, like soldiers, looked in their cold, hard, slippery uniforms, as if they had but one idea among them, and that was a freezer' (56).

Captain Cuttle's catchphrase, 'When found, make a note of', is a reminder both of the inaccuracy of his quotations from the catechism and other sources and of the importance of reading as an interpretive act; despite his parodic renderings of half-remembered texts, he adapts what he has read appropriately for emotional use. But if Cuttle's literary shortcomings are treated with affection, it is fitting that Perch, the purveyor of false stories, should be the mouthpiece for Dickens's most overt attack on the devaluing of literary values. In a comic interlude, Captain Cuttle offers to stand him a drink and proposes 'Wal'r! as the toast:

> Mr Perch, who seemed to remember having heard in infancy that there was once a poet of that name, made no objection; but he was much astonished at the Captain's coming into the City to propose a poet; indeed, if he had proposed to put a poet's statue up – say Shakespeare's for example – in a civic thoroughfare, he could hardly have done a greater outrage to Mr Perch's experience'. (252)

While it promulgates the claims of iconic authors such as Shakespeare the novel is also concerned with private writing, including letters, ensuring that all readers have access to the imaginative world at some level. The status of letters in the novel is variable and contingent. On leaving school the hapless Toots would be expected to assume the lifestyle of a gentleman in wealthy circumstances; such is the damage done by his 'education' that he is incapable of fulfilling this role convincingly. However his imaginative faculty has survived and takes the form of writing himself imaginary letters from distinguished figures. Towards the end of his time at Blimber's he 'had license to pursue his own course of study; which was chiefly to write long letters to himself from persons of distinction' (162).

More disingenuous figures also write letters based on fantasy or agreed conventions, such as Mrs Skewton's letters of invitation to Dombey in which she implies that Edith is in love with him, as a means of counteracting her chilly behaviour in person. The dubious value of Mrs Skewton's writing is further undermined after her first stroke, when she feebly gestures for pen and paper, only to write 'Rose-coloured curtains' (559), signalling that she wants her bed curtains to set off her complexion for the doctor. Rob the Grinder's efforts to spy on Florence and Susan are stymied by his inability to read his own writing, 'There was no danger of these documents betraying anything, if accidentally lost; for long before a word was dry, it became as profound a mystery to Rob, as if he had had no part whatever in its production' (347). Good characters too are at the mercy of the postal system and the goodwill of landladies, as Sol Gills discovers when Mrs McStinger fails to pass his reassuring letters on to Captain Cuttle, who therefore assumes that he must have died overseas.

This increased attention to the role played by letters quite possibly derives from the new ways in which Dickens himself was using his correspondence with friends and readers to shape his novels. Throughout the 1840s he had been using his huge correspondence to test out reader response as he wrote consecutive numbers, often reminding correspondents of the status he wished them to accord his characters, for instance telling Forster that Dombey will see the worth of his daughter 'whom Mr Dombey has used – and so has the boy himself to, for that matter – as a mere convenience and handle to him' (To John Forster, [25–26 July 1846]. Pilgrim 5. 589–93. 589). In the same letter he discusses his idea for letting Walter fall as Carker the Junior had done and asks 'Do you think it may be done, without making people angry?' ([25–26 July 1846]. Pilgrim 5. 589–93. 593).

Charting readers' responses as he writes, he notes in subsequent letters that 'Dombey is a prodigious success. Enthusiastic bulletins reach me daily' (To Thomas Beard, 21 October 1846. Pilgrim 5. 639) and 'Paul's death has amazed Paris' (To John Forster [10 February 1847]. Pilgrim 5. 24). The importance of retaining readers' belief in the characters is nowhere more evident than in his willingness to change the projected plot (as he famously did again when revising *Great Expectations* in 1861). Responding to criticisms as the numbers appeared, he wrote to Forster in December 1847 to say that he had received a 'note from Jeffrey this morning, who won't believe (positively refuses) that Edith is Carker's mistress. What do you think of a kind of inverted Maid's Tragedy, and a tremendous scene of her undeceiving Carker, and giving him to know that she never meant that?' ([21 December 1847]. Pilgrim 5. 211–12. 211)

If he was prepared to take readers' advice on particular points, Dickens was determined to retain control over the final view of his novel, even attempting to direct the course of future criticism. Despite a large sale,

Dombey and Son had disappointing profits, but he insisted, '... I have a strong belief that, if any of my books are read years hence, *Dombey* will be remembered as among the best of them ...' (To John Forster, [22? September 1849]. Pilgrim 5. 610–11. 611). As the idea of Forster one day writing his biography had already been raised by this point, letters such as this can quite literally be seen as an attempt to guide later readers to the 'correct' valuation of his work.

In the novel itself the exploration of reading practices and the value placed on writing and print is finally resolved through Harriet Carker's reading of the Bible to the dying Alice Marwood. In this post-transformation scene, the narrator makes it clear that the New Testament is the one supremely authoritative text, with the power to transform human relations and specifically to link the printed word to human action. Where the *Carol* can stand in for Dickens himself on a shelf or even in a designated place by the fire, the Bible can reach non-literate audiences who are unable to see meaning in print, by literally transforming the face of the interpreter. In this scenario the message becomes legible in the face of the reader, as Alice asks Harriet to position her in such a way 'that I may see the words in your kind face' (871).

From his tentative appeals to potential purchasers of the journals in which his sketches first appeared to the authoritative pronouncements of *Dombey and Son*'s moralising narrator, Dickens consistently engages with his prospective readers as imagined individuals, in order to shape their response to his texts. One way in which he does this is through paratextual material, including prefaces to new editions incorporating reader response. As Dickens seeks to mythologise his own relationship with readers, the narrative persona appears on the margins of the published text, in his series of prefaces to different editions, directly addressing the reader, in ways that already start to break down boundaries between letters and fiction. Increasingly he also develops his daily correspondence as a means of gauging reader response, positioning individual readers in relation to the written page. This may involve placing himself in the imagination before his correspondent or imposing new meanings on an already published text. A letter can even take on semi-magical qualities, as when he tells Macready that in sending him *A Christmas Carol* to read in America, 'It pleases me to think that it will bring you Home for an hour or two' (3 January 1844. Pilgrim 4. 9–13. 12). But within the fiction itself, these 'ideal' readers are encouraged to imagine for themselves what remains unstated or is considered inexpressible by the narrator, a technique Dickens would famously develop in *David Copperfield*.

Note

1. To John Forster, [1 November 1843]. Pilgrim 3. 587–8.

2 The Hero of His Life

While Dickens's famously autobiographical novel apparently closes the gap between writer and reader, it is also engaged in new and subtle ways of mythologising the figure of the author. *David Copperfield*, published in volume form in 1850, raises the question of just what a literary biography might look like, even assuming the appropriateness of publishing details of a writer's life, a subject on which Dickens himself expressed deep ambivalence. Inevitably interest in his life increased with his growing fame, although he consistently resisted attempts from interested correspondents to secure biographical details. Given the care with which his own letters are crafted, it is perhaps surprising to find one writer castigated on the grounds that 'He writes about his books, rather as if he saw his future biography in his mind's eye, with this letter in it' (To Charles Knight, 4 September 1850. Pilgrim 12. Appendix A 626).

Despite the bonfire at Gad's Hill on which he burned 'the accumulated letters and papers of twenty years' (To W. H. Wills, 4 September 1860. Pilgrim 9. 302–304. 304) in the autumn of 1860 (and which secured the privacy of his correspondents rather than himself), Dickens was not consistently opposed to the publication of biographies; indeed he wrote a number of letters to Forster praising biographies he had been reading and acceded to the parents' request that he write a biographical preface to the collected poems of Adelaide Procter (1825–1864) in 1866. It is with great zest and a level of self-congratulation that he tells the story of the discovery of his friend Brian Procter's daughter Adelaide behind the poetic pseudonym of the mysterious 'Miss Berwick'.

The preface to *Legends and Lyrics,* published for the first time as a single volume, begins with a discussion of Procter's first submission of her work to *Household Words*, under her chosen pseudonym Mary Berwick, in the spring of 1853. Dickens recalls seeing:

> a short poem among the proffered contributions, very different, as I thought, from the shoal of verses perpetually setting through the office of such a Periodical, and possessing much more merit. Its authoress was quite unknown to me. She was one MISS MARY BERWICK, whom I had never heard of; and she was to be addressed by letter, if addressed at all, at a circulating library in the western district of London. (ix)

In recounting the story, Dickens as narrator self-consciously separates his admiration of the initial verses from his later knowledge of the writer's identity, stressing both her skill and her business-like qualities:

> How we came gradually to establish, at the office of *Household Words*, that we knew all about Miss Berwick, I have never discovered. But we settled somehow, to our complete satisfaction, that she was governess in a family; that she went to Italy in that capacity, and returned; and that she had long been in the same family. We really knew nothing whatever of her, except that she was remarkably business-like, punctual, self-reliant, and reliable: so I suppose we insensibly invented the rest. For myself, my mother was not a more real personage to me, than Miss Berwick the governess became. (ix)

This account deliberately distances Procter from any suggestion of nepotism, as the daughter of Dickens's friend. More importantly, it quarantines her professional standing as a writer – in which she is both talented and independent, a combination Dickens insistently claimed for the writing community – from her more recognisably feminine attributes, as an implicitly respectable family governess. It is possible that Dickens is also making a tongue-in-cheek allusion to the mystery surrounding the Brontë sisters, who famously worked as governesses while publishing under impenetrable pseudonyms.

Comparison of the preface with a letter from Dickens to Procter herself shows that this anecdote has been worked up partly for the purpose of mythologising the writer. On discovering her identity in 1854, after inadvertently praising 'Miss Berwick's' contribution to that year's Christmas number to her mother with Procter herself standing nearby, he immediately wrote to reiterate his praise and to share the joke that his sub-editor Wills had invented the governess story:

> From the first, I have always had an especial interest in that Miss Berwick, and have over and over again questioned Wills about her. I suppose he has gone on gradually building up an imaginary structure of life and adventure for her, but he has given me the strangest information! ... You must have felt enormously wicked last Tuesday, when I, such a babe in the wood, was unconsciously prattling to you. But you have given me so much pleasure, and have made me shed so many tears, that I can only think of you now in association with the sentiment and grace of your verses. So pray accept the blessing and forgiveness of Richard Watts, though I am afraid you come under both his conditions of exclusion. (To Miss Adelaide Anne Procter, 17 December 1854. Pilgrim 7. 486–87)

Both versions of the story are amusingly told, but what is at stake in the preface is the way in which a female writer should be read. The false identity of Miss Berwick, whose post office address aligns her with potentially illicit correspondence, is sanctioned by the assumption that as a governess, she is educated, and her reluctance to receive letters at her employer's home address is no fault of her own. This respectability, despite her dubious preference for a post office address, is presumably inferred from the quality of her initial letter, as well as the enclosed poem. Dickens's willingness to include the work of this unknown contributor is vindicated when she turns out to be the middle-class daughter of his old friend 'Barry Cornwall', himself a poet writing under a pseudonym. But this discovery undermines the more romantic myth of the writer as obscure and friendless, allowing Dickens to rehearse his view of the professional qualities of the author in question.

His biographical introduction to her collected *Legends and Lyrics* gives some indication of how he thought a literary life should be constructed, and interestingly he does include two of her personal letters, despite his insistence on burning his own private correspondence by this time for fear of its being published after his death. In a letter to her parents he tells them that he has aimed to write what Procter herself would have sanctioned, 'It is brief, and I have aimed at perfect simplicity, and an avoidance of all that your beloved Adelaide would have wished avoided' (to Mrs Procter, 26 September 1865. Pilgrim 11. 96–97. 97). In part this shaping of the preface is suggestive of the poet's right to control, even posthumously, the way in which they are presented to the public. The brevity also allows this form of biography to frame and condition a response to the poems as distinct from the personality of the writer.

The most regular poetic contributor to *Household Words*, Adelaide Procter is proffered as a template for what Dickens thinks a writer should be, personally and professionally. Her early death does not bring her within range of Dickens's fragile girl-women such as Little Nell or Dora Spenlow, and she is not described in the terms he famously applied to Christiana Weller before her marriage, as being somehow too spiritual to live. His continuing association of talent with frailty is in evidence as late as 1860, in the warning to a father to curb his 12-year-old daughter's literary enthusiasm, 'Excuse my recommending you in the strongest manner (I dare say unnecessarily) gently to restrain that talent rather than otherwise. There is very little danger of its perishing, but it may be stronger than the young life with which it is as yet associated' (To Robert Fletcher, 23 January 1859. Pilgrim 9. 200–201). But even without taking into account his imaginative engagement with the deaths of young women, Dickens's response to Procter is notably unsentimental.

This careful positioning of the female writer is ironic given the ambivalent position she occupied in her lifetime. A member of the feminist Langham Place group, she was apparently the favourite poet of Queen Victoria; while she wrote for and about 'fallen' women, she was also a denizen of the keepsake annual. Working within a Romantic tradition, she based a highly successful writing career on poems about failure and thwarted affection, many of which appeared anonymously in *Household Words* before being collected in two series of *Legends and Lyrics* (published in 1858 and 1861 respectively). Some of her most popular poems, such as 'A Lost Chord' and 'Cleansing Fires', were later set to music for the drawing room market.

'A Lost Chord' takes musical expression as a type of the creative and divine, describing the speaker fretfully playing the organ and touching a beautiful chord by chance, while 'my fingers wandered idly / Over the noisy keys'. Since this moment of transcendence, 'I have sought, but I seek it vainly, / That one lost chord divine, / Which came from the soul of the Organ, / And entered into mine'. This sense of a tantalising glimpse of unattainable possibilities is of course a keynote of *David Copperfield*, Dickens's favourite among his own novels. 'Cleansing Fires' offers an alternative perspective on the same idea, resonating with David's efforts to temper his 'undisciplined heart' before he can become worthy of Agnes:

> Let thy gold be cast in the furnace,
> Thy red gold, precious and bright,
> Do not fear the hungry fire,
> With its caverns of burning light:
> And thy gold shall return more precious,
> Free from every spot and stain;
> For gold must be tried by fire,
> As a heart must be tried by pain!

In his twentieth century depictions of Victorian culture, E. F. Benson repeatedly satirises Procter's popularity as a drawing-room favourite after her poetry was set to music, memorably describing 'A Lost Chord' and other drawing-room favourites like it, as 'test cases for tears' (20). Mary Cholmondeley likewise insists on the femininity of Procter's work, satirising the appropriation of 'Cleansing Fires' by superficially romantic figures such as Lady Newhaven in *Red Pottage* (1899):

> It is doubtful whether until this moment Lady Newhaven had known what suffering was. She had talked freely of it to others. She had sung, as if it were her own composition, 'Cleansing Fires.' She often said it might have been written for her.
>
> In the cruel fire of sorrow, [*slow, soft pedal*]
> Cast thy heart, do not faint or wail, [*both pedals down, quicker*].
> Let they hand be firm and steady, [*loud and hold on to last syllable*].
> Do not let thy spi-rit quail, [*bang! B natural. With resolution*].
> Bu-ut... [*hurricane of false notes, &c &c*].
> But now, poor thing, the fire had reached her, and her spirit quailed immediately (214–15).

Clearly Dickens could have presented Procter as an inoffensive, but ultimately sentimental, purveyor of feminine verses, as Benson later chose to do; equally he could have reconfigured her as the pure heroine of one of his own novels. But nothing in his letters written during her lifetime, or in his published comments after her death, gives this impression.

This professional and unromantic view is reinforced in two letters to Wills, clearly not intended for publication and written before Procter's identity became known. Despite his later claim that he himself had 'discovered' Miss Berwick, the first of these letters suggests that in fact Wills rather than Dickens himself may well have been the one who was so struck by the initial poem submitted in the spring of 1853. Dated February of that year, Dickens's letter refers to a poem identified by the Pilgrim editors as Procter's 'Friend Sorrow', in less than flattering terms, complaining that 'There are awful haltings in the Poem, but I have made the best of it' (To W. H. Wills, 17 February 1853. 26). In October 1854, two months before (as luck would have it) praising her contribution of 'The Third Poor Traveller' in front of her, Dickens remarked to Wills of another poem, identified by the Pilgrim editors as 'My Picture', that it 'is of the shadiest quality … but all the meaning that is in it, comes out of it – which is something' (6 October 1854. Pilgrim 7. 432–33. 432). As in the case of other contributors (including on occasion the hapless Wills himself), Dickens could be ruthless in his assessment of particular offerings, complaining in 1856 about a poem of Procter's, 'Pray, *pray*, don't have Poems unless they are good. We are immeasurably better without them. "Beyond", is really Beyond anything I ever saw, in utter badness' (To W. H. Wills, 2 October 1858. Pilgrim 8. 673–75. 673). His faith in Will's judgement seems not to have increased by 1862, when he warned him, 'On no consideration put in any Poem that I have not seen. When I come upon a strange Poem in print and publication, my distress is abject' (To W. H. Wills, 4 November 1862. 155–56. 156).

Despite his professed admiration for Procter's work, Dickens stresses in his preface to *Legends and Lyrics* itself that the writer should not be identified too closely with the moribund sentiments of particular poems, suggesting a level of anxiety about her poetic persona as a distorted reflection of the writer herself. As her biographer, he himself shares something of David Copperfield's anxiety about the responsibility of first-person narration, apparent in his having to convince himself that writing about her death is not the same as making it happen, 'it is natural that I should linger on my way to the close of this brief record, avoiding its end. But, even as the close came upon her, so it must come here' (xv).

Throughout the preface, Dickens implicitly refutes the gendered status of the writer, attributing particular qualities to Procter as a professional rather than as a woman. A more recent biographer notes that, '… Dickens does award Procter an adult and womanly status. He avoids romanticising and infantilising Procter and is keen to dispel the illusion of the recessive poetess' (Gregory, 198–99). Indeed towards the end of the preface his own identification with the subject becomes suspiciously like a kind of transference, as he describes her failing health in the face of her unremitting philanthropic and literary work, 'To have saved her life, then, by taking action on the warning that shone in her eyes and sounded in her voice, would have been impossible, without changing her nature. As long as the power of moving about in the old way was left to her, she must exercise it, or be killed by the restraint' (xv). For all his disapproval of women with a 'mission' in his novels, the subtle disengagement of the writer from prescribed gender norms is characteristic of Dickens's correspondence with female contributors to *Household Words*.

In discussing his own life Dickens was not consistently hostile to the idea of a biography. Significantly he puts off rather than rebukes one correspondent asking for details of his life in a letter of 1864, 'I beg to assure you that I have never seen published any "reliable materials" for a Biographical account of myself. I never supply any, as I think it may be time to pursue the subject when my life is over' (To William Riddle, 28 July 1864. 415). His will specifically refutes any desire for a commemoration of himself as an author, on the grounds that he rests his claim to remembrance on his published work. But as an evidently bewildered Forster would finally reveal, parts of Dickens's abandoned autobiography, several chapters of which he had sent him in ms, made their way largely unaltered into *David Copperfield*.

To a modern reader it makes perfect sense that Dickens's ambivalence about revealing details of his life in the autobiographical fragment should be resolved by this simple expedient of embedding it in a fictional narrative. But Forster himself had received this information in strict confidence and was clearly still shocked by its publication when he wrote after Dickens's death, 'The idea of *David Copperfield*, which was to take all the world into his confidence, had not at this time occurred to him; but what it had so startled me to know, his readers were afterwards told with only such change or addition as for the time might sufficiently disguise himself under cover of his hero' (vol 1. 19–20). If, as Maria Chialant argues, 'this short piece of autobiography, in order to become visible at all, had to camouflage itself as biography' (77), it is worth noting that the fragment is actually presented in three different aspects: the fictional autobiography of the writer David is assumed to be in fact an equally fictional biography written by Dickens; after Dickens's death his first-person account is framed by Forster's biography inflected by the references to *David Copperfield* contained within it. Interestingly Forster later reuses the idea of Dickens taking readers into his confidence to reclaim a level of private relationship, reinstating himself in the role of mediator between Dickens and the public in reminding the reader that he himself has withheld particular details, in the apparently uncontroversial context of the writing of the second number of *Dombey and Son*, 'I do not admit the reader to his full confidence' (vol 1. 404).

Some readers at least suspected the personal elements of David Copperfield's experience, although their perspicacity would not be confirmed until Forster's *Life of Dickens* began appearing between 1871 and 1874. Forster himself remembered that at the time of *David Copperfield*'s first publication, 'there was withal a suspicion, which though general and vague had sharpened interest not a little, that underneath the fiction lay something of the author's life' (vol 2. 98). But as late as 1870 G. A. Sala was able to say of the novel:

> rather absurdly, I think – it is supposed to possess strongly autobiographical features; although it is patent that its author never had a stepfather who ill-treated him; never ran away from home, to be brought up by an eccentric aunt; never groaned under the sway of a brutal flogging schoolmaster like Crinkle [sic]; was never employed to wash bottles in a wine merchant's cellar; and was never articled to a proctor in Doctors Commons. (61–62)

Dickens's insistence that his readers should confine their attention to his published work is not quite the same as rejecting their interest in his life or personality. Rather he seeks to direct public interest towards his literary output as the embodiment of his character; this insistence on imaginative work as a reflection of character is a feature of his letters to family members, evident in one lecture to his son Henry in which he is admonished to work with earnestness and determination, 'Look at some of my Manuscripts at Gad's, and think of the patient hours devoted year after year to single lines' (To Henry Dickens, 11 February 1868. 46–48. 47).

In writing an account of his own childhood however Dickens adopts a series of fictional strategies, aimed at imaginatively relocating a neglected child at the centre of the narrative, much as he would do throughout his novels. In the autobiographical fragment entrusted to John Forster he emphasises how he 'felt my early hopes of growing up to be a learned and distinguished man, crushed in my breast' (Appendix A, *David Copperfield*, 60[1]). Nonetheless he derived solace from the memory that his young companions treated him as a gentleman despite his outward condition. But the status of Dickens's fragment is highly problematic, not least in its self-conscious use of emotive language in the presentation of himself as hapless victim of both family circumstances and his mother's ostensible lack of maternal feeling at this period. Rosemarie Bodenheimer has perceptively cited 'the fictionality of Dickens's self-creation' ('Dickens and the Writing of a Life' 54) in his autobiographical accounts and correspondence, as in his novels, as a major source of his fascination. Certainly the fragment deploys a number of strategies familiar from Dickens's fiction, including its offer to the reader of limited intimacy (while the tone is overtly emotional the episode related is incomplete and not fully contextualised), and the sense of an ultimate order that explains and shapes his early experience as the prelude to his triumph over adverse circumstances and ultimate rise to fame. As Nicola Bradbury notes, 'Together with the intimacy of indignation is a kind of analytical poise, and a pride in the detail and flourish of recall' (20). Max Saunders's comment on aesthetic autobiography that 'The autobiographical needed to be poetized or fictionalized, turned into *art*, before it could provide an adequate representation of the artist's subjectivity' (74) is equally applicable here.

Again anticipating the practice of later writers in its conscious appeal to an imagined reader, the fragment invites the reader's participation through an insistence that his suffering as a boy is 'utterly beyond my power to tell. No man's imagination can overstep the reality' (*David Copperfield*, Appendix A 862). In a discussion of *David Copperfield* Gareth Corderey notes that 'David's hypersensitivity triggers memories so intensely that past becomes present' (372). In the context of the fragment itself, Bodenheimer similarly suggests that the presentation of the child's suffering erases the temporal gap between the event itself and the moment of retelling it, in order to give the writer power over the past:

> The outraged narrator of the fragment seems to be trying hopelessly to be making up to the abandoned child for that failure of parental feeling and appreciation during and after the period of his father's imprisonment for debt. If they would not provide the appropriate protection or the necessary remorse and horror, he would, in retrospect, do it for them. (52)

The fragment's adaptation (in parts, a simple transfer of passages) in the pages of *David Copperfield* further complicates its status and raises questions about the authority of the fictional voice in the novel. For instance, while both David and the narrator of the fragment accord their memories of working in London the power to intrude unexpectedly on their adult selves for no known reason, David strongly suggests that the events he describes have never before been written down. 'No one has ever raised that curtain since. I have lifted it for a moment, even in this narrative, with a reluctant hand, and dropped it gladly' (*David Copperfield* 210). In fact the immediacy of David's voice both echoes and is undermined by Dickens's fragment. Despite David's evident trustworthiness, this is not as he claims the first time these events have been written down, in that beyond the world of the novel a version of them already exists. The fragment even uses the same image to describe the act of voluntary recall, 'I have never, until I impart it to this paper, in any burst of confidence with anyone, my own wife not excepted, raised the curtain I then dropped, thank God' (*David Copperfield*, Appendix A 869). By contrast it now seemed to Forster, as he later expressed it, that Dickens was taking the novel reading world into his confidence (*David Copperfield*, Appendix A, 858).

For readers who come to the novel with no awareness of its personal elements, the experience of then reading the autobiographical account framed in Forster's *Life of Dickens* is necessarily coloured by an existing sympathy with the fictional David. As readers have noted, Dickens makes little effort to understand his mother's position in blaming her for his suffering in Warren's. Partially resolving this question of his mother's 'betrayal', his condemnation of her unflinching practicality in the fragment is nostalgically reworked in the novel as sympathy for her lack of judgement. In the novel David's mother is dead before he is sent to work at Murdstone and Grimsby's. Indeed her death provides the catalyst for his banishment, leading in turn to 'a series of substitutions [Emily and Dora] that exposes and punishes the mother's guilt without jeopardizing the idealized woman she retrospectively becomes' (Poovey 92).

But regardless of the justice or otherwise of Dickens's account, or its framing first in the novel and later in Forster's *Life*, the authority of the fragment is *already* compromised by its very mode of composition. After all this is a document written by and about a public figure, with a known audience. Inevitably Dickens's childhood experience is filtered through his later consciousness of his own position as a famous writer. It is the very existence of this audience that enables the writer's autobiography to be written in the first place, so that paradoxically the present status of the writer, rather than the convincing presentation of his memory, legitimises and gives authority to his account of the past.

It is in this context that the Warren's Blacking episode can be best understood. As in the overtly fictional account, the personal experience of the narrator, what he terms 'the secret agony of my soul' (*David Copperfield*, Appendix A 860), is of considerably greater significance than the condition of the working boys who have no hope of education and therefore escape. It is precisely such an identification with the labouring boys of his own age that Dickens dreads decades later and depicts himself as having managed to avoid even at the time. Throughout this account he remains determinedly the young gentleman. Notably while his fiction goes to great lengths to comprehend the sufferings of the urban poor, his earliest eponymous heroes such as Oliver Twist and Nicholas Nickleby share their plight only for a time and often with the same sense of being in a false position on display in the unpublished fragment. The arguably skewed focus of the narrative, in which the young Dickens is made to occupy a central position rather than appearing as one of a number of boys (while the fictional David is one of 'three or four' boys, such is the narrator's self-focus in the fragment, it is never made clear how many children of either gender Warren's employed), resurfaces in the self-scrutiny of David Copperfield. Mary Poovey suggests that by this point 'David is no longer a special child, valued for who he is, but just another cog in the laboring unit "boys", the subordinate member of a crew in which everyone is simply an instance of the lowest common denominator, labor' (91–92). However, the narrator makes it clear that David *does* remain special; his intense suffering at the time derives precisely from the failure of surrounding adults to recognise him as the hero of his altered life, a status that can only be recovered through written narrative many years later.

'I Believe He Dreams in Letters': *David Copperfield*

While the fragment contains fictional elements, David Copperfield is technically the first of Dickens's fictional autobiographers, incorporating life material in to his text in such a way that it does not have to be recognised or acknowledged. Importantly he is able to shape the presentation of his own life and define his status in relation to the reader, in ways not available to previous characters.

First-person narrators in Dickens have considerable opportunities for influencing the reader, and David Copperfield surely plays with this idea in his famous opening line, in which he says that the pages of his manuscript alone will reveal whether he is or is not the hero of his own life. This narrative tease is, on the face of it, diametrically opposed to Thackeray's presentation of Arthur Pendennis at around the same time as fallible but essentially lovable, 'We are not presenting Pen to you as a hero or a model, only as a lad, who, in the midst of a thousand vanities and weaknesses, has as yet some generous impulses, and is not altogether dishonest' (*Pendennis* 217). In an obvious sense, as Sadrin points out, in *David Copperfield* 'all the references to reading and writing that crop up throughout the book are so many reminders that at two different levels this is the novel of a professional novelist' (2). Notably David begins with the claim that this is an account of his life, but also draws attention to the way that he as a writer is planning to craft it, 'to start my life with the beginning of my life' (1).

Like the self-consciously literary narrating voice of Wordsworth's *Prelude* posthumously published in the same year as the novel, David is allowed to craft a compelling subjectivity in which he involves the reader in the stages of both his life and his composition. However his status is shown to be provisional and unstable at various points, as he is first comically deflated by his aunt Betsy's disappointment in him for being born a boy, and later insists that Steerforth is his personal hero, while his own early dreams of fame are confined to lugubrious fantasies (on his escape from Murdstone and Grimsby's) that his death in a ditch will be reported in the local press. Andrews rightly stresses that 'We are taught empathically to respect the loving trust of the child and his rich imagination; and gentle laughter plays its part in this sentimental education' (*Dickensian Laughter* 96). But the sheer range of characters and their complex interactions reinforce the sense in which David himself is not the only contender for 'hero' status, nor is he automatically the arbiter of such questions. Something of this tension is suggested by Barbara Hardy's analysis of the novel as 'the story of many lives told by one character able to observe and enter imaginatively into them all. [David] is not detached like Master Humphrey or confined in point of view like Esther or always at the centre of his story like Pip. The portrait of himself as the artist is made part of an otherwise typically Victorian novel of multiple action' (48).

Like Dickens himself, his first-person narrators tend to struggle with questions of self-disclosure, just as 'Dickens felt compelled to play hide and seek with his readers about personal matters which ostensibly had nothing to do with the work of fiction in question but which in fact might transform it – put it, as the saying goes, in a new light – if they cracked the code' (Gordon 189–90). Before the reader gets to the first line of *David Copperfield*, with its puzzling question as to who the hero of this eponymous novel really is, Dickens has already introduced a riddle of his own. Under the heading 'Preface', he seemingly confides that the story of his own life is contained somewhere in the following pages:

> I do not find it easy to get sufficiently far away from this Book, in the first sensations of having finished it, to refer to it with the composure which this formal heading would seem to require. My interest in it, is so recent and strong; and my mind is so divided between pleasure and regret – pleasure in the achievement of a long design, regret in the separation from many companions – that I am in danger of wearying the reader whom I love, with personal confidences, and private emotions. London, October, 1850. (unpaginated)

Similar self-deprecation is a recurring feature of the narrative style in *Sketches by Boz*. Here however the deployment of limited intimacy, in which Dickens both 'loves' his unknown reader and emphasises that there are secrets he will ultimately withhold, carries more weight than the suggestion that the same reader might be 'wearied' by such confidence. In letters to individuals Dickens did reveal something of the codification of the book, writing to one friend in 1859, 'Do you care to know that I was a great writer at 8 years old or so – was an actor and a speaker from a baby – and worked many childish experiences and many young struggles, into Copperfield? Don't consider yourself bound to say so, because *I* say so. I merely want to infuse some personal leaven, however little, into this barren note' (To Mrs Howitt, 7 September 1859. Pilgrim 9. 118–19. 119).

In light of the 'danger' that Dickens may confide private history to the reader, it is even possible to interpret David's question as a hint in the direction of autobiographical revelation – the following pages may indeed show to a curious reader that Dickens himself, rather than David, is the hero of the life he relates. Given Dickens's insistence on the reality of his characters, this suggestion allows the surreal possibility that the fictional David regards his creator and not Steerforth as his hero. In a more private communication to Forster written at around the same time, Dickens had already anticipated the ending of the novel with conflicting emotions, telling him, 'I am within three pages of the shore; and am strangely divided, as usual in such cases, between sorrow and joy. Oh, my dear Forster, if I were to say half of what *Copperfield* makes me feel tonight, how strangely, even to you, I should be turned inside-out! I seem to be sending some part of myself into the Shadowy World' (To John Forster, [21 October 1850]. Pilgrim 6. 195). This confessional letter becomes the unseen frame for Dickens's tantalising invitation to the first readers of *David Copperfield*, to conflate real and fictional authors.

Equally, David's question informs the relation of personal development to romance, melodrama and fairy tale, with which the text is preoccupied. Literary models for the development of character include the fatally alluring promise of the fisherman's daughter becoming a lady, a version of a trope already available through such sources as Hans Andersen's story 'The Little Mermaid' (first published in 1837), as well as the ability to discern right and wrong through melodramatic typecasting (a course of education made available to the reader and largely missed by the young David himself). In this sense, the hero's status may depend on his being able to translate character in literary or theatrical terms, as when he meets Steerforth for the first time since leaving school. David is unaware that just before their encounter in the inn they have both been watching the same play, which has left Steerforth cynically unmoved. David himself is still so absorbed in what he has seen that he fails to see anyone entering the room; subsequently he imbues Steerforth with the emotion caused by the play, mistakenly making his old friend, rather than himself, the hero of his heightened feeling:

> I was so filled with the play, and with the past – for it was, in a manner, like a shining transparency, through which I saw my earlier life moving along ... in the then condition of my mind, where the play was still running high, his former protection of me appeared so deserving of my gratitude, and my old love for him overflowed my breast so freshly and spontaneously, that I went up to him at once... (280).

Like Dickens in his preface, David gives no indication as to how the play is like a 'transparency' of his earlier history. Shortly before his seduction of Emily, the more analytical Steerforth (who is not normally associated with the world of reading) comments gloomily that 'At odd dull times, nursery tales come up into the memory, unrecognised for what they are' (313). As in *Dombey and Son*, the source of these 'nursery tales' is left open and therefore available for appropriation by the reader, allowing them to insert the missing names of stories they themselves may have read as a child. The clear implication, in a novel so concerned with the application of reading to moral action, is that the adult who recalls these tales should be able to profit from their hidden meaning, but this moment of perception is not sufficient to deter Steerforth from his destructive course.

Throughout the novel David has enabled a concern with the status of the written word and how it is processed or ignored. As Price has so insightfully demonstrated, his first experiences of the written word are more mixed than readers tend to remember from the powerful images of him as a voracious reader. In fact, 'Writing disintegrates into two extremes: on the one hand, insufficiently tangible abstractions like David's memories and fantasies; on the other, excessively visual objects like Micawber's bills or women's account books, and excessively tactile objects like volumes used to poke, prod, or otherwise impress a child' (Price 95). At certain points in the story the written word itself loses its solidity, but elsewhere it is threatening, even physically dangerous. The placard a young David is forced to wear at Salem House is tangible enough, and he bitterly recalls, '… I knew that the servants read it, and the butcher read it, and the baker read it; that everybody, in a word, who came backwards and forwards to the house, of a morning when I was ordered to walk there, read that I was to be taken care of, for I bit' (*David Copperfield* 75). In his final confrontation with Steerforth, even the benevolent Mr Mell uses an exercise book to hammer on a desk in his frustration, and David recalls that 'It was my book that he struck his desk with' (91). Far less guilt-ridden than David, Pendennis is the subject of a comedic rendering of the same idea, blushing as Warrington praises his novel *Walter Lorraine* while playfully tapping him on the check with the manuscript (473).

The child's apprehension of fairy tale resolutions is sustaining, but insufficient fully to override such traumatic experiences of the world. It is only when David's future seems secure that he can confidently describe life as 'more like a great fairy story, which I was just about to begin to read, than anything else' (267), or luxuriate in the emotional vicissitudes of the Mrs Crupp period when 'I was alone in the world, and much given to record that circumstance in fragments of English versification' (376). When he first contemplates escape from the Murdstone regime, he imagines himself 'going away somewhere, like the hero in a story, to seek my fortune: but these were transient visions, day dreams I sat looking at sometimes, as if they were faintly painted or written on the wall of my room, and which, as they melted away, left the wall blank again' (128–29).

While fiction and the stage apparently offer only temporary relief, David nonetheless accords himself a particular status through aligning himself with the characters he reads about. Even as an adult he has, as John suggests, an emotional need for heroes and villains (*Dickens's Villains* 178). As Price points out, he uses his habit of reading to characterise himself as separate from the Murdstones, and 'Although David's "fancy" can take in the wildest counterfactuals, the one possibility to which his imagination never stretches is that his taste for reading might be shared' (83).

Notwithstanding this presentation of himself as a privileged partaker in the world of the imagination, David himself involves others in his reading. His favourite memory of Little Emily involves just such engagement, 'The best times were when she sat quietly at work in the doorway, and I sat on the wooden step at her feet, reading to her' (*David Copperfield* 137). Like Emily in this scene, David's implied reader is invited to occupy his own former position of imaginative but vicarious participant in heroic adventure. Occasionally this entails privileged access to events the story has not yet reached (and by implication, access to the mind of the fictional writer), as when David recalls seeing Emily almost stumble and fall and admits that he has sometimes thought it would have been better for her to die at this point; having written this much, he pauses to remark critically, 'This may be premature. I have set it down too soon, perhaps. But let it stand' (35). This passage, despite David's deprecatory 'let it stand', is carefully positioned to engage the reader's sympathy with Emily before her fate overtakes her. It is all the more surprising that it was inserted at proof stage to repair a shortage in the number, but as Philip Davis argues, 'This strange and disturbing flash-forward sets a marker not only for the plot but also for the revisions. For here Dickens is finding space, and then filling it with a wholly different dimension' (66). Specifically he is both gesturing towards a future plot development and reminding the reader how easily that plot might have been different. As Davis comments, 'Dickens loves to create those impossible thoughts that send a witness's mind spinning' (67); importantly by raising the possibility of a different future no longer available to the narrating David (because in this alternate version it will never happen) Dickens is able to 'create in the writer an inner reader of what he writes' (68). In a letter to William de Cerjat in 1849, Dickens writes that:

> I had previously observed much of what you say about the poor girls. In all you suggest with so much feeling of their return to virtue being cruelly cut off, I concur with a sore heart. I have been turning it over in my mind for some time, and hope, in the history of Little Em'ly (who *must* fall – there is no hope for her) to put it before the thoughts of people, in a new and pathetic way, and perhaps to do some good. (To W. W. F. de Cerjat, 29 December 1849. Pilgrim 5. 682–84. 682)

Unlike the already fallen Martha, who is first seen as a sinister shadow trailing her old friend, Emily herself is presented in a state of innocence on numerous occasions, encouraging the reader to engage with her despite David's cryptic warnings that she is destined for a dubious fate. This technique is adapted as a means of presenting the feminised David himself, when his innocence is threatened by contact with the 'meanest phases' of the London streets, and this knowledge is maliciously exposed by Uriah Heep very much as Rosa Dartle threatens to proclaim Emily's history when she finds her in shabby but respectable lodgings after Steerforth's desertion. Philip Horne argues that 'The appalling exposure of the child-narratee to moral risk must be established; but for the adult narrator to retain the reader's trust and respect, in the domesticated economy of *David Copperfield* it seems that this moral risk must also be asserted emphatically to have produced no moral damage' (171).

Until he himself becomes an author, David's claim to the reader's consideration rests, more even than on the injustice of his sufferings, on his imaginative faculty. Crucially, the reader is challenged to see even the young David as central to the tragic events unfolding around him and to acknowledge his status in the story, in opposition to the way in which he is presented by his own hero Steerforth and by the various adults who have failed him. His development is presented as important, long before the reader learns that he is now famous, as he signposts particular stages in comments such as, 'The reader now understands as well as I do, what I was when I came to that point of my youthful history to which I am now coming again' (54). Parted from his books at Salem House, he retells the plots to the other boys in the dormitory at night, admitting later that 'What ravages I committed on my favourite authors in the course of my interpretation of them, I am not in a condition to say, and should be very unwilling to know' (*David Copperfield* 88).

In one sense, 'in the presence of a "litter" of paper, ink, and other school supplies, but the absence of printed storybooks, oral transmission turns David himself into a walking reprint series' (Price 104). But crucially the necessity for improvising at Steerforth's command also liberates David to reshape and embellish the stories he tells. With an instinctive apprehension of the power of narrative, the child David (as attested by the adult narrating self), processes his experience through fiction, as when he puts Murdstone into all the bad parts in the books he reads, or in his feeling for Peggotty, 'It was a sort of comical affection too; and yet if she had died, I cannot think what I should have done, or how I should have acted out the tragedy it would have been to me' (*David Copperfield* 59).

The ability to act out literary scenes is suggestive of an imaginative survival skill in this context but also stands as a reminder that who reads is as important as how and what they read. Where David romantically harnesses 'the glorious host' (53) of his father's old books as a survival strategy, Uriah Heep uses books to learn how best to manipulate his employer, and David describes him as 'reading a great fat book, with such demonstrative attention, that his lank forefinger followed up every line as he read, and made clammy tracks along the page (or so I fully believed) like a snail' (227).

When Heep is exposed Micawber becomes a reader of his own text and unlike David himself at this point of the story knows what will happen next before the audience does. The crafting and delivery of this letter offer a humorous commentary on the relations between novel writer and intended reader, as Micawber's composition and delivery are received and framed by the writer David. As Wu Di observantly points out, 'It is noteworthy that, in the record of David's life, none of the other texts he reads, including the classics, are ever quoted at length, whereas Micawber's letters are always quoted in full' (175). Just as readers themselves are engaged by the disasters afflicting the Wickfield household, so Micawber notably lingers over his pecuniary difficulties. David observes that 'The relish with which Mr Micawber described himself, as a prey to these dismal calamities, was only to be equalled by the emphasis with which he read his letter; and the kind of homage he rendered to it with a roll of his head when he thought he had hit a sentence very hard indeed' (731). Much of the comedy of this scene is manufactured through periodic repetition of the name Heep, which David presents in capital letters to suggest the weight Micawber's voice accords to it. After a while, the reader is told that whenever he feels the name of Heep coming on, he literally alters his manner, and the capitalisation of the name for emphasis even allows him to draw the reader's attention to a spontaneous pun outside the letter itself, '"Approach me again, you – you – you HEEP of infamy," gasped Mr Micawber, "and if your head is human, I'll break it"' (731).

As so often in Dickens's fiction, the reader is literally taught how to read and respond to the text; vicariously enjoying Micawber's performance through David's relation of it, readers can watch the mechanics of his delivery as he creates suspense or signals loathing of the figure he exposes. With wry affection David comments that 'Mr Micawber's enjoyment of his epistolary powers, in describing this unfortunate state of things, really seemed to outweigh any pain or anxiety that the reality could have caused him' (732) and that when everyone thinks he has finished, he sets off again and 'proceeded, with a mixture of the lowest spirits and the most intense enjoyment, to the peroration of his letter' (737). Nonetheless Micawber is, as he knows, a genuinely effective orator and as he reaches the charges against Heep, David admits that 'We all held our breath, I think. I am sure Uriah held his' (733). Di argues persuasively that Mr Micawber's letters have a vital function in the novel in serving 'as a touchstone for David's maturation as a reader and observer' (176) as he learns to read more critically. As Dickens himself presented friends with copies of his books, admitting that he had been more affected by the imaginary events than anyone else could be, at the end of his performance, 'Much affected, but still intensely enjoying himself, Mr Micawber folded up his letter, and handed it with a bow to my aunt, as something she might like to keep' (738).

Like Micawber and of course like David himself, Steerforth is capable of assuming different roles with sensitivity and conviction, but in his case the acting is tendentious, allowing him to disguise rather than comprehend or share his own feelings. David sees this as a game with hindsight, but a more perceptive reader may concur with John's comment that on the contrary, 'The poignant part of Steerforth's story is that he is an actor even in childhood; he experiences himself from the outside, so to speak' (*Dickens's Villains* 177). He cannot emulate David's innocent goodness largely because of his higher degree of self-consciousness, an affliction from which David himself suffers when he becomes a schoolboy for the second time, after his escape from Murdstone and Grimby's.

All this time the narrator of *David Copperfield* claims to be writing for his own exclusive perusal, but like Dickens himself, he repeatedly reminds his readers of the physical act of writing, in ways that suggest the status of the published author. Implicitly this demonstration of David's public identity is also a reminder that texts are finally unreadable except by the writer. To quote Thackeray again:

> We have said before, could we know the man's feelings as well as the author's thoughts – how interesting most books would be! – more

interesting than merry. ... certainly each man who lives by the pen, and happens to read this, must remember, if he will, his own experiences and recall many solemn hours of solitude and labour. What a constant care sate at the side of the desk and accompanied him! Fever or sickness were lying possibly in the next room: a sick child might be there, with a wife watching over it terrified and in prayer; or grief might be bearing him down, and the cruel mist before the eyes rendering the paper scarce visible as he wrote on it, and the inexorable necessity drove on the pen. What man among us has not had nights and hours like these? But to the manly heart – severe as these pangs are, they are endurable: long as the night seems, the dawn comes at last, and the wounds heal, and the fever abates, and the rest comes, and you can afford to look back on the past misery with feelings that are anything but bitter.

(*Pendennis* 734)

In recalling his neglected childhood, the adult David admits that his suffering after his mother's death, 'seems to cast its gloom upon this paper as I write' (145). Conflating the moment of coming upon Dora in her garden with the act of writing the scene, he assures readers that 'I tingle again from head to foot as my recollection turns that corner, and my pen shakes in my hand' (383). The acquirement of the art of shorthand is carefully documented, as David apologetically congratulates himself on his efforts, 'I feel as if it were not for me to record, even though this manuscript is intended for no eyes but mine, how hard I worked at that tremendous short-hand' (590).

Such meta-textual strategies are familiar to readers of Dickens's letters, but this level of power becomes unsettling to the fictional writer himself, when he is forced to relate the story of Emily's flight and has to reassure himself that 'It is no worse, because I write of it. It would be no better, if I stopped my most unwilling hand' (436). At this point the fictional narrator comes into direct conflict with the author Dickens, who has previously decided that the character '*must* fall – there is no hope for her' (To W. W. F. de Cerjat, 29 December 1849. Pilgrim 5. 682–84. 682).

Despite the highly private events he describes, critics have long noted David's reticence in certain respects, significantly in his decision not to refer to his own work. He pointedly remarks that 'It is not my purpose, in this record, though in all other essentials it is my written memory, to pursue the history of my own fictions. They express themselves, and I leave them to themselves' (671). Lyn Pykett argues that his decision not to discuss his own fiction is just one instance in which he 'avoids the personal, and conceals even in the process of disclosing, or, to put it another way, discloses by concealment. The narrator of *David Copperfield* never fully discloses himself to any other character, to the reader, or even to himself, but rather he represents such self-disclosure as a rhetorical impossibility' (116). An alternative interpretation of this silence on the subject of his own books is offered by Hardy, who argues that:

> Dickens's relationship with his readers was so close and familiar that when he says David's novels will supply the rest, in other words, can speak for themselves, it is a knowing allusion, a kind of special *occupatio*, and some readers are bound to see fiction go transparent at this point, to let the real novels show through – especially as we are told virtually nothing about the fictitious fictions. (47)

This 'transparency' accords with the permeable boundaries Dickens creates between his fiction and his private correspondence, in which readers are encouraged to make connections between real people and characters, actual events and fictional plots. This strategy replaces a 'private' Dickens with a narrator whose life is open to scrutiny, albeit he controls the terms in which it can be read. In essence David manages to have it both ways, offering the reader a literary account of his life that, like any biographical account, partakes of the rules of fiction. His elevation of ostensibly 'real' events over fiction directly reverses Dickens's own insistence that his readers should remember him for his work and not seek to find out details of his life. But the point remains the same – the reader is to accept as a moral certainty that the writer of a work of fiction is knowable through the particular text being read, and should not be subject to external criteria (even a reading of his other books) unless he himself has brought them to his reader's attention.

This control over the authorial persona ceases to be possible when Dickens is humorously invoked in a novel by another writer. *The Newcomes* comically places a newly successful Pendennis in a position where he is asked questions in free indirect speech about the relative status of living authors, at a time when Thackeray himself was routinely compared to Dickens by partisans on either side:

> Who is the greatest author now alive? You will tell me when you come upstairs after dinner: - and the young lady sails away following the matrons, who rise and ascend to the drawing-room. Miss Newcome has been watching the behaviour of the author, by whom she sat; curious to know what such a person's habits are; whether he speaks and acts like other people; and in what respect authors are different from persons 'in society'. (310)

In personal letters, the two identities become difficult to separate, as Dickens discusses the writing process. Hoping to visit Broadstairs in the summer of 1850, he wrote, 'Between Copperfield and Household Words, I am as busy as a bee. I hope to go down to that old image of Eternity that I love so much, and finish the former... to its hoarse music. May it be as good a book as I hope it will be, for your children's children's children to read!'

(To W. C. Macready. 11 June 1850. Pilgrim 6. 112–13. 113). To other friends he wrote openly that 'Je suis fort occupé, en ecrivant le dernier livraison de Copperfield – meilleur (j'espere [sic] et je crois) de tous mes livres, *à present*'[2] (To Count Alfred d'Orsay. 1 October 1850. Pilgrim 6. 184–85. 184), flattering Mary Boyle with an apparent 'confidence', 'To let you into a secret I am not quite sure that I ever did like, or ever shall like, anything *quite* so well as Copperfield (22 July 1852. Pilgrim 6. 720–21. 721).

But despite his author's admiration, David is not the only one to be the hero of his own life: the elevation of the ordinary figure into something important is a feature of all Dickens's fiction, even in this unique presentation of a middle-class boy who becomes famous. Writing in *Cassell's* in 1912 Arthur Waugh wrote, 'David Copperfield among the empty bottles; Pip in bondage to Mrs Gargery; Lizzie Hexam by the riverside fire – all his youthful heroes and heroines are heroic, not so much by virtue of their own nobility, as through the sympathy they evoke for their helpless and fettered condition' (349). David's authority depends on his extraordinary status as a successful writer, but by routinely presenting himself as limited in scope and perception, he enables the status of other 'ordinary heroes' whose writing may never be published other than through his means in writing the story of his life.

While the first-person narrator ostensibly controls the telling of his own story, the novel uses letters and letter writing as a key motif of the text. Throughout the novel, the status of letters varies depending on who is writing them and in what context, as characters comment on, appropriate, or refer to each other's letters. Betsy Trotwood wryly comments of Mr Micawber, 'I believe he dreams in letters!' (755), while David remarks to the reader, 'I am not sure whether I have mentioned that, when Mr Micawber was at any particularly desperate crisis, he used a sort of legal phraseology: which he seemed to think equivalent to winding up his affairs' (416). After their encounter at the theatre, Agnes writes to David warning him against his 'bad angel' Steerforth, advice he ignores with fatal consequences. It is however on Agnes's advice that David writes to Dora's aunts after her father's death. During the ensuing interview 'Miss Lavinia turned my letter, so as to bring the superscription towards herself, and referred through her eye-glass to some orderly-looking notes she had made on that part of it' (583), mimicking the legal inspection of official documents.

Letters by other characters do not depend for their status on the ability to articulate meaning, which is after all provided by David's frame narratives. Peggotty's letters are not given in full, but the reader is told that they are blotted performances and that 'the blots were more expressive to me than the best composition; for they showed me that Peggotty had been crying all over the paper, and what could I have desired more?' (241) Emily's parting letter to her uncle, by contrast, is rendered as an overtly emotional document composed in correct English; it is also, however, the tangible sign that she is knowingly about to commit a sin against her home, and the reader finally learns that it is the culminating letter of a series, beginning with a letter Steerforth passes on to her through the offices of Littimer and the unsuspecting Miss Mowcher.

The letter Betsy Trotwood sends to Mr Murdstone is never seen but can be assumed to be a formal document, albeit a sinister one in the mind of the fearful child David. Conversely, a later letter from Agnes goes beyond the page, and 'was like her cordial voice in my ears. What can I say more!' (477) This sense of intimate exchange will find its ultimate expression in David's publication of his first novel, an event that conveys a coded reminder to Dickens's own friends that his books are to be received as personal messages. David's friends certainly accept this substitution, as he is told that 'my old friends heard of my growing reputation, and read my book as if they heard me speaking its contents' (679).

This technique serves to create a multi-layered perspective and also to further the plot or heighten tension at particular points. Murdstone's exchange with Betsy Trotwood is mediated through her communication of it to David and intensifies his suspense as he wonders whether he will be returned to his stepfather; for Micawber, letters are a form of theatre but also lead to his fateful employment by Uriah Heep, who answers his advertisement in the press; David's impassioned letters to Dora are fatally discovered by Miss Murdstone, and he writes to Julia Mills 'something in the style of Mr Micawber' (539).

In one of their last days together, Steerforth hands David a letter from Peggotty telling him that Barkis is dying, but persuades him to spend a day at Highgate before going to see his old nurse. Steerforth somewhat insensitively responds to the news with a pietistic commonplace, shading quickly into a declaration of callous selfishness, 'the sun sets every day, and people die every minute, and we musn't be scared by the common lot. ... Ride on! Rough-shod if need be, smooth-shod if that will do, but ride on! Ride over all obstacles, and win the race!' (415)

David does not know that this is his last chance to redeem his friend and dissuade him from his plan to elope with Emily, and (reprising his pusillanimous behaviour when Steerforth insulted Mr Mell) the opportunity is lost when he fails to focus his attention on his own feeling of unease. Bodenheimer's analysis of knowing and refusing to know is significant in this context, as she argues that 'The innocent are curiously deaf to the linguistic strategies of the schemers, and their lack – or suppression – of suspicion is often self-serving. For Dickens knowingness is at once corrupt and essential to survival; the tension between the two is rarely resolved in his art' (*Knowing Dickens* 33).

As David recalls this fateful conversation, he was about to remonstrate with his capricious friend, when 'my mind glanced off' (415) to another subject. Having left Steerforth, he ruminates on his strange behaviour and 'wished, for the first time, that he had some worthy race to run' (416). But he has also been carrying about a letter from Mr Micawber, which he has forgotten until it 'tumbled on the floor' (416). This minor incident is sufficient to interrupt David's thoughts, as he reads that 'the undersigned is Crushed' and that Traddles's 'friendly acceptance' is not provided for, leaving David 'sorely distressed' (416) on his friend's account. In a somewhat disingenuous move, David refocuses the reader's attention (and his own) on the plight of one friend largely in order to avoid his own failure to remonstrate with another, a failure that will contribute to the disaster shortly to overtake the Peggotty household.

Dickens was himself forced to change the direction of his story, after receiving a distressed letter from Mrs Jane Seymour Hill, the woman on whom he admitted he had based Miss Mowcher. Writing immediately to apologise, he told her that 'I do not mean it to be a very good character now, but I will make it so, and oblige the Reader to hold it in a pleasant remembrance – if that will give you any relief from this – by me quite unexpected and unforeseen distress' (To Mrs Jane Seymour Hill. 18 December 1849. Pilgrim 5. 674–75). What he had clearly not taken into account, as he implied in his letters discussing this incident, was that the success of his fictional creations involved not only an increase in his own fame, but a concomitant notoriety for the originals who were not otherwise publicly known. On the same day he told Forster, 'I have had the queerest adventure this morning, in the receipt of the enclosed from Miss Mo[w]cher! It is seriocomic, but there is no doubt one is wrong in being tempted to such a use of power' (To John Forster. [18 December 1849]. Pilgrim 5. 676). By February he complained that he was 'repairing Miss Mowcher's injury – with a very bad grace, and in a very ill humour' (To Miss Burdett Coutts, 12 February 1850. Pilgrim 6. 35).

Running parallel to its preoccupation with letters is the novel's critique of the law, a theme that Dickens would develop in *Bleak House*. Official documents have less moral authority in the satirical passages where they mainly appear; however, they too are amorphous in meaning, as David calculates that the evidence in a case that falls to the lot of Spenlow and Jorkins is 'just twice the length of Robinson Crusoe' (377); and even the official documents penned by Spenlow himself take on a new meaning after his death, when 'his handwriting of yesterday was like a ghost' (541). In one notable instance, words fail to transfer themselves from the spoken to the written medium at all, when it is ascertained that despite his many lectures to David on this very subject, Spenlow has died without leaving a will. But even the opaque language practised by the parliamentary and legal figures, and more joyously by the feckless Micawber, becomes a component of David's literary development. During Micawber's time in the Marshalsea, David characteristically tells the reader that:

> I set down this remembrance here, because it is an instance to myself of the manner in which I fitted my old books to my altered life, and made stories for myself, out of the street, and out of men and women;

and how some main points in the character I shall unconsciously develop, I suppose, in writing my life, were gradually forming all this while. (163)

David gives numerous instances of street characters and London scenes, which he uses to sharpen his observational skills and develop his imagination. But the seemingly unpromising incident he specifically wishes to recall at this point is Micawber's writing of a petition to the House of Commons, for an alteration in the law of imprisonment for debt. Such scenes serve an important function in showing that words can be meaningless but nonetheless serve an innocent purpose as distraction or social facilitation. In a benign reworking of the meaningless parliamentary speeches he reports, David admits that during his first interview with Dora's aunts, 'I think I observed, myself, that it was highly creditable to all concerned. I don't in the least know what I meant' (581).

The subtle and powerful control over language exhibited by the successful author is shown here, by the fictional author himself, to be at times a simple question of smoke and mirrors. This aspect to David's fame is comically underscored when he is trumped by Mr Micawber, now a dignitary in Australia, at the end of the novel. Micawber's speech is followed up by a letter published in the *Port Middlebay Times*. At the very end of the novel Micawber has finally succeeded in becoming, like David, the hero of his own life. Micawber implicitly asserts his own status by choosing to publish a letter to David in the press, rather than simply posting it, although his somewhat farcical excuse is that Peggotty is shortly going to England and can take charge of it in person. In the letter he makes it clear to David that he represents the town of Port Middlebay, while reminding his fellow citizens that the famous author is a personal friend of his:

> though estranged (by the force of circumstances over which I have had no controul) from the personal society of the friend and companion of my youth, I have not been unmindful of his soaring flight. ... I cannot, therefore, allow of the departure from this place of an individual whom we mutually respect and esteem, without, my dear sir, taking this opportunity of thanking you, on my own behalf, and, I may undertake to add, on that of the whole of the Inhabitants of Port Middlebay, for the gratification of which you are the ministering agent. (851)

In this celebratory curtain call at the end of the novel David is upstaged by Mr Micawber, who makes his final appearance as an invited public speaker and as a writer of published letters. This reversal of status is given more serious treatment in *Pendennis*, where Thackeray acknowledges that Pendennis's opportunities have enabled him to win fame where Warrington's greater talent has been thwarted by circumstances, before concluding in a parody of the famous emancipation slogan, '... let us give a hand of charity to Arthur Pendennis, with all his faults and shortcomings, who does not claim to be a hero, but only a man and a brother'. (785)

David Copperfield became part of Dickens's own mythology, as the most private text he wrote but one that was adapted for public circulation. While writing the novel he had written to Forster on one occasion that 'I have been very hard at work these three days, and have still Dora to kill. But with good luck, I may do it tomorrow' ([20 August 1850]. Pilgrim 6. 153). While this perfunctory treatment is apparently inconsistent with his professions of attachment to his characters, it stands as a reminder that Dickens valued professional organisation as much as literary genius. Nonetheless the personal element in the text continued to resurface in sometimes unexpected ways.

Writing to his old lover Maria Beadnell (now Mrs Winter) when she unexpectedly contacted him a few years later, he identified her unhesitatingly with the figure of Dora. He clearly takes it for granted that she has read the novel, as he tells her that on seeing her writing on the envelope, 'I opened it with the touch of my young friend David Copperfield when he was in love' (10 February 1855. Pilgrim 7. 532–34. 533). In a subsequent letter he writes that 'I have a strong belief – there is no harm in adding hope to that – that perhaps you have once or twice laid down that book, and thought "How dearly that boy must have loved me, and how vividly this man remembers it!"' (To Mrs Winter, 15 February 1855. Pilgrim 7. 538–39. 539)

Writing to the theatrical manager Arthur Ryland, with whom he seems to have had no intimate relationship whatever, Dickens takes him too into his confidence, in turning down an invitation to read from the book, 'I don't mind confiding to you that I never can approach the book with perfect composure (it had such possession of me when I wrote it), and that I no sooner begin to try to get it into this form, than I begin to read it all and to feel that I can't disturb it' (29 January 1855. Pilgrim 7. 514–15. 515). Writing the opening chapters of *Great Expectations* in 1860, the apparently very different character Pip is carefully checked against the equally self-doubting child David for possible overlap, suggesting Dickens's commitment to both characters but also his own fear that writing a first-person child narrator would inevitably act as a trigger and he would be tempted to write David's story (and his own) all over again. As he wrote to Forster, 'To be quite sure I had fallen into no unconscious repetitions, I read David Copperfield again the other day, and was affected by it to a degree you would hardly believe' ([early October 1860]. Pilgrim 9. 325). In his *Life of Charles Dickens*, Forster justifiably took these two novels as a benchmark of his friend's achievement, claiming with implicit confidence that:

> It may be doubted if Dickens could better have established his right to the front rank among novelists claimed for him, than by the ease and mastery with which, in these two books of *Copperfield* and *Great Expectations*, he kept perfectly distinct the two stories of a boy's childhood, both told in the form of autobiography. (vol 2. 285)

Dickens himself admitted that *David Copperfield* had always remained his favourite among his own novels. Its importance to him is indirectly signalled in the sheer speed at which he was able to re-read it, suggested by the letter to Forster in which he implies that he has taken only a day to get through it. Even assuming that he has read only the early chapters, the inference is that he knows the book so well as to remind himself of its sense with ease at any distance of time.

As he suggests in his letter to Maria Winter, the novel would become a touchstone for Dickens's state of mind over the few years after its first publication. In June 1854 he described writing it as 'the so happy and yet so unhappy existence which seeks its realities in unrealities, and finds its dangerous comfort in a perpetual escape from the disappointment of heart around it' (To John Forster [? January – 17 June 1854]. Pilgrim 7. 354). By the following year, David's famous 'unhappy want or loss of something' has been expanded beyond the pages of the novel itself, adding an additional point of reference never offered by David himself, to reference Dickens's own unhappiness, 'Why is it, that as with poor David, a sense comes always crushing on me now, when I fall into low spirits, as of one happiness I have missed in life, and one friend and companion I have never made?' (To John Forster, [3 and ?4 February 1855]. 523).

A further side effect of David's success was the creation of a test case for other meta-fictional heroes. When Thackeray returned to the debate over the status of fictional authors and their published texts in *The Newcomes* a few years later, he took Clive Newcome as the ostensible 'hero', but Pendennis was reinstated in his central role through the delayed admission that he himself is the narrator guiding the other characters, 'It was in the days of my own youth, then, that I met one or two of the characters who are to figure in this history, and whom I must ask leave to accompany for a short while, and until, familiarized with the public, they can make their own way' (*The Newcomes* 7). Jerome K. Jerome's partly autobiographical novel *Paul Kelver* (1902) includes a fictionalised encounter between Dickens and the boy hero who wants to be a writer when he grows up and whose final sobering realisation that he will never write as well as his 'hero' is the keynote of the book.

Notes

1. While the fragment is included in Forster's *Life*, the appendix to David Copperfield is cited here for ease of reference.
2. 'I am very busy writing the last number of Copperfield – best (I hope and believe) of all my books, *to date*' [emphasis in original].

3 First-Person-Narrators and Editorial 'Conducting'
Limited Intimacy and the Shared Imaginary

In Dickens's early fiction the most apparently ordinary figures can become heroes through the directive focus of a narrative lens, while David Copperfield's accession to literary fame renders his initially obscure personal history compelling as a myth of the writer's development. In the later fiction less trustworthy figures are also enabled to write their own stories, as the increasingly sophisticated deployment of unreliable first-person narrators is used to blur the boundaries between public and private modes, domesticating the act of writing and complicating the apprehension of the writer's experience as literary myth. The boundaries between public and private writing are further contested in the fictionalising tendencies of many of Dickens's letters, even as readers are encouraged to take the fiction as a form of personal correspondence.

From their inception and naming, to the posthumous publication of letters alluding to them, Dickens's characters take up a number of positions on the trajectory from manuscript to print. As the novels become more carefully thought out from the 1840s, each character is plotted in writing, often in the form of letters to friends and advisers such as Forster. The manuscript of the novel refines the development of the character, a process that continues even after the script is printed by professionals at proof stage. During and after publication of the novel in parts and later in volume form, Dickens continues to reshape the characters, through writing about them in personal letters to friends, and often to interested strangers. This investment stresses the apparent physicality of characters beyond the confines of their respective stories, even as the emphasis on writing underscores the sense in which they are imaginative creations. Within the fiction itself, Elaine Freedgood notes Dickens's own insistence on the materiality of his text in both *Bleak House* and *Great Expectations*, as he draws the reader's attention to the physicality of handwriting and tombstone inscriptions, raising the question, 'Is the labour of the writer restored to the product of his labour with this insistence on the materiality of the letters of his text?' ('Material' 384)

At particularly busy periods, the mass of letters requiring attention takes on a sublime aspect, as when Thomas Baylis is told that 'I have been away for a month, reading, and I write this present missive up to the chin in a raging sea of correspondence' (19 December 1861. Pilgrim 9. 543–44. 543).

First-Person-Narrators and Editorial 'Conducting' 105

The writing of letters themselves sometimes appears to be the most important topic, with proffered news or messages being relegated to a subordinate point on Dickens's imaginative register. In one he explains that if Mamie and Georgina knew he was writing 'they would charge me with many messages of regard. But as I am shut up in my room, in a ferocious and unapproachable condition, owing to the great accumulation of letters I have to answer, I will tell them at lunch that I have anticipated their wish' (To Thomas Baylis, 2 July 1862. Pilgrim 10. 98).

On occasion Dickens contrives to materialise something that he acknowledges does not or will not exist in reality. In a continuation of the imaginative substitution of one text for another, discussed in chapter one, his most privileged friends are increasingly asked to accept fiction in place of letters:

> After I have been believing such things with all my heart and soul – two results always ensue. First, I can't write plainly to the eye. Second, I can't write sensibly to the mind.
>
> So, Copperfield is to blame, and I am not, for this wandering note. And if you like it, you'll forgive me? (To the Hon Mrs Richard Watson, 24 September 1850. Pilgrim 6. 179)

Providing a template for and in some cases developing the 'intimacy' Dickens claimed between himself and his public, on occasion his correspondents are even encouraged to conflate novels and letters, finding hidden meanings in the fiction or literally being asked to accept that a published novel can substitute for a personal communication, '… I really think so often of my friends in writing my books, and have the happiness of knowing they think so much of me in reading them, that I have a sort of stupid sense as if they served for letters …' (To W. F. de Cerjat, 20 December 1852. Pilgrim 6. 828–30. 828). As in the letter to Haldimand discussed in the last chapter, this rather vague avowal gives the recipient of this letter very little sense of where in the published fiction he ought to look, if he wants to find further missives there.

Four letters of 5 July 1856 do stress the specialness to be inferred by the individual correspondent, in the offer (or not) of substituting fiction for personal correspondence. Washington Irving is assured that 'If you knew how often I write to you individually and personally in my books, you would be no more surprised in seeing this note than you were in seeing me do my duty by that flowery julep… at Baltimore' (5 July 1856. Pilgrim 8. 150–51). Neatly reversing the terms of this coded writing, Dickens wrote apologetically to Walter Savage Landor on the same day, to tell him that 'I write to you so often in my books, and my writing of letters is usually so confined to the numbers that I *must* write, and in which I have no kind of satisfaction, that I am afraid to think how long it is since we exchanged a direct letter. … that you *do* write, and that pretty often, I know beforehand. Else why do I read *The Examiner*?' (5 July 1856. Pilgrim 8. 152–53). In this context, the level of intimacy offered to Hans Christian Anderson appears far less intense than might be inferred from the letter itself, dated the same day, in which he is told that 'I love and esteem you more than I could tell you on as much paper as would pave the whole road from here to Copenhagen' (5 July 1856. Pilgrim 8. 145). Finally, an affable letter to the Duke of Devonshire seems to offer a piece of inside information even as it refutes the ability of individual readers to find biographical clues in the fiction. In this letter he jokingly confides the historical source of Flora Finching and that:

> I am so glad you like Flora. It came into my head one day that we have all had our Floras (mine is living, and extremely fat), and that it was a half serious half ridiculous truth which had never been told. It is a wonderful gratification to find that everybody knows her. Indeed some people seem to think I have done them a personal injury, and that their individual Floras ... are each and all Little Dorrit's. (5 July 1856. Pilgrim 8. 149–50. 149)

Despite Dickens's instructions these private letters themselves become printed, public texts through posthumous publication. Indeed readers may feel that they have a right to access letters including allusions to their favourite characters, an appropriation that reaches its apogee when the fragment becomes part of the published text in *David Copperfield*. This perpetual movement of the characters, between private correspondence and printed fiction, significantly challenges the boundaries between private writing and publicly accessible text.[1] In perceiving published fiction as equivalent to direct address, readers form an intimate relationship with the writer, although Dickens does not necessarily encourage the concomitant control over his text assumed in the case of a poem by his contemporary Elizabeth Barrett Browning by an admiring Mary Cholmondeley, who wrote in her diary, 'I wonder whether she felt it to be <u>hers</u>, she who wrote it, as intensely as I know it to be <u>mine</u> who only read it' (11 June 1895).

The changing status of Dickens's letters on any subject and regardless of personal relationship, purely because of his fame, is nowhere more obvious than in an exchange with a member of the Post Office who returned an early complaint about the service, soliciting a new letter in return. Dickens answered good humouredly agreeing to this proposal that 'I have therefore put my juvenile complaint to the Post-Office, into the fire, and send you this instead. Thinking you might like this all the better if it were associated with one of my books, I transcribe a few words from David Copperfield, on the opposite side' (To unknown correspondent, 1 May 1855. Pilgrim 7. 604–605. 604). In rooting this exchange in one of his books, Dickens both acknowledges the source of his correspondent's interest and reminds him of its accepted parameters.

At least one early critic picked up on the significance of the way in which writing by published authors became accessible to the public, suggesting that the permeable nature of the manuscript / print divide could be used to understand the imaginative process itself. Writing in *The North British Review* in 1851, David Masson suggested that readers should consult available specimens of Dickens's handwriting to compare his novelistic style with that of Thackeray:

> If Messrs Bradbury and Evans would furtively supply us with a page of the manuscript of "Copperfield," together with a page of the manuscript of "Pendennis," we should probably be able, on comparing the two, and examining the state of their penmanship, to detect some characteristic differences in the habits of composition of the two novelists, and to say which of them is, on the whole, the more careful and trained, and which the more easy and fluent writer. Nay, even without having such an unusual facility afforded to us, we might, by way of a first attempt in the graphiological art, try to infer something or other (and we advise our readers to infer it) from a comparison of the free and somewhat dashing penmanship of Dickens, as exhibited to the public in the printed specimens, with the neat and elegant writing of those stray autographs of Thackeray, which, in exploring the albums of our fair friends, we have occasionally seen. (59)

Masson goes on to suggest that the reader can actually gain 'some insight into the mechanism of an author's style' by reversing the process and copying out printed passages by hand. Excerpting passages from *David Copperfield* and *Pendennis* respectively, he urges readers to test this theory, assuring them that:

> By this means the critic attaches himself, as it were, to the author in the act of composition, and is able to discover much – not only haste or slovenliness, if there is any; not only superfluous expression, false metaphor, or bad punctuation; but also the tricks of association, the intellectual connexions and minute flights by which the author leaps from thought to thought and from phrase to phrase. (59)

Given his enormous correspondence, it would have been impossible for Dickens to restrain intrusive interest in his handwriting, and indeed he turned instinctively to the image of physical writing as a sign of integrity on at least one occasion. Infuriated by a hostile review in *The Edinburgh Review* in 1857, he retaliated with a rebuttal in *Household Words* in which he aligned his status as the journal's editor with his authorship of the particular article. Stating rather unnecessarily that 'The name of Mr Dickens is at the head of this page, and the hand of Mr Dickens writes this paper' (415), he implicitly substitutes his own manuscript for characterless print in reminding the reader that he has literally written this response, which appears without an appended name but under the large type 'Conducted by Charles Dickens'

('Curious Misprint in the Edinburgh Review' 415). In 1865, for the first and last time, he bestowed a manuscript on a reviewer, because as he put it 'as you have divined what pains I bestowed upon the book, perhaps you might set some little value on the Manuscript, as your corroboration' (To E. S. Dallas, 30 November 1865. Pilgrim 11. 117–18. 118).

The status and function of *Household Words* in this context is closely aligned with the authority of Dickens as both writer and critic. Dickens's account of planning his new journal echoes his descriptions of beginning a new novel, in the metaphor of 'floating ideas', which would be damaged by premature explanation, 'I do great injustice to my floating ideas (pretty speedily and comfortably settling down into orderly arrangement) by saying anything about the Periodical now …' (To John Forster, [7 October 1849]. Pilgrim 5. 621–23. 621). He does however go on to explicate some of its aims, such as the inclusion of 'A history of remarkable characters, good and bad, *in* history; to assist the reader's judgement in his observation of men, and in his estimates of the truth of many characters in fiction' (622). It is worth noting that in this account of 'remarkable characters' as a guide to the reader's judgement, history is to serve primarily as a means of interpreting and valuing fictional characters.

Much as Dickens presents himself from the 1840s, most overtly in the *Carol*, as infiltrating the homes of readers, the central conceit of the new journal depends on a figure who is in knowable in theory but never seen in practice:

> … I want to suppose a certain SHADOW, which may go into any place, by sunlight, moonlight, candlelight, and be in all homes, and all nooks and corners, and be supposed to be cognisant of everything, and go everywhere, without the least difficulty. A kind of semi-omniscient, omnipresent, intangible creature. … I want the compiled part of the paper to express the idea of this Shadow's having been in libraries, and among the books referred to. I want him to loom as a fanciful thing all over London. … I want to express in the title, and in the grasp of the idea to express also, that it is the Thing at everybody's elbow, and in everybody's footsteps. At the window, by the fire, in the street, in the house, from infancy to old age, everyone's inseparable companion. … Now do you make anything out of this? which I let off as if I were a bladder full of it, and you had punctured me. (7 October 1849. Pilgrim 5. 621. 622–23)

Douglas-Fairhust describes the effect of Dickens's oeuvre as unifying individual readers, so that 'Whether his readers were scattered in space or brought together by one of his public performances, the same words transformed thousands of distinct individuals into a united audience' (182). However Helen Small's reminder that reading 'is rarely, if ever, an undifferentiatedly collective experience' (263) reflects Dickens's own awareness that his readership was in practice varied and indeed provisional. It was surely for this reason that as Catherine Waters comments, 'Offering an irresistible compound of entertainment with instruction, Household Words shares its winning formula with the nineteenth-century advertisement, which also attempts to combine the rhetorical and the informative' (*Commodity Culture* 24). In other words, advertisements succeed by being both persuasive and essentially directive, much as the journal seeks to guide and control the response of its readers.

Creating a further layer of complexity, Dickens's letters to potential contributors suggest the difficulty of balancing business and literary imperatives. Explaining the house style in 1852, Dickens told a correspondent that 'the constant endeavour is, to adapt every paper to the reception of a number of classes and various orders of mind at once' (To C. M. Young, 21 July 1852. Pilgrim 6. 719). This is a different approach from collapsing differences between readers. However in advising a contributor to *All the Year Round*, which succeeded *Household Words* in the aftermath of his separation from his wife and subsequent break with Bradbury and Evans, Dickens wrote 'If you can find it in your heart to make the attempt, only fancy throughout that you are doing your utmost to tell some man something in the pleasantest and most intelligent way that is natural to you – and that he is on the whole a pleasant and intelligent fellow too, through rather afraid of being bored – and I really cannot doubt your coming out well' (To Thomas Beard, 25 March 1861. Pilgrim 9. 395). In a less flattering formulation, another correspondent was told in 1861 that 'Wills has no genius, and is, in literary matters, sufficiently commonplace to represent a very large proportion of our readers' (To Sir Edward Bulwer Lytton, 15 May 1861. Pilgrim 9. 415).

If Dickens was occasionally dismissive of his sub-editor and his readership, his strategies in soliciting contributors are carefully thought through, and interestingly he stresses professional engagement over cultural constructions of gender. In soliciting a story from Elizabeth Gaskell in 1850, for instance, he accords her the gender-neutral status of 'writer', before a phrase in which she becomes the 'authoress' of a particular novel, 'I *do* honestly know that there is no living English writer whose aid I would desire to enlist, in preference to the authoress of Mary Barton' (To Mrs Gaskell, 31 January 1850. Pilgrim 6. 21-22. 22). Here Dickens is characteristically both the editor in search of capable help and the reader who represents public taste.

His willingness to position himself as reader as well as writer is even more obvious in a letter attempting to secure the work of Anne Marsh, in which he suggests that her books constitute a secret in his possession, akin to a personally addressed letter, as he tells her:

> You have interested my leisure hours so often and so long, and have given me so much heartfelt pleasure by your writings, and by your generous approval of mine, that I cannot address you as a stranger. ... If I were to endeavour to tell you how much I have been moved and

affected by your books, I should almost feel as if I were parading the secrets of my heart. And yet I cannot help saying that they alone are the occasion of my writing to you, and that if I write in the perfect confidence that you will forgive me for the trouble to which I put you, the blame must lie on their heads. (22 February 1850. Pilgrim 6. 43–44)

Given that this letter is overtly written to solicit material for the new journal, it is hard to see what could have motivated him to write to her, *other* than a knowledge of her novels. But just as Dickens's readers are encouraged to feel a sense of community, both with him as the writer and with each other, so Marsh is invited to enter a quasi-emotional rather than a strictly contractual relationship. In this formulation, business considerations are presented as secondary, while the labour of writing itself is displaced by a vision of reading, specifically associated not with work but with 'my leisure hours'. This association of reading with leisure is inherently unstable for a writer and more particularly for an editor whose work will involve reading numerous manuscripts and preparing them for publication.

Household Words became an arena for the display of new fiction and journalism by different authors, and Dickens's position as 'Conductor' of the journal added a new dimension to his relations with other authors. After *Household Words* was superseded by *All the Year Round* in 1859 he was obliged to console Charles Lever in the dual capacity of editor and friend, for the failure of *A Day's Ride*. Having initially encouraged him not to 'be afraid to trust the audience with any thing that is good. Though a very large one, it is a fine one' (9 March 1860. Pilgrim 9. 219), he was obliged to start writing *Great Expectations* in parallel, in response to falling sales, and his embarrassment is both palpable and almost certainly offered with deliberate tact in the letter of explanation to the unfortunate author, 'I set such a value on your friendship and have such a high sense of your generosity and delicacy, that I hate to write – dread to write – can't write – this letter! And more than that; I carry it to my desk upon my shoulder like Christian's load, and shall not have laid it down until I hear cheerfully from you. So even to have written it, is no relief' (To Charles Lever, 6 October 1860. Pilgrim 9. 321–22. 322). Another letter distances the editor from his own excisions of a writer's text, suggesting that his pen controls his hand rather than the other way round, 'My daring pen shall have imbued its murderous hand with ink, before you see the Proof' (To Miss Marguerite Power, 25 September 1860. Pilgrim 9. 317–18).

There is a slight uneasiness about business arrangements, perhaps deliberately made visible, in a letter to G. H. Lewes, attempting to secure work from George Eliot by proxy:

> Of my personal feeling and wish in the matter, and of the extent to which I have it at heart as an artist, to have such an artist working with me, I have no right to say more in this connexion. I never can

overcome the delicacy and difficulty that arise in me, the moment I have to make any mention of writing, in any other character than as a writer. Only tell me, therefore, whether you will see Wills, and when?

Now, thank God! I subside into the personage who smoked his cigar in the chair before the fire, last Thursday, and can send my kindest regard and truest sympathy in all things, without a fettered mind. (To G. H. Lewes, 4 November 1859. 160–61)

In their distancing from the financial questions that would need to be discussed at some point, these initial, carefully crafted letters to prospective writers are suggestive of friendship offerings that set the relations between editor and writer on an equal footing for their future guidance. In this respect they differ markedly from the professional correspondence with Wills, in which Dickens can be both directive and dismissive of particular contributions.

Nonetheless it is salutary to remember that Dickens was not always to be seen as the unassailable judge of the work of others. As Mary Boyle recalled, 'Charles Dickens, himself a hero, was a hero-worshipper, and in all of my experience I never knew a man so utterly exempt from the slightest tinge of professional jealousy' ('Dickens's "Dearest Meery" Remembers' 86). Notably he shows a willingness to be edited himself, both within the context of *Household Words* and in his fiction (in his critical study of 1898 Gissing palpably shudders when he is forced to discuss Bulwer Lytton's influence on the ending of *Great Expectations*). During one unedifying exchange with Harriet Martineau over factory reform, Dickens wrote to Wills:

Miss Martineau, in this, is precisely what I always knew her to be, and have always impressed her on you as being. ... I do suppose that there never was such a wrong-headed woman born – such a vain one – or such a Humbug.

If you think any little thing I have put in too hard, consult Forster. If you both think so, take it out. Not otherwise. (6 January. Pilgrim 8. 9–10. 9)

Dickens's writing itself appears as a point of discussion and debate between characters, in a number of novels of the 1840s and '50s, and this in itself becomes potentially problematic in the context of the journal, notably in the famous debate between Captain Brown and Miss Jenkyns in *Cranford*, over the relative merits of Dickens and Johnson. Writing to Gaskell about the serialisation of Cranford in *Household Words* in 1851, Dickens apologised for having substituted Hood's poems for *The Pickwick Papers* in the proofs of that month's number, which he told her could not now be recalled. He pointed out to her that 'Any recollection of me from your pen, cannot (as I think you know) be otherwise than truly gratifying to me; but with my name on every page of Household Words there would be – at least I should feel – an impropriety in so mentioning myself' (to Mrs Gaskell, [4] December 1851. 548–49. 549).

As an editor Dickens also became involved in the assessment of work sent in by contributors on behalf of their friends. For a number of years previously, he had been regularly approached for advice on the publication of mss of various sorts, as in the case of John Overs. In his capacity as editor of *Household Words*, the constant flow in to the office of unsolicited work added considerably to this correspondence. His response to some of these potential contributors, and to friends writing on their behalf, develops a theory of authorship combining professional standards with a mythology of the standing of the writer. One writer was advised in 1853:

> for ever and a day to dismiss the Gentle Reader as a monster of the Great Mud Period, who has no kind of business on the face of the literary Earth; to remember if she sit down to write for a journal like this, that she is just an English woman writing the English language for a large English audience, and to consider whether she cannot get on in such an aim without German lines and French words; to forget herself as utterly as the Gentle Reader, and only to remember what she is describing. (To unknown correspondent. 28 February 1853. Pilgrim 7. 33–34. 34)

As much as anything, Dickens's letters to and about these writers show his concern to sustain the selective status of the journal. Returning a submission passed on by Elizabeth Gaskell he fumed, 'People don't plunge into Churches and play the Organs, without knowing the notes or having the ghost of an ear. Yet fifty people a day will rush into manuscript for these leaves only who have no earthly qualification but the actual physical art of writing' (To Mrs Gaskell, 21 February 1853. Pilgrim 7. 27).

The infusion of contributors' work with Dickens's own style was the source of inevitable tension at certain points and was also problematic in the sense that Dickens himself was apt to resent any perceived encroachment on his signature style. As early as 1847 he had complained in a letter to Emile de la Rue:

> You write of one man imitating the Inimitable! By Heaven they all do – to an extent that is perfectly inconceivable! I cannot take up a Magazine or story book of any kind, but I see the most palpable and blundering imitation of myself over and over again – coupled, very likely, with some disparagement of myself by the same hand. (24 March 1847. Pilgrim 5. 41–43. 41–42)

After working his way through a parcel of mss sent to the office of *Household Words* in 1850, he told Angela Burdett Coutts, 'extremely dreary they were – all with a drone of imitation of myself in them, which pervaded the whole parcel' (14 August 1850. Pilgrim 6. 147–48. 147).

Such complaints applied to both new would-be contributors to the journal and novelists as successful as Harriet Beecher Stowe, Dickens remarking acidly of Uncle Tom's Cabin that 'She (I mean Mrs Stowe) is a leetle unscrupulous in the appropriation way. I seem to see a writer with whom I am very intimate (and whom nobody can possibly admire more than myself) peeping very often through the thinness of the paper' (To the Hon. Mrs Richard Watson, 22 November 1852. Pilgrim 6. 807–809. 808). Even the hapless Wills is adjured on one occasion to avoid such imitation in his contributions to the journal. Criticising a proposed contribution, Dickens tells him that 'You are always getting into the footsteps, too, of a writer I know; and when your own shoes might otherwise leave a plain bold mark, they get so entangled with the prints of his, that the reader, following on the track of both, gets confused and bothered' (13 April 1855. Pilgrim 7. 590–91. 591). Perhaps surprisingly, there is at least one instance on record of Dickens apparently encouraging imitation. Asked by Mrs Watson whether a particular contribution is his own, he responds that 'The Walk is not my writing. It is very well done by a close Imitator'.[2]

As his own fame increased Dickens was able to impose new meanings on his earlier fiction, through writing prefaces to new editions. Robert Patten has explained that 'paratexts can define for readers the genre they will be consuming: romance, horror, legend, fantasy, sci-fi, satire, history, memoir, and so forth. And the author's preface, written before the book is ever published, tries to mediate between the author's intentions and the reader's expectations, to say how this work came about and what it expects to accomplish' ('Publishing in Parts' 16). He also uses the physical form of serialisation to reinforce connections between different bodies of work, telling Henry Austin that 'I will shew you tomorrow a few lines of Sanitary Preface I have done, to the cheap Oliver. I have gone to the expence [sic] of printing it to "sew up" with Copperfield at the end of this month – with the patriotic view of "sewing up" at the same time, Sir Peter Laurie' (21 March 1850. Pilgrim 6. 69–70).

But he was forced to make a public declaration, when a printed 'exposé' of the Catholic Maynooth College, including possibly titillating details, found its way in to the July number of the journal, and one irate reader complained to *The Times*. Dickens protested immediately, 'It is unnecessary for me to assure you that nobody connected with the publication of Household Words has the least knowledge of this disgraceful publication, or has had the least part in placing it where your correspondent found it' (To the Editor of the Times, 9 July 1852. Pilgrim 6. 708–9. 708). The subsequent investigation found that the likely culprit was a bookseller, who had access to copies of the journal after it left the office for ultimate delivery to the wholesaler. But the incident suggests an unsettling echo of Dickens's earlier protests over piracy of his work, as his carefully revised and crafted prose was doctored and placed in uncongenial contexts, under his name but without his consent.

In the novels first-person narrators are not wholly able to control the representation of their stories and may struggle to find a role for themselves. David, Esther and Pip are all very different but uniquely placed to show the status of character narrators before they publish and become famous (David) or have a reason to relate their stories (Esther, Pip) and to persuade the reader to invest emotionally in characters who may never become writers. Of the three, David alone implies in the first lines of his story that he has a recognisable status, but is promptly quashed by the Murdstones and by his pseudo 'aristocratic patron' figure Steerforth, who exploits his imaginative faculty for his own entertainment. Nonetheless all three narrators are driven by the need for self-expression. Hardy observes that 'Dickens's uncharacterized and anonymous narrators are generally reticent, but given to rare interventions like the discussion of "streaky bacon" in *Oliver Twist*' (45). However this division between first person and omniscient does not account for the status of private documents written by characters within texts, which prove to be a key feature of Esther Summerson's narrative in particular.

The instinct to frame events – literally to place oneself in the picture – is demonstrated when Pip waits for his first meeting with Herbert in their London lodgings 'I had nearly maddened myself with looking out for half an hour, and had written my name with my finger several times in the dirt of every pane in the window, before I heard footsteps on the stairs' (159). Crucially, first-person written narratives are not only vehicles for the writers' own words, but also filters for other characters such as Skimpole; as Horne observes, 'Esther's treatment of Skimpole reminds us that punctuation – as anyone knows who has had to transcribe an interview from a recording – is a potent tool, a form of editing, even a form of rewriting' (157).

First-person narratives are not necesarily, as might be expected, determined primarily by gender. Both David and Esther worry about the writing itself and about who are the heroes or central figures in their respective narratives, while Pip queries the status of published writing, through satirical portrayals in the town newspaper and the mysterious book read by Mrs Pocket (which turns out to be a guide to the upper classes). All three powerfully articulate the very lack of confidence by which they feel their writing to be hampered, building their narratives at the intersection of private experience and public or social engagement. *Bleak House* uniquely offers both first- and third-person accounts of letters and documents crossing or catapulting characters across the boundary from private to public and back. In each case, the narrative is constructed at least partly through the apparently transparent medium of personal letters. The fallibility of first-person narrators is attested by Thackeray when, undermining the authenticity of Pendennis's account in *The Newcomes*, he concludes that:

> no doubt, the writer of the book, into whose hands Clive Newcome's logs have been put, and who is charged with the duty of making two octavo volumes out of his friend's story, dresses up the narrative in

his own way; utters his own remarks in place of Newcome's; makes fanciful descriptions of individuals and incidents with which he never could have been personally acquainted; and commits blunders which the critics will discover. (296)

In Dickens's novels handwritten letters are shown to be as untrustworthy as print, as *Bleak House* and *Great Expectations* attest.

'No Natural Power Over a Pen': *Bleak House*

Bleak House finished serialisation in September 1853, just as Bradbury & Evans were about to start bringing out the first numbers of *The Newcomes*. Towards the end of Thackeray's novel, in which he replaces his earlier attack on *Oliver Twist* with several scenes praising its interest for his fictional readers, a short passage appears containing yet another allusion to Dickens's fiction, in what is surely a passing swipe at Esther Summerson:

> To break her heart in silence for Tomkins who is in love with another; to suffer no end of poverty, starvation, capture by ruffians, ill-treatment by a bullying husband, *loss of beauty by the smallpox*, death even at the end of the volume; all these mishaps a young heroine may endure (and has endured in romances over and over again), without losing the least dignity, or suffering any diminution of the sentimental reader's esteem. (595. Emphasis added)

Of course there is more to Esther's story than simply a sentimental plot about the vindication of the illegitimate heroine's innocence. In his innovative use of dual narrators, Dickens enables a displacement of his own narrative authority as the two perspectives alternate in the telling of public and private events and slowly converge towards the end of the novel. The preface comically insists on its own authenticity, claiming that a recent speech by a Chancery Judge 'seemed to me too profound a joke to be inserted in the body of this book, or I should have restored it to Conversation Kenge or to Mr Vholes, with one or other of whom I think it must have originated' (unpaginated). As the preface makes clear in this invitation to believe in the external reality of Kenge and Vholes, a triumvirate of imagination, memory and knowledge must be brought in from outside the novel, in order to help readers to understand it.

The central motif of both narratives is provided by the self-generating business of the Jarndyce v Jarncyce Chancery suit, in which:

> Dickens's basic representational strategy is to seize upon a ceremonial emblem or motif associated with Chancery practice, wrench it out of its context, and recombine it with ideas or motifs that suggest the primitive shapelessness or the gothic cruelty of the dark ages.

> Moreover, unlike pictorial satire, which can operate only with images and within a framed space, *Bleak House* unfurls the juxtapositional aesthetics of graphic satire across the vaster and more complex discursive domain that the novel form made available. (Sen 54)

The response to the novel was not universally favourable. Sean Grass argues that 'during the 1830s and 1840s Dickens was treated roughly far less often than he, or any writer so prominent, had a right to expect. The turning point in Dickens's fortunes with reviewers was *Bleak House*, arguably his most powerful novel' (107).

Dickens himself always claimed not to read hostile reviews, but from the very start of his career his fiction consistently weighs the value of different responses to literature. No exception to this rule, *Bleak House* is preoccupied to the point of obsession with the status of the written word in general. As critics have noted, it also 'makes detectives of most of its characters and all of its readers' (Pykett. *Charles Dickens*. 136), being, as John Gordon puts it, 'built out of moments where the reader must decide on the spot (and then, probably, reconsider, on a later spot) which way to go, which way is realer' (187). It is at its very centre, a novel about the difficulty of knowing whom to trust, in a world where words are portentous and misleading or conversely trivial and unwittingly fatal. Notoriously (and despite Dickens's unfortunate portrayal of Miss Mowcher in *David Copperfield*) this is the novel in which Leigh Hunt was the only person not to recognise himself in Harold Skimpole, an insult Dickens can hardly have ameliorated in his subsequent letter, when he told him that 'when I have felt it was going too close I stopped myself, and the most blotted parts of my MS. are those in which I have been striving hard to make the impression I was writing from, *un*like you' (To Leigh Hunt, [? Early November 1854] Pilgrim 7. 460–61. 460).

As Sen points out, the third person narrative voice both details fictional events and directs its satire to a socially aware reader:

> In these circumstances it is not surprising that immediately after Krook's death by Spontaneous Combustion, that is, immediately after the most obviously fictional event in *Bleak House*, Dickens can effortlessly discard his role as storyteller for that of public speaker addressing the queen herself on behalf of the people (57).

In addition to commenting on topical events, the novel carefully positions itself within the emerging body of fiction by the same author. In the final line of the preface Dickens obliquely references the popularity of his previous work, which he claims has already been surpassed by the serialised story some readers are about to encounter for the first time. In this characteristic address, readers are invited to meet the author in the pages of the novel, much as its characters are represented as actual figures who pass their jokes on to Chancery Judges, 'I believe I have never had so many readers as in this book. May we meet again!' (unpaginated).

This intimate relationship is almost immediately thrown into doubt by an uncharacteristically terse narrator, who (unlike the typical mid-century narrators of Thackeray and Trollope, for instance) shows no sustained awareness of the reader and who alternates with the self-deprecating Esther. In a rare acknowledgement of the first-person narrative running alongside its own, the third-person account makes one possibly satirical reference to Esther's habit of stylistic repetition, in the opening of chapter 7, 'While Esther sleeps, and while Esther wakes'. Pamela Gilbert observes that if the sentimental tradition works by invoking familiar patterns, and by taking the reader as more aware or able to make connections than the characters themselves (48), 'The traditional feminine narrative voice had been non-ironic, and more closely aligned to the sentimental one, although also more detached. Dickens, however, adopted a more traditionally masculine satirical voice as a counterpoint to his scenes of sentiment' (47). This division reaches its most extreme form in the shared narration of *Bleak House*. This structure means that '*Bleak House* begins fantastically and ends fancifully. Moreover, as a novel with two narrators it begins and ends twice. In between, the power of Dickens's fancy and fantasy conjures into being a host of different and disparate voices' (Pykett. *Charles Dickens*. 138).

Paradoxically these narrators, who barely acknowledge each other's presence in the text, share a compulsive interest in writing, including the illicit reading of private documents. According to Daniel Hack, 'There is reference in the novel to the handwriting or writing activity of no fewer than twenty named characters' (38). But if the two narrators never quite touch, the worlds they describe repeatedly overlap. The novel's central motif of the documents in Jarndyce and Jarndyce appears in both narratives, refracted through images of reading and writing that include the composition and appropriation of wills and letters, autobiography and fiction. While some of these papers (including both legal transcripts and personal correspondence written by Captain Hawdon) are subjected to close and repeated scrutiny, others such as the barrows of paperwork in Jarndyce and Jarndyce or the documents carried about by Miss Flyte, invert the vaguely defined status of generic fairy tales in previous novels, in that they are fatally pervasive without being particularised. This lack of particularity serves a double function here, in that the papers are presented by the third-person narrator as a deliberate obfuscation of the facts they purport to establish. Miss Flyte herself narrowly avoids using her own papers to blow her nose during a visit to Esther, '"Dear me!" said she, putting her hand into her reticule, "I have nothing here but documents, my dear Fitz Jarndyce; I must borrow a pocket-handkerchief"' (520).

Written materials associated with Chancery are apparently chaotic and often remain unread. Nonetheless they form a pattern of connection between Chancery suitors. There is a clear warning in the description of Gridley's room, where 'A table and some shelves were covered with manuscript papers, and with worn pens, and a medley of such tokens' (371). In a series of tableaux leading to his early death, Richard is later seen 'poring over a table covered with dusty bundles of papers which seemed to me like dusty mirrors reflecting his own mind' (724). Like Krook himself, he becomes a compulsive collector of these documents. Highlighting the damaging nature of this habit, Victoria Mills notes that 'Fictional collectors are often addictive personalities. Dorian Gray alternates collecting with a developing opium habit, Krook in *Bleak House* drinks as avidly as he collects and Richard Carstone, collector of useless documents from the ongoing court case Jarndyce v Jarndyce, often appears with the flushed face of the addict' (42).

If then an interest in text is potentially unhealthy and damaging rather than liberating, the novel demands that the reader reconsider the basic question, what does it mean to be able to read and write? Tulkinghorn derives his power from the close guardianship of family secrets (represented and reinforced by the papers he secrets in locked boxes). Such papers can literally be used as weapons, as when Guppy and Jobling return to Krook's shop after his death, where they find the Smallweeds in residence 'and Mrs Smallweed on the level ground in the vicinity, snowed up in a heap of paper fragments, print and manuscript, which would appear to be the accumulated compliments that have been sent flying at her in the course of the day' (586). In a less direct form of aggression, according to Miss Flyte, the Lord Chancellor's wife '"leads him a terrible life. Throws his Lordship's papers into the fire, my dear, if he won't pay the jeweller!"' (522)

At the most basic level the question of literacy has obvious implications for working-class characters in the novel. Jo characteristically hovers between bathos and moral weight in his final revelation of the limits of the written word, asking Snagsby to apologise to Esther for his having infected her, and deriving comfort from the idea that the words will be written 'wery large' (675). Disguised as a working-class woman, Lady Dedlock instinctively feels that her final letter to Esther will not be treated seriously if she leaves it at the post office, telling Guster 'it would be rubbed out and not minded and never sent' (843). The girl Esther sees married in Lincolnshire makes a mark in the register to avoid shaming her husband, who cannot yet write his name. The comic description of Charley's progress, elsewhere in the novel, stands as a reminder of just how difficult this is, 'Writing was a trying business to Charley, who seemed to have no natural power over a pen, but in whose hand every pen appeared to become perversely animated, and to go wrong and crooked, and to stop, and splash, and sidle into corners, like a saddle-donkey' (448).

Even the ability to write only constitutes a level of power if the recipient of the written text is able to read. Playfully confusing the terms of reference, Jarndyce comments on Mrs Pardiggle's tract that 'he doubted if Robinson Crusoe could have read it, though he had had no other on his desolate island' (122). Characters who are illiterate, such as the brick makers and Krook, may also be dishonest or violent. Nonetheless the inability to read is poignantly linked to dispossession and powerlessness; at the metaphorical level the inability to interpret what is seen alters the relations between other senses, rendering the subject voiceless as well as blind. Jo the crossing sweeper is surely, as Judith Flanders claims, 'One of Dickens's most compelling characters' (49), but is famously not allowed to give evidence at the 'inkwich' because he is uneducated; the third-person narrator points out that the 'blindness' to text involves the inability to 'hear' the written word in the act of reading:

> It must be a strange state to be like Jo! To shuffle through the streets, unfamiliar with the shapes, and in utter darkness as to the meaning, of those mysterious symbols, so abundant over the shops, and at the corners of streets, and on the doors, and in the windows! To see people read, and to see people write, and to see the postmen deliver letters, and not to have the least idea of all that language – to be, to every scrap of it, stone blind and dumb! (236)

When Smallweed tells George, 'We have never been readers in our family. It don't pay. Stuff. Idleness. Folly. No, no!' (318), he is therefore (for once) missing a trick. The narrator's condemnation distinguishes between the 'disability' of the illiterate Jo and the damaging impact of this deliberate rejection of reading. As a breed the Smallweeds are in a degenerative state, resembling monkeys rather than human beings:

> During the whole time consumed in the slow growth of this family tree, the house of Smallweed, always early to go out and late to marry, has strengthened itself in its practical character, has discarded all amusements, discountenanced all story-books, fairy tales, fictions, and fables, and banished all levities whatsoever. Hence the gratifying fact, that it has had no child born to it, and that the complete little men and women whom it has produced, have been observed to bear a likeness to old monkeys with something depressing on their minds. (308)

Krook remains illiterate precisely because, accepting the power of the written word, he fears that any teacher will deliberately mislead him. Guppy remarks that 'It's a monomania with him, to think he is possessed of documents. He has been going to learn to read them this last quarter of a century' (475). At the other end of the social scale, Volumnia also has an eye to the papers of others, taking the first opportunity to check what she can expect from Sir Leicester Dedlock's will:

> Certain it is that she avails herself of the present opportunity of hovering over her kinsman's letters and papers, like a bird; taking a short peck at this document, and a blink with her head on one side at that document, and hopping about from table to table with her glass at her eye in an inquisitive and restless manner. In the course of these

researches she stumbles over something; and turning her glass in that direction, sees her kinsman lying on the ground like a felled tree. (792)

Nor is the belief in literature itself as universally redemptive in this novel as it is elsewhere in Dickens. Esther's affectionate but unflattering nicknames include Dame Durden and Mother Hubbard (significantly the rhyme itself designates this figure as 'Old Mother Hubbard); Skimpole's whimsical introduction of his Beauty daughter, his Comedy daughter and his Sentiment daughter, draws the reader's attention to the constrained roles he has selfishly imposed on them for his own aesthetic enjoyment. As Esther quickly realises, Skimpole also draws on types of the Romantic Child to justify his irresponsible behaviour and mask his opportunistic appeals for money. This claim becomes particularly repugnant to characters such as Esther in light of his callous (by implication pseudo-aristocratic) indifference to genuinely poor children such as the hardworking Charlie and Jo, who have retained their essential innocence and goodness despite being exposed to the most deprived areas of London.

Like *David Copperfield*, *Bleak House* is concerned with private writing as much as with canonical or public texts. Again like David, both narrators include numerous references to letters. Jarndye's rather disconcerting proposal to Esther is carefully mediated through a letter delivered by Charley, and she ratifies it in terms used by David Copperfield and Dickens himself, when she says that the act of reading is like hearing the voice of the writer, 'It was not a love letter though it expressed so much love, but was written just as he would at any time have spoken to me. I saw his face, and heard his voice, and felt the influence of his kind protecting manner, in every line' (638). Esther's rendition of the letter as reported rather than direct speech is key to the reader's interpretation of it. She herself governs the tone by literally telling the reader what it 'expressed'. Even so, it is an uncomfortable scenario for the reader, who is able to trust Esther's interpretation and Jarndyce's motive only through a prior knowledge of the character of each.

Elsewhere in the novel letters have less positive connotations. Caddy is coerced into endless circular correspondence for her 'telescopic' mother, who teaches her what is useful for this purpose at the expense of basic housekeeping – when Esther teaches her to sew, she remembers that 'She was clumsy enough with her needle, poor girl, and pricked her fingers as much as she had been used to ink them' (439). Tellingly Kenge speaks of Mrs Jellyby, who fails so palpably to fulfil her role as guardian of the domestic hearth, while 'standing with his back to the fire, and casting his eyes over the dusty hearth-rug as if it were Mrs Jellyby's biography' (44). Jarndyce welcomes his wards to Bleak House with identical letters in order to avoid intimate speech (although he later tells Esther that her influence has instigated a change in him and he is increasingly able to talk seriously to his wards face to face), as 'a relief to you possibly, and to me certainly' (74); he himself receives numerous begging letters, carefully crafted to elicit a

First-Person-Narrators and Editorial 'Conducting' 121

particular response but shutting down the possibility of reciprocal questioning. As Esther remarks, 'It appeared to us that some of them must pass their whole lives in dealing out subscription-cards to the whole Post-office Directory – shilling cards, half-crown cards, half-sovereign cards, penny cards' (112). When Smallweed writes to George foreclosing on his debt, George is instinctively reluctant to open the letter and instead assesses its danger by inspecting the envelope:

> He looks at it at arm's length, brings it close to him, holds it in his right hand, holds it in his left hand, reads it with his head on this side, with his head on that side, contracts his eyebrows, elevates them; still cannot satisfy himself. He smooths it out upon the table with his heavy palm, and thoughtfully walking up and down the gallery, makes a halt before it every now and then, to come upon it with a fresh eye. Even that won't do. 'Is it,' Mr George still muses, 'blank cartridge or ball?' (496)

Meanwhile George himself has put off writing to his mother until he feels that it is now too late. Having finally capitulated and shown Hawdon's letter to Tulkinghorn, with disastrous results, George establishes his moral character beyond further doubt by repeating the original indiscretion, in a letter to Esther in which he explains what was in the original and how he was duped by the lawyer. In a novel so dependent for its plot on the misuse of private letters, this indiscretion constitutes a minor act of heroism, as Esther surely recognises.

Esther and Jarndyce both correspond with Richard as his moral breakdown begins, and Richard rejects their concern, writing 'coldly, haughtily, distantly, resentfully' (516) to his guardian. When Esther visits Richard in Deal, 'He was writing at a table, with a great confusion of clothes, tin cases, books, brushes, and portmanteaus, strewn all about the floor' (646–67). In a breakdown of the Dickensian metaphor of the letter as quasi-magical vehicle of communication, he crushes the letter he was writing when she comes in:

> 'Have you been at the trouble of writing all that, and am I not to read it after all?' I asked. 'Oh my dear,' he returned, with a hopeless gesture. 'You may read it in the whole room. It is all over here'. (647)

Esther, who retains a full sense of the value of letters, is anxious to receive this one even though she can now speak to the writer in person, but Richard poignantly directs her attention instead to the disordered state of his room. The letter, in its various unfinished drafts, is literally 'all over here'; more importantly, the disarray in which he is living should tell her what was in the letter – that it is 'all over' with him here.

Towards the end of the novel, Lady Dedlock writes to Esther to express the love she cannot show in public, counteracting Guppy's unsolicited letters in which he implicitly threatens to expose her as Esther's mother. The writing of letters may be dangerous – or as Bucket expresses it, 'green'; equally letters can substitute for dangerous speech or even physical contact, as when Ada writes to Esther during her period of quarantine. Esther derives considerable solace from this communication, as the first use to which she puts her restored vision, 'my sight strengthening, and the glorious light coming every day more fully and brightly on me, I could read the letters that my dear wrote to me every morning and evening, and could put them to my lips and lay my cheek upon them with no fear of hurting her' (514).

The novel perpetuates its links between legal discourse and personal feeling when Guppy records his proposal to Esther in a pocket book and refers back to it when he wishes to remind her that she rejected it before her illness left her less marriageable. While this proceeding may be deeply insensitive, it allows Esther to record without comment Guppy's dependence on her honour – they must both know that his notes made for his own reference at the time of the proposal can have no legal weight without her attestation. The Dedlock plot, which hinges on Lady Dedlock's inadvertent mark of recognition when she sees Hawdon's writing after he transcribes a legal document later sent to Tulkinghorn, is conversely based on a deep lack of trust between domestic and legal characters. In an effort to gain definite knowledge from a betrayal of emotion, when George initially refuses to hand over Hawdon's last letter to him, Tulkinghorn abruptly shows him an affidavit in Jarndyce and Jarndyce in the same hand. Only George's refusal to engage in any direct communication saves him from falling into this trap (refusing to co-operate, he does not of course see the writing), much as Jarndyce is preserved from the contamination associated with Chancery by avoiding the court altogether.

Esther's narrative situates itself against the public world of Chancery, as she repeatedly insists on her domestic relations and limited scope of action. However it is already contextualised by the public but equally closed world whose power she invokes, as she becomes the chronicler of Richard's tragic story. Hardy argues that:

> Esther's is subtle story-telling, and it is a pity that such a bold idea as making a woman tell so much of the story should be at all undermined by the author's delight in domestic virtue. However, he does not confine her sensitive register to the domestic sphere but takes her into the public world of Chancery, making her the most outspoken and socially subversive of his three sustained narrators. (*Dickens and Creativity* 55)

This most self-effacing of Dickens's narrators nonetheless controls the reader's experience of written text for much of the novel, and this includes raising questions about the vehicle and significance of her own writing. Esther, 'if she asserts herself as the main character of her narrative, goes on pretending right up to the end that she is relating Rick Carstone's tragic story. ... Esther is the true heroine of the book, but then, she is the heroine of a novel which has grown out of the one she had been appointed to write...' (Sadrin 12–13). When Jarndyce and Ada compliment her she tells the reader that 'I must write it, even if I rub it out again, because it gives me so much pleasure' (448). Presumably Esther is supposed to be writing in pencil, reinforcing the fragility and impermanence of her record. She ends the novel very much as Dickens began it, with an expression of love for her unknown reader; unlike the public-facing male author of course, she limits herself to one intimate confidant and has no plans to meet again on the page of subsequent texts, 'The few words that I have to add to what I have written, are soon penned; then I, and the unknown friend to whom I write, will part for ever. Not without much dear remembrance on my side. Not without some, I hope, on his or hers' (910).

But the course of her narrative has already destabilised the authority of the written word. In a last satirical comment on Skimpole, she confides in the reader that following the coolness between himself and Jarndyce 'He died some five years afterwards, and left a diary behind him, with letters and other materials towards his Life; which was published, and which showed him to have been the victim of a combination on the part of mankind against an amiable child' (864). The published 'Life' is essentially a public and masculine form, but it is largely based on letters and diaries, implicitly feminised private documents that have already been subverted by both Esther and the third-person narrator. Such documents are either preserved by chance, in which case they arguably accrue inappropriate weight and may not offer a representative view of the subject or as in this case, they have been tendentiously collected – or even written – precisely because they present the subject as he wishes to be seen.

Bleak House constantly reverts to the familiar theme of the failure or refusal of words. By extension, character interaction can be governed by what is not written or is not available for reading. The disappearance of the Hawdon / Honoria love letters in Krook's combustion dramatically withholds a written exchange from the reader, which several characters know to have existed. But the draft letters Richard writes to Esther and then throws round the room, and the line Esther considers writing and rubbing out again, subtly remind the reader of alternative versions of events, which may never be written at all. Her own incomplete narration of events drives the reader to complete the last sentence of the novel for her, breaking off just before she can agree with her husband's assertion, presumably that she is prettier than she ever was.

The readers of the novel are free to complete the sentence for themselves, as the missing phrase operates to engage active reading practices up until the very last line. As in his letters about *David Copperfield*, Dickens in turn shows himself willing to share 'confidences' with friends about the personal memories he has incorporated in the novel, which in turn are to inform the

124 *First-Person-Narrators and Editorial 'Conducting'*

imaginative response of his readers. In one letter he urges a correspondent to participate in the walks he himself has presumably taken as part of the writing process:

> Convey yourself back to London by the agency of that powerful Locomotive, your imagination, and walk through the centre avenue of Covent Garden Market from West to East:- that is to say, with your back towards the church, and your face towards Drury Lane Theatre. Keep straight on along the side of the Theatre, and about halfway down, on the left side of the way, behind the houses, is a closely hemmed-in grave yard – happily long disused and closed by the Law. I do not remember that the grave-yard is accessible from the street now, but when I was a boy it was to be got at by a low covered passage under a house, and was guarded by a rusty iron gate. In that churchyard I long afterwards buried the 'Nemo' of Bleak House. (To Miss Palfrey, 4 April 1868. Pilgrim 12. 91)

In the autumn of 1853 Dickens was complaining to Lavinia Watson about the desolate air of London out of season, but was able to tell her that he had gone:

> wandering about to look for some ingenious portmanteau; and near the corner of St James's street, saw a solitary Being sitting in a trunk shop, absorbed in a book which on closer inspection I found to be Bleak House. I thought this looked well, and went in. And he really was more interested in seeing me when he knew who I was, than any face I had seen in any house – every house I knew, being occupied by painters – including my own. (21 September 1853. Pilgrim 7. 154–45. 154)

Like the literary detectives of *Bleak House* itself, Dickens has by his own account been driven to find out *what* the man is reading, before approaching him. His reward is to discover that the reader's willingness to value him in person is precisely relative to the book that is physically between them at that moment.

'Considerably worried and scratched by every letter': *Great Expectations*

The haunting opening of *Great Expectations* echoes the assurance of David Copperfield's narration in its handling of the child's early confrontation with a strange and potentially hostile world, leading Sadrin to comment suggestively that 'As we read these lines, we soon realize that we are attending nothing less than the birth of a writer: self-authored in the midst of the world that he has just conjured up' (96). Unlike David and like Esther, Pip is not a professional writer and has only one story to tell. But his narrative opens up a debate about the status and function of literacy, as the theme of reading creates parallels between obvious and also less likely pairs of characters including Joe / Magwitch, Wemmick / Jaggers, and Wopsle / Pip. These clues are scattered across the text, accruing significance in the reader's mind in the same way that Pip must impose a level of order on his narrative trajectory in order to reassess his place in the world of the novel.

The opening of the narrative contains an implicit warning against the undirected imagination, invoking David Copperfield's 'undisciplined heart' even as it sheers off from the earlier novel's celebration of the power given by reading, 'impersonating my favourite characters... - as I did – and ...putting Mr and Mrs Murdstone into all the bad ones – which I did too' (*David Copperfield* 53). Chartable lineage is reworked as boundless potential for reinvention through Pip's early reading in the churchyard, as 'Like all budding autobiographers, it is the book of his origins that he is first given to read. And, of course, he rewrites it. There is little else he could do' (Sadrin 97).

It soon becomes clear that for Pip the imagination is not initially a symbol of hope or means of salvation, but rather the first of many traps into which he is thoughtlessly decoyed in the course of the novel. He will almost lose his life to the vengeful Orlick when he allows himself to be duped by the anonymous summons to the marshes, which he learns too late has been penned by Compeyson. It is surely significant that Magwitch's old enemy uses disguised writing to deceive his last victim; as Orlick gloats, 'I've took up with new companions, and new masters. Some of 'em writes my letters when I wants 'em wrote – do you mind? – writes my letters, wolf! They writes fifty hands; they're not like sneaking you, as writes but one' (390–91).

Clearly the unreflecting Orlick fails to see that Compeyson has as much to gain in writing this letter as he does himself, or in other words that he writes the letter not 'when I wants 'em wrote' but in accordance with his own plans for the destruction of Magwitch. But the questionable nature of written language is a feature of the text from the first passage of Pip's narrative. Like David, Pip's earliest memories include the churchyard where his parents are buried, and so:

> As I never saw my father or my mother, and never saw any likeness of them... my first fancies regarding what they were like, were unreasonably derived from their tombstones. The shape of the letters on my father's, gave me an odd idea that he was a square, stout, dark man with curly black hair. From the character and turn of the inscription, '*Also Georgiana Wife of the Above,*' I drew a childish conclusion that my mother was freckled and sickly. (3)

With adult self-awareness the narrating Pip admits that '... I read "wife of the Above" as a complimentary reference to my father's exaltation to a better world; and if any one of my deceased relations had been referred to as

"Below," I have no doubt I should have formed the worst opinions of that member of the family' (39). The sparsity of the text Pip is given to read, and which forms his only imaginative connection with his dead parents, is the first of a series of linked metaphors suggesting deprivation or emotional starvation – it is surely significant that when he is turned upside down by Magwitch moments later, nothing falls out of his pockets, given that the literature of childhood routinely uses the contents of a boy's pockets as an imaginative motif.

As for David, the process of learning to read is a formative part of his childhood experience, although in Pip's case it is notably less idyllic, 'Much of my unassisted self, and more by the help of Biddy than of Mr Wopsle's great-aunt, I struggled through the alphabet as if it had been a bramble-bush; getting considerably worried and scratched by every letter' (40). At this stage Pip has not disentangled the ability to read, a mark of status, from the critical faculty of interpreting and assessing the worth of what is read. One of his more comic memories is of learning to read by means of a popular song with a bow wow chorus, when 'in my desire to be wiser, I got this composition by heart with the utmost gravity; nor do I recollect that I questioned its merit, except that I thought (as I still do) the amount of Too rul somewhat in excess of the poetry' (99). Later he will reconsider the conflation of class culture with moral superiority through the brutally parodic rise of Magwitch, who tells him that 'A deserting soldier in a Travellers' Rest, what lay hid up to the chin under a lot of taturs, learnt me to read; and a travelling Giant what signed his name at a penny a time learnt me to write' (317). In a poignant shift from previous invocations of the imaginative child, the Giant of fairy tale has become an exploited employee in a freak show, signalling Magwitch's own exclusion from the world of literary fancy but also providing him with the basic education he has failed to gain through other channels.

Perhaps surprisingly, the character who apparently derives most enjoyment from reading is the barely literate Joe, whose instinct to connect experience with the written word stops short at the recognition of his own name, largely because Mrs Joe 'an't over partial to having scholars on the premises ... and in partickler would not be over partial to my being a scholar, for fear as I might rise. Like a sort of rebel, don't you see?' (44) Even here the reflective Pip is forced into a minor act of disloyalty, acknowledging the reader's greater understanding by spelling the name correctly when Jo does not, '"Give me," said Joe, a good book, or a good newspaper, and sit me down afore a good fire, and I ask no better. Lord!" he continued, after rubbing his knees a little, "when you *do* come to a J and a O, and says you, "Here at last, is a J-O, Joe," how interesting reading is!"' (42)

A less subtle reminder that access to 'literature' is tied to both wealth and material status comes from Joe himself, when he expresses regret that the memorial poem he composed himself was never carved on his father's tombstone, 'As I was saying, Pip, it were my intentions to have had it cut over him; but poetry costs money, cut it how you will, small or large, and it were not done' (43). The words 'Whatsume'er the failings on is part, Remember reader he were that good in his hart' directly contradict everything he has told Pip about his father, reinforcing the danger of Pip's attribution of characteristics to his own parents based purely on their tombstones.

A less naïve character, the worldly Pumblechook does not attempt to translate life into literary terms, which he bypasses altogether. However he too instinctively bases his fantasies of Pip's future on an invocation of the material object, in this case the child himself. As the narrator bitterly recalls, 'The miserable man was a man of that confined stolidity of mind, that he could not discuss my prospects without having me before him – as it were, to operate upon …' (88). As Pykett reminds us, 'The Pip who narrates is the product of other people's dreams and fantasies and a character in other people's stories. The story that he tells is, in part, the story of how he learns that this is the case' (*Charles Dickens* 171). But fittingly the novel ends with the humiliation of Pumblechook, and the serio-comic reconciliation of Joe's masculine strength with the rudiments at least of the culture he has previously rejected. When Pip visits the forge he finds Joe writing as if he were launching a physical assault on the page:

> At my own writing-table, pushed into a corner and cumbered with little bottles, Joe now sat down to his great work, first choosing a pen from the pen-tray as if it were a chest of large tools, and tucking up his sleeves as if he were going to wield a crowbar or sledge-hammer. It was necessary for Joe to hold on heavily to the table with his left elbow and to get his right leg well out behind him, before he could begin, and when he did begin, he made every down-stroke so slowly that it might have been six feet long, while at every up-stroke I could hear his pen spluttering extensively. (424)

If serio-comic resolution is offered by this scene in the forge, miscommunications and misapprehensions throughout the novel centre on the stories told about Satis House and its reclusive owner.

Much of Pip's distress arises from his failure to position himself in relation to others, according to the very limited codes within which he has been taught to operate. Sadrin argues that:

> from the moment he enters Satis House, Pip acts like someone who has inadvertently found his way into a work of fiction which he improves, as he reads on, with his own marginal notes. As long as he remains an outsider… his metaphorical embellishments are rather harmless and do not alter the meaning of the book. Real misconstructions begin when he finds himself changed overnight into a young man with great, yet greatly unexpected, expectations, and, urged by circumstances to take himself for a fairy-tale hero, forces his way into the wrong book and the wrong literary genre. (115)

In fact Pip lacks the literary acumen to interpret the motifs of death and decay that seem so disturbing to his own reader, years after the early events of the novel are supposed to have taken place. Far from being harmless, his embellishments after his first day at Miss Havisham's signal the beginning of his own corruption, as Joe is quick to warn him in his admonishment that he should tell no further lies.

The narrative that follows is an account of Pip's inevitable fall when he ignores the unsophisticated honesty of his first mentor. This trajectory places him in the class of young men who make false starts, of whom the most obvious exemplar was Martin Chuzzlewit and the least reprehensible, David Copperfield. These mistakes are redeemable, unlike the sins of the middle-aged figures who appear alongside them. In a discussion of worldliness and social hypocrisy in the novels, Andrews suggests that for instance:

> Young David tries on his man-of-the-world personae watched with affectionate amusement by his older narrating self. Few of young David's masks fit well or stay on for very long. The mask of the mature hypocrite is a very different matter. When, in *Martin Chuzzlewit*, Pecksniff gets drunk at Todgers's it is as if his mask, without quite falling off, keeps slipping at a grotesque angle, occasionally exposing something of the real face. The two faces tilt apart and recombine. (*Dickensian Laughter* 115)

Pip's lack of self-awareness as a young man places his mistakes somewhere between the wholesome folly of a young David Copperfield and the licentious hypocrisy of an ageing Pecksniff. He misunderstands Miss Havisham's testamentary intentions because, both naïve and selfishly ambitious, he projects his own fantasies into the gap between what he is told and what remains unspoken. But if a lack of education has impeded Pip's ability to interpret the Gothic tropes literally saturating the figure of Miss Havisham, the reader slowly comes to understand that written communication itself is flawed in the novel. After Mrs Joe is battered by Orlick she is reduced to writing on a slate and:

> As she was (very bad handwriting apart) a more than indifferent speller, and as Joe was a more than indifferent reader, extraordinary complications arose between them, which I was always called in to solve. The administration of mutton instead of medicine, the substitution of Tea for Joe, and the baker for bacon, were among the mildest of my own mistakes. (111)

Having attained the culture of a gentleman, Pip discovers that writing is no less deceptive when he and Herbert substitute record keeping for actual economy:

> Each of us would then refer to a confused heap of papers at his side, which had been thrown into drawers, worn into holes in pockets,

half-burnt in lighting candles, stuck for weeks into the looking-glass, and otherwise damaged. The sound of our pens going, refreshed us exceedingly, insomuch that I sometimes found it difficult to distinguish between this edifying business proceeding and actually paying the money. In point of meritorious character, the two things seemed about equal. (252)

Again it is Magwitch who undermines the attribution of value to meaningless words, when he asks Pip to read to him in foreign languages. A bewildered Pip remembers that 'While I complied, he, not comprehending a single word, would stand before the fire surveying me with the air of an Exhibitor, and I would see him, between the fingers of the hand with which I shaded my face, appealing in dumb show to the furniture to take notice of my proficiency' (310). In contrast to the self-deceiving Pip, Magwitch attains a level of dignity when he rejects literature altogether as a means of interpreting his experience, explaining that 'I am not a going fur to tell you my life, like a song or a story-book. But to give it to you short and handy, I'll put it at once into a mouthful of English' (316). Pip on the contrary persistently filters his experience through literary tropes – when he belatedly realises that he is not the hero of his own story, he can only make amends by repositioning himself in his narrative as the Prodigal Son of both Joe and Magwitch.

Poignantly, this realisation of literary structures as inherently limited involves a subversion of Dickens's own trademark celebration of home. It is a critical commonplace that the fiction's celebration of an idealised domestic space is bizarrely at odds with the fully realised broken homes inhabited by key characters from Gabriel Varden to Lizzie Hexham; however this contradiction is not normally *articulated* in the novels. Pip's famous guilt about becoming 'ashamed of home' is contextualised by his previous commitment to this ideal even as he understands its inherent tensions. Unlike Esther Summerson or David Copperfield, he does not necessarily see the substitution of an ideal home for an imperfect one as the resolution to the dilemma. Estella's contempt (her own extraordinary home notwithstanding) is so damaging because it exposes the complicity of the private space of home in circumscribing identity, through the imposition of class boundaries. Up until this point, Pip explains, 'Home had never been a very pleasant place to me, because of my sister's temper. But, Joe had sanctified it, and I had believed in it' (97). He might have said with equal meaning that before this exposure of his particular home as socially inferior, 'Dickens's other orphan narrators had sanctified it, and I had believed in it'.

In contradistinction to Estella's reluctant participation in Beggar My Neighbour, the only card game Pip knows how to play, Joe takes pride in the teaching of his wife's young brother and is willing to learn from him in a reciprocal relationship that Miss Havisham deliberately short-circuits in her manipulation of both children. Significantly one of the most affectionately rendered scenes in the novel is Joe's early interaction with Pip in the abortive attempt to learn to read. In a full-length study of the novel Mary

Hammond points out that even after the 1850 Public Libraries Act many readers continued to buy novels, and even by 1861 'An important adjunct to this culture of borrowing – drawing on much earlier precedents of course, but surprisingly long-lasting – was the practice of sharing; of spreading all or part of a new Dickens novel around groups of readers or listeners as part of a social event' (26). Tellingly Andrews has suggested that in his focus on physical detail 'Dickens provides the script for silent internal performing by his reader' (*Dickensian Laughter* 30), allowing them to become readers 'aloud', and this translation of experience into drama may be a character's only means of articulating particular concerns. In his last novel, *Edwin Drood*, when Rosa wants to admit her frustration to her fiancé, she tells him of her birthday ball at the Nun's House and how she refused to dance with the girl who impersonated Edwin himself. Seeing his displeasure, she counters that he is as tired of her as she is of him, a scenario she can actively enjoy when she experiences it as performance. When he demands, 'Did I say so, Rosa?' she instantly responds, "Say so! Do you ever say so? No, you only showed it. Oh, she did it so well!" cries Rosa, in a sudden ecstacy with her counterfeit betrothed' (17).

In the course of his narration, however, Pip repeatedly draws attention to the connections made between literary or dramatic motifs and the experience of (sometimes credulous) readers and audiences. In *Great Expectations* Wopsle processes his responses to the world through dramatic representation, coming to represent the many characters in this novel who are determined by the script they have chosen or that has been chosen for them. But this habit is presented in far from elevating terms, as Pip notes that in the excruciating performance of Hamlet he and Herbert go to see, the king has a cough and 'The royal phantom also carried a ghostly manuscript round its truncheon, to which it had the appearance of occasionally referring, and that, too, with an air of anxiety and a tendency to lose the place of reference which were suggestive of a state of mortality' (231).

While the novel is set in the first two decades of the 19th century, even the supposedly uncompromising depiction of criminality and the law is of course pervaded by the reader's own awareness of the 1860s sensation craze. Pip's impression of Jaggers is derived partly from his book collection, 'There was a bookcase in the room; I saw, from the backs of the books, that they were about evidence, criminal law, criminal biography, trials, acts of parliament, and such things' (193). But this possession of book objects is paralleled and subtly undermined by the infiltration of Wemmick's curiosities, which include 'several manuscript confessions written under condemnation – upon which Mr Wemmick set particular value as being, to use his own words, "every one of 'em Lies, sir"' (191). In this context Pip's own story is resolved as notably anti-climactic, when he literally loses his 'expectations' and instead realises a small capital from his rather less glamorous exertions in an office.

One of Dickens's most benign self-deceivers, Herbert parallels Pip in misplacing himself in the story of Satis House, recalling incorrectly that he beat Pip severely in their juvenile fight. Projecting his own generosity onto his friend, Herbert defines him as 'a good fellow, with impetuosity and hesitation, boldness and diffidence, action and dreaming, curiously mixed in him', precipitating a rare moment of self-awareness on Pip's part, as he 'stopped for a moment to consider whether there really was this mixture in my character. On the whole, I by no means recognised the analysis, but thought it not worth disputing' (227).

This direct challenge to the status of Pip as literary hero forces the reader once again to question what sort of story they are reading. In Horne's analysis, 'when the reader's trust is not a founding premise of a novel, as it mostly is with omniscient narration, it has to be earned by a first-person narrator who is a character among others, and whose reliability must not be compromised by exaggeration or too obvious an axe to grind' (167). But if 'Dickens actually compels us to read *Great Expectations* as we do mystery tales or uncanny stories which, contrary to fairy tales, are usually written in the first person in order precisely to create mixed feelings in the reader, uneasily torn between suspicion about the tale and regard for the teller' (Sadrin 116), Pip's unspoken refutation of Herbert's idealistic view offers a rare moment of humility that reclaims him as the reader's primary reference point, despite his flaws.

Dickens himself was sufficiently unsure of his writing to seek advice from Bulwer Lytton, who famously advised him to change the original ending of the novel and allow at least the prospect of Pip's ultimate union with Estella. This story is sufficiently well known from Dickens's own admission that 'Bulwer was so very anxious that I should alter the end of Great Expectations – the extreme end, I mean, after Joe and Biddy are done with – and stated his reasons so well, that I have resumed the wheel, and taken another turn at it. Upon the whole I think it is for the better' (To Wilkie Collins, 23 June 1861. 428). Despite the mixed responses to this change, Dickens would continue to seek advice from the same source during the late stages of *Our Mutual Friend*:

> I am looking forward to sending you the proofs complete, about the end of next month. It is all sketched out, and I am working hard at it, giving it all the pains possible to be bestowed on a labour of love. Your critical opinion two months in advance of the public will be invaluable to me. For you know what store I set by it, and how I think over a hint from you. (To Sir Edward Bulwer Lytton, 20 July 1865. Pilgrim 11. 72–73. 73)

Implicitly Bulwer Lytton is being asked to play two closely related roles: the imaginative reader whose critical acumen will detect any weakness in the story and (despite his questionable success) the professional author whose awareness of public taste will be useful even at late proof stage in suggesting minor corrections. This role is subtly different from the editorial role played by Dickens as he worked through, amended and corrected the proofs of successive numbers of *All the Year Round*; nonetheless Dickens shows perhaps surprising humility (some readers have seen it as misjudgement) in deferring to the criticisms of his friend.

Within the text of *Great Expectations*, it is surely significant that despite his own corruption, Pip does still define himself as a reader, suggesting his potential for redemption when he strategically assures his own reader that 'Notwithstanding my inability to settle to anything – which I hope arose out of the restless and incomplete tenure on which I held my means – I had a taste for reading, and read regularly so many hours a day' (285). But his awareness of books as status objects stands as a further warning against defining character purely in literary terms. While one of the Pocket children is removed crying from the garden, Pip observes that 'Mrs Pocket read all the time, and I was curious to know what the book could be' (171). This unusual association of reading with the failure to comfort a child is explained when 'It turned out that the book I had seen Mrs Pocket reading in the garden, was all about titles, and that she knew the exact date at which her grandpapa would have come into the book, if he ever had come at all' (175), a snobbish obsession that anticipates the link between Mrs Pocket and Bentley Drummle, 'who was so sulky a fellow that he even took up a book as if its writer had done him an injury, [and] did not take up an acquaintance in a more agreeable spirit' (185).

Status is achieved in these circles when characters can claim connection with the names entered in books such as *Burke's Peerage* – the absurdity of this identification with class structures is a source of comedy in this scene, although it permeates the narrative. Pip is more sensible of its application to his own situation when he learns of Pumblechook's tendentious claims to have been his early patron, a lie that is also given weight through the written word. In a distorted parallel with Mrs Pocket's book (an expensively bound volume that would increase her status only if her grandfather were listed), the local paper is registered as an item of ephemera, which does accord Pip a level of celebrity within an equally limited social circle. The waiter significantly draws his attention to an article claiming:

> Our readers will learn, not altogether without interest, in reference to the recent romantic rise in fortune of a young artificer in iron of this neighbourhood (what a theme, by the way, for the magic pen of our as yet not universally acknowledged townsman TOOBY, the poet of our columns!) that the youth's earliest patron, companion, and friend, was a highly-respected individual not entirely unconnected with the corn and seed trade, and whose eminently convenient and commodious business premises are situate within a hundred miles of the High-street. (211)

Of course the status of the paper in the reader's mind varies according to what it reports, and Pip later admits to an irrational fear of its authority when he avoids reading newspaper announcements of Estella's marriage, 'Why I hoarded up this last wretched little rag of the robe of hope that was rent and given to the winds, how do I know! Why did you who read this, commit that not dissimilar inconsistency of your own, last year, last month, last week?' (349)

Challenges to the authority of the written word and indications of its untrustworthiness are hallmarks of the later novels. In his own letters Dickens manipulates the apparent authenticity of the letter in particular, giving Georgina Hogarth a template letter with which to fend off his widowed sister in law Helen Dickens, whom he was anxious to avoid seeing himself. Drafting a notably blunt paragraph to the effect that he wished to avoid all personal communication, he suggested that 'You may add – as you like – either that you do, or that you do not, know the reason for this', before relenting and including an additional few lines that could be used independently of the first part of the letter, 'This last paragraph marked with a bracket, will be all you have to say for me, if you don't like to say the rest' (To Georgina Hogarth, 1 August 1866. 228).

While the narrative of *Great Expectations* is similarly crafted in order to meet the expectations of the paying public, it is likely that the reader places a degree of confidence in Pip precisely because he shows himself to have outlived his early selfishness and to a degree even displays in the course of his narration the qualities Herbert attributes to him. While his character may be deeply flawed, the apparent honesty of his narration invests him with a disproportionately high level of authority, and the reader is moreover likely to feel complicit in his thankless rejection of Joe and initial aversion to Magwitch. Pip positions himself in a long tradition of monitory address, rooted in the graveyard tradition, when he insists that the readers trace their own personal experience through the vicarious act of following his history. His unusual assumption of a quasi-religious authority at this point directs the reader to disengage from the text itself and apply its lessons to their individual experience, 'Pause you who read this, and think for a moment of the long chain of iron or gold, of thorns or flowers, that would never have bound you, but for the formation of the first link on one memorable day' (66).

Ultimately Pip both affirms the importance of literary expression as a means of validating experience and questions its efficacy, when he apologies that 'I must give one chapter to Estella. It is not much to give the theme that so long filled my heart' (273). Only by writing this ordered account of his life is he able to process its significance, as he suggests when he finally turns to the reappearance of Magwitch, 'And now that I have given the one chapter to the theme that so filled my heart, and so often made it ache and ache again, I pass on, unhindered, to the event that had impended over me longer yet' (284–85). Like Pip himself, Magwitch rewrites the central history but is himself neither a literary character nor a figure of moral authority. Like Pip,

Magwitch is thwarted in his efforts to engineer a particular outcome, one that is in fact based on the wrong script. In its tracing of the corruption and ultimate redemption of the central character *Great Expectations* stands as a corrective to the tracts forced on Magwitch by sanctimonious prison visitors (a theme familiar from Mrs Pardiggle's behaviour in *Bleak House* and resumed in Dickens's next novel, *Our Mutual Friend*). But when Pip finally accepts the flawed Magwitch, readers can in turn accept that he is writing a narrative different from the ones exposed as false in his story and so accept the authenticity of his experience, even as it is shown to be self-consciously literary after all.

These first-person narratives highlight ways in which preface / fiction / real author have permeable imagined boundaries and how the reader participates in and extends the affective feeling depicted in the novels. In a revealing letter to an *All the Year Round* contributor Dickens explicitly describes the process by which readers translate the ethos of fictional narrators and characters into real-life situations, telling him:

> a writer of fiction has always to consider how he can tempt his readers into wholesome considerations into which they would not submit to be dragged, and that some of the deepest wounds he gives often come of what seem to be his lightest touches. Besides; in his Art as in all other things, the greater includes the less. If it be his happy privilege to awaken in many breasts a noble tone, and a scorn of all meanness and false pretence, both must comprehend, in time, a whole catalogue of individual meannesses and false pretences that he has never named in detail. (To George Holme, 14 March 1870. Pilgrim 12. 491–92)

This extension of the imaginative response may also operate on the writer himself, as one part of a story begins to infiltrate the depiction of apparently unrelated scenes; there is a latent possibility that the textual rendering of a theme or character may even splinter into fragments, at its most acute when Dickens worries that he will allow a young David Copperfield to hijack the story of the less obviously appealing Pip, to the detriment of both, and at its most creative when the captivating Dora resurfaces as the serio-comic Flora. This fear of cross-contamination (an effect that actually does surface throughout Dickens's private letters) of course makes for considerable creative mileage in his claim that he had destroyed the original ms of his autobiography because he was unable to write down the Maria Beadnell episode. Typically conflating himself and his personal history as 'the subject' of the writing, he told her in 1855 that 'A few years ago (just before Copperfield) I began to write my life, intending the Manuscript to be found among my papers when its subject should be concluded. But as I began to approach within sight of that part of it, I lost courage and burned the rest' (To Mrs Winter, 22 February 1855. Pilgrim 7. 543–45. 543–44). The story cannot be told at all without the inclusion of this youthful amour, but it can be told differently in order to include the central incident in a different story with a better ending.

Despite the construction of a character behind the speaking voice, the availability of intimate relations between readers and first-person narrators is not a given. It is not always possible for the readers to be certain of their positioning as confidants rather than simply voyeurs, particularly where direct address is not a feature of the narration or when it is intermittent. David would have the reader believe that his narration is intended for no eyes other than his own even as he consciously crafts his version of events, while Pip's relations with the reader are based on a carefully inflected tone that veers with his progress between the apologetic and confessional and the morally bracing. Even Esther talks about us as the 'unknown' friend, a reminder that she and the reader have not met on equal terms but also that she knew 'someone' was there all the time. While first-person narrators present themselves as knowable and known, at least by other characters within the stories they tell, the reader is finally thrown back for a sense of mutual affection on the writer of the meta-textual prefaces.

Notes

1. This insight was almost certainly the result of talking to PhD student Vicki Callanan. We agreed that if I had indeed stolen the idea from her, she would overlook it and I would acknowledge it.
2. Identified by the Pilgrim editors as G. A. Sala.

4 Decoding the Text

It is not just first-person narrators who chart an increasing mistrust of the written word as a means of shaping and validating experience. In common with the emerging sensation genre, Dickens's major novels of the 1850s and '60s share a focus on the falsification, appropriation or misappropriation of personal letters and other documents. In a particularly extreme example, *Great Expectations* takes the anonymous letter as a plot device used in the planned murder of Pip by the vengeful Orlick. A key concern from *Bleak House* onwards is how private and legal documents are decoded and reinterpreted, often by readers for whom they were never intended and in ways never meant by the writer. There are of course notable similarities between this novel and *Little Dorrit*. Clennam's illegitimacy and strict upbringing are reminiscent of Esther's experience, and the discovery of sexual transgression is vital to both plots.

Little Dorrit also revisits the theme of public documents as so much waste paper, which Dickens had memorably developed in the Chancery passages of the previous novel. In the stories of Dorrit and Doyce, who both become enmeshed in the workings of the Circumlocution Office, the reader is offered alternative responses but premised in each case on the futility of resistance to this institution. Clennam's temporary mania for speculation links him to Richard Carstone in *Bleak House*, and his despair is evidenced by the disarray in which he leaves his papers, 'The usual diligence and order of the Counting-house at the Works were overthrown. Unopened letters and unsorted papers lay strewn about the desk' (594).

As a public figure himself, Dickens had been writing the status of his imaginative processes into his own letters from the 1840s onwards. An intriguing letter to a Mrs Nichols in 1864 reprises the letter in which he reminded Angela Burdett Coutts that the pen he used to write to her was in fact the very same he had been using to write *Martin Chuzzlewit* earlier in the day, telling her that 'To-morrow afternoon I will send you a pen that I will bring down purposely – with which I have been at work all day on my new book' (To Mrs Nichols, 29 March 1864. Pilgrim 10. 377). Letters about the process of composition thus continue to create part of a multi-layered text, with a hierarchy of readers who have access to varying levels of meaning.

Dickens inserts himself into the novel as it is experienced by readers, as when for instance he includes a meta-fictional awareness of the emerging canon of his own novels within the published text. The preface to *Little Dorrit* ends with the reminder that, 'In the preface to Bleak House I remarked that I had never had so many readers. In the preface to its next successor, Little Dorrit, I have still to repeat the same words. Deeply sensible of the affection and confidence that have grown up between us, I add to this Preface, as I added to that, May we meet again!' (xxii). By February 1856 he was able to tell Georgina Hogarth that 'the first No. of Little Dorrit has gone to 40,000, and the others are fast following' (8 February 1856. Pilgrim 8. 48–49. 49).

As ever in Dickens, the narrative creates layers of meanings accessible to different readers. Mrs Watson apparently picked up on the significance of the St Bernard convent scene and was rewarded with the answer, 'I did write it for you, and I hoped, in writing it, that you would think so. All those remembrances were fresh in my mind – as they often are – and gave me an extraordinary interest in recalling the past. I should have been grievously disappointed if you had not been pleased, for I took aim at you with a most determined intention' (To the Hon. Mrs Richard Watson, 7 October 1856. Pilgrim 8. 201–203. 201).

Dickens also references his own previous novels in subtle ways. In an echo of the earlier novel *David Copperfield* as well as Dickens's own letters mythologising his response to Gad's Hill as a child, Mr F's aunt mysteriously announces within the novel itself, 'There's mile-stones on the Dover road!' (224) While this allusion is not further translated for the reader, her cryptic comment may derive significance from her association with Flora Finching. Flora, the satirically updated portrait of David Copperfield's Dora (significantly her name even rhymes with that of her earlier incarnation), written after Dickens had met Maria Beadnell again in middle age, is comically obsessed with retelling the story of her relationship with Clennam and implying that they are still in love. The link between novels is satisfying in itself, but readers acquainted with this story of Dickens's own youth are then able to infer a veiled rebuff – the once-abandoned David whose escape from obscurity begins with a journey down the Dover Road to the haven of his aunt's house has safely passed this particular milestone on the road. In a moment of affectionate nostalgia Dickens nonetheless conceded privately that 'There are some things in Flora in number 7 that seem to me to be extraordinarily droll, with something serious at the bottom of them after all. Ah, well! was there not something very serious in it once?' (To John Forster, [7 April 1856]. Pilgrim 8. 82). Perceptive or well-informed readers can then decode or find different meanings by linking novels to each other.

Again, it is instructive to read Thackeray against this invitation to join hierarchical reading practices. Pendennis as the narrator of *The Newcomes* digresses at one point to comment on secrets within marriage, the existence of which may be rendered visible by literary texts:

> I think of a lovely reader laying down the page and looking over at her unconscious husband, asleep, perhaps, after dinner. Yes, madam,

a closet he hath: and you, who pry into everything, shall never have the key of it. I think of some honest Othello pausing over this very sentence in a railroad carriage, and stealthily gazing at Desdemona opposite to him, innocently administering sandwiches to their little boy – I am trying to turn off the sentence with a joke, you see – I feel it is growing too dreadful, too serious. (151)

In this passage the written word cannot be retracted but needs to be 'turned off with a joke' just as an ill-advised remark in conversation necessitates a witty distraction. In both *Little Dorrit* and *Our Mutual Friend*, Dickens's writer characters likewise change their minds about the versions of events they have written, and writing becomes unstable or dangerous as a result. Significantly Dickens returns to a literary image of his own – the blank wall in *David Copperfield* now becoming a page – in effacing the past, after the breakdown of his marriage. In answer to an attempt at intercession between him and Catherine, Dickens told Angela Burdett Coutts that 'a page in my life which once had writing on it, has become absolutely blank, and that it is not in my power to pretend that it has a solitary word upon it' (To Miss Burdett Coutts, 12 February 1864. Pilgrim 10. 355–57. 356).

A few years earlier he had literally destroyed the written pages of his personal letters, a feat he ironically recorded in several letters to friends, 'Yesterday I burnt, in the field at Gad's Hill, the accumulated letters and papers of twenty years. They sent up a smoke like the Genie when he got out of the casket on the seashore; and as it was an exquisite day when I began, and rained very heavily when I finished, I suspect my correspondence of having overcast the face of the Heavens' (To W. H. Wills, 4 September 1860. Pilgrim 9. 302–304. 304). Something of the difficulty he felt in controlling the circulation of his own letters comes across in his remark to another correspondent a few years later that 'the extraordinary abuse of confidence in the posting about of private letters which I have of late years constantly observed, has moved me to two courses; firstly, to destroy all the letters I receive from private friends, as soon as I have read them; and secondly to write as short letters as I possibly can' (To R. J. Lane, 25 February 1864. Pilgrim 10. 363).

Notwithstanding this intention, the length of Dickens's extant letters is not notably different after the date of the bonfire at Gad's Hill, and he continued to comply with requests for autographs and signed *cartes de visite*. Writing to one concerned correspondent only a few months after the bonfire, he assured him that 'I have never taken the least offence against the Managers of your Institution, and that I have never had the faintest cause for any, and that I regard it with the most cordial interest and good will. My books were sent by my direction, straight from the Publishers; and this is the sole cause of my not having written in them'. To reinforce the point, he includes some specially written text, 'On the other side, I send you a few words, which can be inserted where you think best' (To G. Hewitt, 20

May 1861. Pilgrim 9. 416). Writing to the author Mrs Henry Wood in 1864, he agreed to sign 20 cards, presumably for distribution among her acquaintances, and he was understandably touched to learn that his friend Clarkson Stanfield had died with a recent letter from him under his pillow (To Henry Chorley, 2 June 1867. Pilgrim 11. 374).

Nonetheless the letters he himself received necessarily change their status from the moment of his decision to burn them after reading. While an old school friend is enthusiastically told after a public dinner that 'I perfectly recollect your name as that of an old schoolfellow... If you had made yourself personally known to me at the dinner I should have been well pleased; though in that case I should have lost your modest and manly letter' (To Dr Henry Danson, 5 May 1864. Pilgrim 10. 391), this same letter *is* in a sense immediately lost, in that it is not destined to be preserved.

'Answers to Letters in Faded Ink': *Little Dorrit*

As explored in previous chapters, Dickens's writing about his own process of composition works to engage readers with the as yet unwritten text and creates a hidden dimension to the work itself. His letters in the mid-1850s themselves include the working up of literary anecdotes and images. As he was about to start work on *Little Dorrit* in the spring of 1855, Dickens wrote to one correspondent that 'I am in the first stage of a new book, which consists in going round and round the idea, as you see a bird in his cage go about and about his sugar before he touches it' (To Captain E. Morgan, [19 March] 1855. Pilgrim 7. 571–72). Some weeks later he complained to Angela Burdett Coutts that:

> I am in a state of restlessness impossible to be described – impossible to be imagined – wearing and tearing to be experienced. I sit down of a morning, with all kinds of notes for my new book... resolve to begin – get up, and go out, and walk a dozen miles – sit down again next morning – get up and go down a railroad – come back again, and register a vow to go out of town instantly, and begin at the feet of the Pyrenees – sit down again – get up and walk about my room all day – wander about London till midnight – make engagements and am too distraught to keep them – Couldn't go to the Academy Dinner – felt it impossible to bear the speeches – pleaded Influenza at the last moment – and am at present going through the whole routine, over and over and over again. (8 May 1855. Pilgrim 7. 613–14)

Two days after this dissection of his own state of mind, he told her more laconically, 'Restlessness worse and worse. Dont at all know what to do with myself. Wish I had a Balloon' (10 May 1855. Pilgrim 7. 615). But writing to Wilkie Collins the next day, he has already edited this initial idea as if it were itself a textual motif, 'The restless condition in which I wander up and down my room with the first page of my new book before me, defies all description. I feel as if nothing would do me the least good, but setting up a Balloon. It might be inflated in the Garden in front – but I am afraid of its scarcely clearing those little houses' (11 May 1855. Pilgrim 7. 616). Letters and fiction are finally conflated as creative acts when he tells Burdett Coutts that 'The interlineations in this note, are attributable to my being at work on the new book – which makes me perfectly reckless as to erasures' (29 May 1855. Pilgrim 7. 632–33. 633). On the face of it, this 'recklessness' in amending his letter as he writes, may suggest that he has less time or energy than usual after working on *Little Dorrit* and is therefore less careful in his personal correspondence; conversely, it could also imply that the imaginative process of writing a novel extends to the writing of letters, as he edits his initial phrasing in search of the perfect expression. Either way it was, he told Lady Duff Gordon on 6 October, like 'living the life of an amiable fighting man in training for his next match' (6 October 1855. Pilgrim 7. 716–17. 717).

Little Dorrit is itself combative in the sense that it shows characters struggling to maintain their integrity in a system that is set to crush them. In the context of the struggle for dominance between opposing voices in the world of the fiction, Sen argues that 'in contrast to Thackeray's ability to move between two authorial positions, Dickens, in *Little Dorrit*, entrenches himself firmly outside the charmed circle of the elite' (38). The theme of mis/communication necessarily involves a struggle for control over perspective, a tension that includes juxtapositions of prison and perceptions of open space, secrets and trust and the dignity of work with the enforced leisure of invalids, prisoners and the newly rich Amy Dorrit.

Jonathan Grossman argues that these apparently conflicting perspectives notwithstanding, all the characters are – as the narrator insists – temporarily and spatially connected, so that '*Little Dorrit* represents how individuals within this system, who project an omniscient-like view of it, nonetheless must perpetually confront that their own perspectives are always partial, incomplete and belated. Their difficulty is not... that their modern world is fragmented and disconnected. It is just the opposite. The density and extensivity of people's interconnections exceeds their capacity to grasp them' (195). While tropes of travel and confinement dominate the text, these often suggest the ways in which the written word is circulated or forestalled.

Like *Bleak House*, *Little Dorrit* itself repeatedly stresses different types of reading and writing, and characters' various attempts to control or interpret the written word. Bodenheimer argues that 'Against all perpetrators and dupes of deceptive language, Dickens brings on his homeopathic weaponry: rhetoric vs. rhetoric, his credibility against the credibility – or credulity – of his targets. The linguistic world he creates is a world of rhetorical performances on high horses vying to claim the high ground of credibility' (*Knowing Dickens* 31). This contest for credibility sets the narrator against particular characters and also measures one character against another. Most dramatically, Mrs Clennam refuses to let Rigaud-Blandois relate his version of Arthur's history on the grounds that 'Since it must be seen, I will have it seen by the light I stood in' (646), and it is this desire to control her story herself that propels her from her seclusion and back into the streets, at the end of the novel.

An apparently ambivalent figure such as Pancks, who holds the invidious position of 'jobber' to the false Patriarch Casby, openly presents the ordering of language as a question of skill. He will ultimately expose the way in which Casby's false language derives its effect from his benevolent appearance, but much earlier in the novel he uses documentary evidence to put together a convincing case for the Dorrit family's entitlement to a fortune. The complexities of Dorrit's financial affairs are represented by a series of papers copied from Pancks's notebook, and when Pancks, 'who supported the character of chief conspirator, had completed his extracts, he looked them over, corrected them, put up his note-book, and held them like a hand at cards' (252). Literally translating words into action, Pancks deals the cards to the other players, John Chivery and Rugg.

These struggles for authority over language and writing include both major figures such as Mrs Clennam and apparently unimportant characters, some of whom are never presented to the reader and whose control over the ephemeral text they encounter is limited and transient. Among the powerless working class as in the workings of the Circumlocution Office, the promise held out by writing may be fraudulent and illusory – when Trollope wants to stress that a branch of the Civil Service is punctilious but essentially trustworthy he describes it as 'exactly antipodistic of the Circumlocution Office ...' (*The Three Clerks* 1). In the house where Pancks has his lodging, 'A professor of writing occupied the first-floor, and enlivened the garden railings with glass-cases containing choice examples of what his pupils had been before six lessons and while the whole of his young family shook the table, and what they had become after six lessons when the young family was under restraint' (249). In a more innocent and exuberant display of writing, where Frederick Dorrit lodges, 'the pupils of Mr Cripples appeared to have been making a copy-book of the street door, it was so extensively scribbled over in pencil' (76). Even Maggy reads advertisements on shop doors while out with Little Dorrit and Clennam, and 'When he saw how pleasure brought a rosy tint into Little Dorrit's face when Maggy made a hit, he felt that he could have stood there making a library of the grocer's window until the rain and wind were tired' (87). Significantly Clennam is much better educated than Maggy, but only through her enjoyment can he 'make a library' of the grocer's ephemera and outstay the elements themselves.

Elsewhere in the novel reading and texts are often threatening rather than liberating; on his return to England Clennam recalls 'the dreary Sunday of his childhood, when he sat with his hands before him, scared out of his senses by a horrible tract which commenced business with the poor child by asking him, in its title, why he was going to Perdition?' (24). This scene is renewed when his mother, apparently to avoid any prolonged conversation with him after his long absence, instead 'read certain passages aloud from a book – sternly, fiercely, wrathfully – praying that her enemies (she made them by her tone and manner expressly hers) might be put to the edge of the sword, consumed by fire, smitten by plagues and leprosy, that their bones might be ground to dust, and that they might be utterly exterminated' (29). The context of Mrs Clennam's reading is doubly important in this scene, insofar as she chooses gruesome passages seemingly arbitrarily from the Old Testament and then 'by her tone and manner' appropriates them to her personal use and apparently invests them with greater meaning. Similarly, in her perversion of Christian teaching Mrs Clennam consciously rewrites the coded message sent by her dead husband through Arthur, the 'do not forget' of the watch-paper.

This scene comes immediately after the meditation on Arthur's own memories of childhood, where, to quote Bodenheimer, 'the earlier split between benevolent memory and isolated traumatic return disappears in a newly introspective narrative; here memory is persistent, anxious, and sad, creating depression rather than nostalgia or trauma' (82). But the coded appeal only makes sense to the reader in the final chapters of the novel and is never understood by Arthur himself, who is unable to 'remember' something he was never told. To the unsuspicious eye, this beaded watch-paper appears to be simply a conventional piece of feminine fancy work. The narrator withholds its true significance until Rigaud's denunciation of Mrs Clennam's fraud on the Dorrit family, meaning that the 'do not forget' can only be decoded by the characters originally concerned, or by Amy and ultimately the reader of the novel itself.

The watch itself is revealed to be far less trivial than its status as feminine fancy work might suggest. But much of the novel really is concerned with writing as meaningless display. Most obviously the accumulated documents of Chancery satirised in *Bleak House* have become the endless memoranda of the Circumlocution Office, which are rarely or never seen being actually read by the Barnacles to whom they are addressed. One of Dickens's attributes as a correspondent and responsible director of literary taste is, as he reminds the authors of unsolicited letters, that he actually does read the many letters addressed to him.

To reverse the terms of 'How not to do it' and find a model of 'How to do it', the reader of Dickens's novel, who presumably *does* ingest the written text presented to them, must decode Mr Meagles's parodic references to 'allongers and marshongers' as the French 'Allons' (let us go) and 'Marchons' (let us walk on, or make progress). Ironically Meagles may be speaking with a vague memory of the revolutionary Marseillaise, which begins 'Allons enfants de la Patrie' (Let us go, children of the Fatherland) and includes 'Marchons! Marchons!' in the refrain.[1] This careful reader is asked to sustain a relationship with the narrator rather than follow the many false guides who inhabit the text; the expected responsiveness is rewarded with 'in jokes' at the expense of Mrs General, with her insistence on enunciation over meaning and refusal to believe in uncomfortable facts (this technique for creating intimacy between writer and reader to the exclusion of a particular character would later be developed in Podsnap of *Our Mutual Friend*), when the narrator wryly condemns 'what may be called in these pages the Pruney and Prismatic nature of the family banquet' (539).

Dickens noted that 'Society, the Circumlocution Office, and Mr Gowan, are of course three parts of one idea and design' (To John Forster, [?29–30 March 1856]. Pilgrim 8. 78–79. 79). In fact the narrator goes further than this in suggesting that society with a small s is 'infected' by the principles of the Circumlocution Office, which in turn has its underside in the apathy of the Marshalsea. Flanders notes that Dickens apparently presents a sanitised view of his own family's experience:

> *Little Dorrit* presents a rather orderly, domestic image of the prison, where families lived according to middle-class norms as best they could. But the rules of the prison suggest otherwise: there were fines for taking other people's property; for throwing urine or faeces out of the windows or into other people's rooms; for making noise after midnight; for cursing, fighting, dirtying the privy seat, urinating in the yard, stealing from the taproom and singing obscene songs. (*The Victorian City* 178)

But if the social conditions of the prison are somewhat edited, the narrator is at pains to analyse the lassitude with which its inmates are quickly blighted. The prison, like the official institution, makes great display of writing. As he starts to adapt to life in the prison, Dorrit himself collaborates in the subordination of feeling to words and the replacement of moral action by writing. On the death of his wife, 'he remained shut up in his room for a fortnight afterwards; and an attorney's clerk, who was going through the Insolvent Court, engrossed an address of condolence to him, which looked like a Lease, and which all the prisoners signed' (54).

As he worked on the novel Dickens humorously identified himself with the imprisoned family, telling Hans Christian Anderson that 'I am hard at work on Little Dorrit, and she will hold me prisoner for another nine or ten months' (5 July 1856. Pilgrim 8. 144–45. 145). Ironically, given Dickens's own substitutions of fictional text for unwritten letters, in the novel a progressive symptom of the Marshalsea disease is the ultimate substitution of planned writing for the written page itself. One prisoner insists that he will write petitions until he effects his release, although after 'unloading his mind, and after announcing (as it seemed he always did, without anything coming of it), that he was going to write a letter to the papers and show the Marshal up, he fell into miscellaneous conversation with the rest' (73). The provisional status of writing within the prison is closely aligned with

Dorrit's pleasure in the assumed respect he inspires in his fellow prisoners. The closed circuit of the Marshalsea at first signals the limit of his aspirations and after his release is relegated to a 'forgotten' past. When the family is finally liberated, the other debtors ironically present 'the Father of the Marshalsea' with a piece of writing that loses all value outside the prison walls: 'They got up an address to him, which they presented in a neat frame and glass (though it was not afterwards displayed in the family mansion or preserved among the family papers); and to which he returned a gracious answer' (356).

Characters' relationships to letters and text extend the theme of reading and decoding, as they themselves are represented through, or stand in for, the written word. The inscrutable Merdle is embodied as print, where 'Mr Merdle's right hand was filled with the evening paper, and the evening paper was full of Mr Merdle' (466). His final suicide will also appear in the press. Despite this association with the mass production of print, Merdle finally chooses to kill himself with a knife intended to open letters, lent by another character who rejects domesticity. 'It was an odd thing, Fanny smilingly observed, for her who could seldom prevail upon herself even to write a letter, to lend to a man of such vast business as Mr Merdle' (586).

Less public characters are more easily associated with hand writing, and hardly surprisingly, the begging letter is a key trope of the novel. While the doctor imprisoned for debt assures Dorrit, 'Nobody writes threatening letters about money, to this place. It's freedom, sir, it's freedom!' (53), numerous letters and testimonials are written from the prison. Departing collegians leave money for Dorrit enclosed in letters. The shabby genteel Marshalsea go-betweens 'had a peculiar way of doggedly slinking round the corner, as if they were eternally going to the pawnbrokers. When they coughed, they coughed like people accustomed to be forgotten on doorsteps and in draughty passages, waiting for answers to letters in faded ink, which gave the recipients of those manuscripts great mental disturbance, and no satisfaction' (75).

Where the impact of manuscript letters is stamped on the very bodies of the go-betweens, the self-proclaimed gentleman Rigaud-Blandois imposes his dangerous personality on the written documents he encounters. In his first meeting with the Dorrits he adds his name to the visitors' book on the mountain 'in a small, complicated hand, ending with a long lean flourish, not unlike a lasso thrown at all the rest of the names' (373). His own letter to Mrs Clennam, in which he threatens her with exposure if she refuses to pay him off, is ostentatiously polite. What she of course does not see is the brutal manner in which he uses it to taunt Clennam, now a prisoner in the Marshalsea, with his own powerlessness: 'When he had finished this epistle, Rigaud folded it, and tossed it with a flourish at Clennam's feet' (625).

Handwriting may, as in the visitors' book, indicate the false character of the writer; however this code is often intended to be accepted as common currency. Once released from the prison Dorrit uses his experience of making oblique requests, in proposing a marriage between Fanny and Sparkler, to Merdle:

> In his epistolary communication, as in his dialogues and discourses on the great question to which it related, Mr Dorrit surrounded the subject with flourishes, as writing-masters embellish copy-books and cyphering books: where the titles of the elementary rules of arithmetic diverge into swans, eagles, griffins, and other calligraphic recreations, and where the capital letters go out of their minds and bodies into ecstasies of pen and ink. (502)

Mrs General's referees (in an echo of Snawley's endorsement of Squeers in *Nicholas Nickleby*) write meaningless praise of her abilities in order to get rid of her, and 'one venerable archdeacon even shed tears in recording his testimony to her perfections (described to him by persons on whom he could rely), though he had never had the honour and moral gratification of setting eyes on Mrs General in all his life' (375).

Dickens himself was not above indulging in such minor acts of deception in his own letters. Writing to Mark Lemon in 1856, he jokes that his family will assume from his posture that he is passing on their messages, whereas in fact what he is writing down is his avoidance of this very obligation, 'You may imagine the loves and messages that are now being poured in upon me by all of them, so I will give none of them; though I am pretending to be very scrupulous about it, and am looking (I have no doubt) as if I were writing them down with the greatest care' (7 January 1856. Pilgrim 8. 11–13. 13). As these messages are never delivered, their value and quantity can be imagined by the reader of the letter in line with his own desires. A similar strategy in a letter of 1869 again implies that the flattering messages being withheld by Dickens himself are too numerous to be easily conveyed even by word of mouth between the recipient of the letter and his wife: 'We are delighted to be remembered by your charming wife, and I am entrusted with more messages from Gad's Hill to her than you would care to give or with-hold. So I suppress them myself, and absolve you from the difficulty' (To the Hon. Robert Lytton, 2 September 1869. Pilgrim 404–405).

In her refusal to engage in the false currency of the other characters, Little Dorrit replaces bombastic language with more authentic expression, knowingly rendering herself readable by other characters. In writing to Arthur she naïvely tells him, 'I know you cannot be so glad to hear from me, as I am to write to you' (390). Too self-effacing to believe in the value of her own writing, she suggests in a later letter that he may not even find time to read it:

> As I said in my last that it was best for nobody to write to me, and as my sending you another little letter can therefore give you no other trouble than the trouble of reading it (perhaps you may not find leisure

for even that, though I hope you will some day), I am now going to devote an hour to writing to you again. (459)

Her obtrusion of herself on Clennam's notice goes no further than a subtle reminder of her presence behind the paper, 'I stopped at the last full-stop to read all this over' (461). It is the narrator who awards her the status she will not claim for herself, using this letter as the ending of the 13th number.

In certain instances her insistence on protecting her father arguably leads to moral ambivalence in depriving him of moral responsibility. Pykett for one argues that 'by means of her collusion in his fictions of gentility and her concealment of the harsh truths of her own and her siblings' lives from him, Little Dorrit "varnishes" the cracked surfaces of life just as thoroughly as Mrs General does' (154). But the narrator clearly regards her as essentially ingenuous, providing her with scenes in which she hides her face or suppresses stories rather than engage in the verbal fencing adopted by Fanny. When both the elder Dorrit and Tip approach Clennam through letters entrusted to Maggy 'Arthur read, in Little Dorrit's downcast eyes, to whom she foresaw that the letters were addressed' (218). She resists Maggy's attempts to retell the story of the Princess and the shadow, a transparent allegory of her love for Clennam, because he is emotionally literate enough to interpret it.

This transparency is shared by the hapless John Chivery, whose fantasies of his own death register a desire for the status he knows he will never attain in the social world he inhabits. Like the debtor who is always going to petition for his release but never does, John's writing in theory never gets past his own mind. However, the reader does have access to it, as in an attempt to give permanence to the ephemeral world of text; he perpetually updates a putative headstone that is never actually commissioned. In four different versions charting the course of his failed courtship of Little Dorrit, the wording describes him as 'universally respected' (179), 'Never anything worth mentioning' (185), suicidal (311) and 'MAGNANIMOUS' (613). Even these fantasies are bound by John's definition of himself as a Marshalsea turnkey, an identity he includes in his imagined inscription. When Clennam returns to the prison, the narrator contrives to insert a joke to the reader on this theme, explaining that he 'had been trying to read, and had not been able to release even the imaginary people of the book from the Marshalsea' (614).

But its satirical presentation of literary fantasy notwithstanding, the novel is itself concerned with the decoding and reinterpretation of writing and text, encountered and produced by a range of characters. Despite her position as fraudulent benefactor of the will made by her husband's uncle, it is Mrs Clennam who finally relates the story of Arthur's parentage, and her version is the only one made directly available to the reader. Little Dorrit only learns the truth at her insistence, as Mrs Clennam first reclaims the written history and then hands the envelope straight back to her, telling her to read the contents. In a final act of loving deception, Little Dorrit later asks Clennam to burn the papers unread. As the flames burn up, he asks her, 'Does the charm want any words to be said?' and substituting love for the damaging terms of memory, she replies with an uncharacteristically flirtatious, 'You can say (if you don't mind) "I love you!"' (687).

In this final resolution memory is not suppressed, although it is apparently quarantined through the guardianship of Little Dorrit. Where David Copperfield confidently proclaimed that 'all these things have worked together to make me what I am', the more obviously damaged Clennam is protected from the written secrets of his own life, in which there is no obvious hero.

'A Potent Smell of Burnt Pens': *Our Mutual Friend*

Dickens's last completed novel, like its predecessors, is deeply preoccupied with the power of the written word in promoting imaginative interpretations of everyday experience and with the significance of reading correctly. As Sheila Cordner observes, 'In *Our Mutual Friend*, Dickens asks readers to think about what modes of interpretation are lost in the process of acquiring textual literacy' (89).

One of the novel's most effective serio-comic interludes is provided by the letter from Pleasant Riderhood rejecting Venus's proposal of marriage, on the grounds that she does not wish 'to regard myself, nor yet to be regarded, in that bony light' (84). While working class literacy provides a central motif, the narrator complicates the binary model of middle-class education versus working-class ignorance at various points in the novel. Patrick Brantlinger has convincingly argued that 'somewhere in Dickens's thinking lurks an equation between crime and literacy, instead of between – as might be expected – crime and illiteracy' (72), an anxiety that surfaces in the murderous actions of Bradley Headstone in this novel. Pointing out that 'When Dickens presents illiteracy in later novels, he tends to equate it with innocence rather than crime' (73), Brantlinger goes on to argue that 'This is true both of Joe Gargery's painful reading lessons in *Great Expectations* and of Boffin's in *Our Mutual Friend*' (73). But it is worth noting in this context that the newly wealthy Boffin is not actually taught to read; rather he is subject to the somewhat haphazard interpretations of his protégé Wegg, as he invests himself with a false authority through his assumption of this power over the written word.

At other points in the novel the attainment of literacy is used to redress the balance of power in more subtle ways and to different effect. At the Veneerings' house the otherwise unappealing Charley Hexam unconsciously signals his alert intelligence when he shows more interest in the library than do the owners themselves, as he 'glanced at the backs of the books, with an awakened curiosity that went below the binding. No one who can read, ever looks at a book, even unopened on a shelf, like one who cannot' (18). Lizzie herself, like Joe Gargery in *Great Expectations*, initially refuses more education than her brother can give her second hand, reminding him that

'I can't so much as read a book, because, if I had learned, father would have thought I was deserting him, and I should have lost my influence' (29). This ignorance renders her vulnerable to false teachers later on, when both Eugene and Bradley Headstone seek to manipulate her through the offer of having her taught to read and write.

The narrative is conflicted in its representation of writing, which is shown to be both liberating and unstable, even treacherous in its tendency to be redeployed or misappropriated beyond its intended function and original context. Characters and readers alike must look for clues in what they read, and the potentially deceptive nature of the written word permeates the novel from the start, ironically supporting Gaffer Hexam's distrust. When the mysterious lodger first appears at the Wilfer house and signs an agreement with his new landlord, 'The contracting parties were R. Wilfer, and John Rokesmith, Esquire' (39), and Rokesmith is also the name Harmon signs on the contract he writes for his employment by Mr Boffin. He is finally arrested through the merging of private and public writing, when the Inspector reads the inscription in a book to 'Mrs John Rokesmith. From her husband on her birthday' (760) and identifies it as the writing of 'Julius Handford', who is sought in connection with the murder of John Harmon.

Characters are required to become sophisticated readers in order to understand the situations in which they find themselves. Without access to Sophronia's conversation with Twemlow, in which she asks him to warn Georgiana's parents against her, Fledgeby is wholly unable to decipher Podsnap's letter rejecting the Lammles' friendship. This letter, in which Podsnap pompously asks on behalf of himself and his wife 'to express our united sense of the polite attentions of Mrs Alfred Lammle and yourself towards our daughter Georgiana' only to continue 'Allow us, also, wholly to reject them for the future', is inexplicable to Fledgeby, and just as George stares in bewilderment at the envelope containing Smallweed's letter in *Bleak House*, he instinctively seeks further clues in the paper itself, 'Fledgeby looked at the three blank sides of this note quite as long and earnestly as at the first expressive side' (425). But if the motivation remains unclear to him, his education allows him to apprehend the deliberately insulting register veiled as formal politeness – it is 'expressive' in its very portentousness. That this formal tone is offensive in its politeness is discernible to members of a similar class because it is culturally coded. The working class Headstone is quick to catch this tone, which he knows he cannot reproduce, in his ill-matched verbal fencing with Eugene when he first accosts him in his chambers.

While much of the plot hinges on the impact of education on the working class of London, a keynote of the novel is the distinction between literally being 'able to read' and the possession of emotional literacy. Charley Hexam famously tells his sister at the start of the novel, 'You said you couldn't read a book, Lizzie. Your library of books is the hollow down by the flare, I think' (30), before becoming corrupted by his own utilitarian education.

Some of the most absurd incidents in the novel hinge on the inappropriateness of writing and interpretation, notably when the chapter detailing Bella's idyllic wedding is followed by her mother's reception of her letter, 'I think your father will admit it to be documentary proof of what I tell him' (672). It never occurs to Mrs Wilfer that the written account may be designed to obfuscate her husband's role in the wedding scene it describes rather than simply substituting for a direct experience of that event.

Access to reading and writing is similarly undermined by juxtapositions such as the Boffin / Wegg pairing, in which from an early point 'the man of low cunning had, of course, acquired a mastery over the man of high simplicity' (185). Notably Wegg's trade in ballads and cheap verse as objects of commodity is as undiscriminating as Boffin's own desire for vicarious literary attainment. Much of the time Boffin literally does not know what is being read to him, as Wegg parodically mispronounces and edits book titles and adapts obsolete poems to his own uses. Neither figure shows any awareness of current literary trends, implicitly removing Boffin from the influence writers such as Dickens himself were attempting to exert on a new generation of readers. The significance of this haphazard reading becomes clearer in light of David Vincent's comment that:

> The sheer durability of print, together with the continuing inability of the most dedicated autodidact to control access to new copyright literature, constantly disordered the chronology of publishing in this period. By the second half of the nineteenth century, the literary world of the common reader represented a vast, cluttered, uncatalogued second-hand bookshop. Forms of fiction and verse long thought to be obsolete survived in forgotten corners to be rediscovered by fresh generations anxious to practise their recently acquired skills. (Vincent 222)

Mr Boffin is naïvely impressed by Wegg's status as 'A literary man – *with* a wooden leg – and all Print is open to him!' (49) Wegg in turn plays on this awe of the written word to extract additional payment, claiming that 'When a person comes to grind off poetry night after night, it is but right he should expect to be paid for its weakening effect on his mind' (51). Specifically it is his own inability to read that encourages Mr Boffin to conflate obscurity of meaning with attainment in deciphering words on the page. Rokesmith / Harmon as an educated man, is less impressed with Wegg's adaptations of the street ballads he has formerly tried to sell to passersby, but 'The effect of the poem on the Secretary being evidently to astonish him, Mr Boffin was confirmed in his high opinion of it, and was greatly pleased' (182).

More acute than her husband, Mrs Boffin is so unimpressed by Wegg's reading on the only occasion of her attending that she falls asleep; the reader is subtly reminded that like her husband, she herself cannot write, feathers being used to adorn her headgear rather than for the manufacture of pens, 'several total eclipses of Mrs Boffin's candle behind her black velvet disc, would have been very alarming, but for being regularly accompanied by a potent smell of burnt pens when her feathers took fire, which acted as a restorative and woke her' (59).

Even a comparatively well-educated character like Bella apparently takes to reading only on her marriage and still struggles with print on occasion. While she reads voraciously and indiscriminately in the business sections of the papers in order to have a stock of conversation on her husband's return home, she is comically flawed by the book of cookery and household management, partly because the recipes assume a greater degree of knowledge than she possesses, and the *Complete British Housewife* in any case 'was by no means an expert Briton at expressing herself with clearness in the British tongue' (682).

Nonetheless the narrator refuses to idealise ignorance by aligning it exclusively with either innocence and the imagination or fetishised housewifery. Nor does it preclude characters from strategic plotting. Later in the novel Bradley Headstone makes a fatal mistake about the cunning and aptly named Rogue Riderhood, when 'knowing him to be a very ignorant man who could not write, he began to doubt whether he was to be feared at all' (792). In dealing with Eugene and Mortimer, Riderhood himself shows an exaggerated confidence in the authority of writing, refusing to give them his name unless it is taken down as an 'Alfred David' (affidavit). 'Deferring to the man's sense of the binding powers of pen and ink and paper, Lightwood nodded acceptance of Eugene's nodded proposal to take those spells in hand' (149). But while he is unable to read himself, later in the novel Riderhood easily tracks Headstone down and tricks the pupils into revealing his name, as written on the board.

Other working-class characters are sufficiently literate to decode and apply the records of official mismanagement of the Poor Law, reinforcing Betty Higden's horror of the workhouse. The narrator thunders at one point, 'The shameful accounts we read, every week in the Christian year, my lords and gentlemen and honourable boards, the infamous records of small official inhumanity, do not pass by the people as they pass by us' (325). In this context the working-class reader is more sensitive to the nuances of print than members of the unaffected middle class. In the police station, this disconnection between official record keeping and the reality of the lives of the poor is mirrored in the Inspector's writing against a backdrop of drunken misery. After the supposed murder of John Harmon, Eugene, Mortimer and Harmon himself 'found the Night-Inspector, with a pen and ink, and ruler, posting up his books in a whitewashed office, as studiously as if he were in a monastery on the top of a mountain, and no howling fury of a drunken woman were banging herself against a cell-door in the back-yard at his elbow' (24).

Mr Boffin's confusion about the authority of print is presented as comic, 'What to believe, in the course of his reading, was Mr Boffin's chief literary difficulty indeed; for some time he was divided in his mind between half, all, or none; at length, when he decided, as a moderate man, to compound with half, the question still remained, which half? And that stumbling-block he never got over' (476).

But this apparently needless anxiety is framed by the instability of writing demonstrated throughout the novel and more immediately contextualised by the numerous begging letters he receives, which 'Rokesmith' manages on his behalf, including 'fifty-seven churches to be erected with half-crowns, forty-two parsonage houses to be repaired with shillings, seven-and-twenty organs to be built with halfpence, twelve hundred children to be brought up on postage stamps' (211). The individual letters are still worse, in that they enclose documents 'the non-return of which would be their ruin. That is to say, they are utterly ruined now, but they would be more utterly ruined then' (212). In this way print is forced on the household, as Rokesmith is obliged to engage, on Mr Boffin's behalf, with the written artefacts delivered to his house. Dickens himself received numerous begging letters throughout his career, most of which he attempted to investigate. As Slater puts it, 'The begging-letter writers he had always with him, of course, and here the remarkable thing is the number of individual cases he actually made time to follow up. ... Almost as troublesome as this class of correspondents were the visitors to London bearing letters of introduction to him' (*Charles Dickens* 341). Imaginative writing itself is rendered suspect through these letters, which are intended to deceive the recipient and which take up so much of the secretary's time.

Elsewhere the impecunious Lammles' bluff that they are seeking the ideal residence leads to the circulation of more – unknowingly – false letters:

> Mr and Mrs Lammles' house in Sackville Street, Piccadilly, was but a temporary residence. It had done well enough, they informed their friends, for Mr Lammle when a bachelor, but it would not do now. So they were always looking at palatial residences in the best situations, and always very nearly taking or buying one, but never quite concluding the bargain. Hereby they made for themselves a shining little reputation apart. People said, on seeing a vacant palatial residence, 'The very thing for the Lammles!' and wrote to the Lammles about it, and the Lammles always went to look at it, but unfortunately it never exactly answered. (256)

As elsewhere in Dickens, the status of imagination is complex; as the narrator shows, appeals to the imaginative faculty must be determined by a careful engagement with the target audience, while too complete a dependence on the reading of fairy tales themselves may lead the reader astray. The narrator derides such treatises as *The Adventures of Little Marjory* as supposedly suitable reading for child prostitutes in the Ragged Schools (214) not simply because they are determinedly 'innocent', but also because they are frankly boring. But once she has learned to read, the prematurely adult

Jenny Wren herself makes sense of her relations with Riah by according him roles from the fairy tales through which she has presumably just learned to read, first telling him that he is 'like the fairy godmother in the bright little books!' (434) and later mistakenly casting him as the Wicked Wolf. Finally she learns to use her imaginative faculty to decode what is before her, rather than relying on any given literary template as a guide to the world around her.

Dickens's friends are encouraged to view his letters as a means of encountering him in a quasi-physical sense or even as evidence of his truthfulness, for instance when he is forced to cancel an engagement only because 'my amiable cold took it into its head last night to get into my throat and chest; and I lay coughing all night long – as this present tremulous writing may testify' (To Charles Sumner, 5 February 1868. Pilgrim 12. 37). In the same way, having realised that she was wrong in her relative assessment of Riah and Fledgeby, Jenny delights in the letter a chastised Fledgeby sends to Riah on his resignation from Pubsey & Co. Unlike Riah himself she can interpret the letter in light of Fledgeby's physical suffering, and 'The dolls' dressmaker found it delicious to trace the screaming and smarting of Little Eyes in the distorted writing of this epistle' (728).

Acts of 'false' writing remain the only resource of Young Blight, who likewise makes pretence to Mr Boffin, telling him that he must look through the appointment book and the callers' book before allowing him to see Mortimer Lightwood. Mortimer's failure involves Blight in a form of quasi-imprisonment comparable to the enervating atmosphere of the Marshalsea in *Little Dorrit*. As the narrator explains, 'Wearing in his solitary confinement no fetters that he could polish, and being provided with no drinking-cup that he could carve, he had fallen on the device of ringing alphabetical changes into the two volumes in question, or of entering vast numbers of persons out of the Directory as transacting business with Mr Lightwood' (87). Like *Dombey and Son*'s Toots, Blight compensates for a lack of communication with the outside world by literally writing his own version of reality on an empty page.

Miss Peecher likewise scripts the story of her imagined life, in the absence of any approach from Headstone:

> oftentimes when school was not, and her calm leisure and calm little house were her own, Miss Peecher would commit to the confidential slate an imaginary description of how, upon a balmy evening at dusk, two figures might have been observed in the market-garden ground round the corner, of whom one, being a manly form, bent over the other, being a womanly form of short stature and some compactness, and breathed in a low voice the words, 'Emma Peecher, wilt thou be my own?' (338)

But this transient imposition of fantasy on the experience of daily rejection is cruelly parodied in the nightmarish fantasies of Headstone himself after his attempted murder of Eugene. Giving new significance to Thackeray's trope of the palimpsestic novel, in which the record of the writer's life is more exciting than the fiction he writes, 'If a record of the sport had usurped the places of peaceful texts from Scripture on the wall, the most advanced of the scholars might have taken fright and run away from the master' (555).

The imagined 'record' of Headstone's crime is never materialised on the wall as David's imagined pictures are, even within the text itself. But one way in which the narrator carefully cordons off pleasurable engagement with reading and writing from the acquisition of status is through just such an insistence on the material. Mr Boffin's struggles with writing, like Charley's in *Bleak House*, are rendered physical in the remark 'It is curious to consider, in such a case as Mr Boffin's what a cheap article ink is, and how far it may be made to go' (178). In direct contrast to this childlike readiness to get literally covered in ink, when Young Blight sends a note to the Veneering house on the reappearance of Mr Dolls, 'the Analytical, perusing a scrap of paper lying on the salver, with the air of a literary Censor, adjusts it, takes his time about going to the Table with it, and presents it to Mr Eugene Wrayburn' (627). Mr Boffin seemingly aligns himself with this moral failure, when he begins to haunt book shops for stories of misers. In the denouement to the Wegg plot, it transpires that he is aware of the imaginative value such warning tales will have for Bella, taken in conjunction with her experience of the impact they supposedly have on her benefactor. On his instructions Bella 'would examine the window with the greatest attention, while Mr Boffin would examine her face' (466). William Morris was sufficiently impressed by the character to reference him in his own story of the Thames, *News from Nowhere*, in the minor character Boffin.

Freedgood suggests the way in which the novel's awareness of materiality is itself fragile, as referenced in Dickens's postscript to the novel, in which he writes about rescuing the Boffins from the train wreckage, 'Before mechanical reproduction, there is one writer and one text: both can and could be lost to us. Yet looked at another way, in materializing text and author, this account of the train accident de-materializes character: they "live" only on paper, we are harshly reminded' ('Material' 385). The characters may indeed be dependent for their 'life' on the survival of the page and the reader's willingness to engage with it; nonetheless, that reader's vicarious education is expected to continue beyond the page, as becomes clear in the final scene in which Boffin is revealed as the watchful benefactor, long disguised as a corrupt miser. Her moral education complete, Bella later tells him that 'I want neither you nor any one else to tell me the rest of the story. I can tell it to *you*, now, if you would like to hear it' (775).

'You Readers, Who Ought to Know Everything': *The Mystery of Edwin Drood*

Throughout his fiction Dickens stresses the importance of reading as an index to character, while increasingly questioning the status and authenticity of the written word itself. In *The Mystery of Edwin Drood* reading and

154   *Decoding the Text*

writing become vital clues to character in their bearing on dramatic events, as observations of reading and writing practices range across the spectrum from moral domesticity to potentially lethal manufactured evidence.

In a parallel with *Nicholas Nickleby*'s fixation with presenting the same scene from various standpoints by moving between 'verbal' and written accounts, and John Jarndyce's use of letters to pre-empt embarrassing conversations in *Bleak House*, Rosa's shyly benevolent guardian overtly relies on written notes to guide his conversation. On his first appearance he tells Rosa, 'I made a guiding memorandum or so – as I usually do, for I have no conversational powers whatever' and then 'Mr Grewgious smoothed his smooth head again, and then made another reference to his pocket-book; lining out "well and happy" as disposed of' (68). The reader is of course alive to the irony that Rosa is far from happy and that this subject is far from being 'disposed of'. It is more than tempting to trace this habit to the elderly playwright John Poole, as comically described in a letter of 1865:

> Poole still holds out at Kentish town, and says he is dying of solitude. ... I see him about once in two or three months, and in the meantime he makes notes of questions to ask me when I come. Having fallen in arrear of the time, these generally refer to unknown words he has encountered in the newspapers. His three last (he always reads them with tremendous difficulty through an enormous magnifying-glass) were as follows:
>
> 1   What's croquet?
> 2   What's an Albert chain?
> 3   Let me know the state of mind of the Queen. (To W. C. Macready, 22 April 1865. Pilgrim 11. 33–34. 34)

Grewgious himself, like Jarndyce, must learn to do without this prop in social and intimate situations. The reader in turn must learn to assess particular textual practices, including the possibility of false reading as a symbol of loss or a vehicle of virtuous care.

The engraving PJT above the portal of Grewgious's chambers offers the reader a chance to join the narrator in a sort of parlour game, improving on Grewgious's speculation that the initials stand for 'Perhaps John Thomas, or Perhaps Joe Tyler' (87), with offers such as 'Pretty Jolly Too' (92) or 'Possibly Jabbered Thus' (97). These allusions to commonplace rather than exceptional texts subtly suggest the very imaginative force that Grewgious for one denies possessing (it is habit and a feeling of loneliness, not any lack of perception that prevents him from engaging with PJT as he does with Rosa, the daughter of the woman he himself loved).

In an act of benign hypocrisy, Crisparkle (who has near perfect vision) inhibits his reading of letters in order to flatter his mother, as 'the old lady was exceedingly proud of her bright eyes being so clear that she could read writing without spectacles. Her son was also so proud of the circumstance, and so dutifully bent on her deriving the utmost possible gratification from it, that he had invented the pretence that he himself could *not* read writing without spectacles' (38). His respect for the private thoughts of others is expressed through an epistolary image when he pretends not to hear Neville's reaction on hearing of the engagement between Rosa and Edwin, 'said so evidently to himself, or to anybody rather than Mr Crisparkle, that the latter instinctively felt as if to notice it would be almost tantamount to noticing a passage in a letter which he had read by chance over the writer's shoulder' (48). Significantly Dickens had said of an *All the Year Round* employee dismissed for theft in 1867, 'I never could believe in Johnson, solely (I think) because, often as I have tried him, I never found him standing by my desk when I was writing a letter, without trying to read it' (To W. H. Wills, 2 September 1867. Pilgrim 11. 417).

When Edwin argues with Neville on the night of the dinner at Crisparkle's, his sneering attack on readers, 'I lead a busy life, and I speak under correction by you readers, who ought to know everything, and I dare say do' (55) is one of several instances of bad taste that his disappearance (and perhaps Dickens's death) leave him unable to redeem. But in his defence, inhabitants of Cloisterham are subjected to some dubious claims on the part of self-styled writers. Durdles and Sapsea compete for the authorship of Mrs Sapsea's ludicrous epitaph, which as set out on the page is roughly the shape of a woman's figure and, as the widower stresses himself, potentially imposing as a material object. Handing the ms to Jasper, he urges him to 'take it in your own hand. The setting out of the lines requires to be followed with the eye, as well as the contents with the mind' (27). Jasper is also the auditor when Durdles later claims that he is 'surrounded by his works, like a popular Author' (33).

Comically Miss Twinkleton as the monitor of youth attempts to supervise reading as potentially corrupting. In London 'Rosa soon made the discovery that Miss Twinkleton didn't read fairly' (203), editing love passages to drain them of any subversive content. When she stumbles on some books of sea voyages it is their educative value (like Magwitch in *Great Expectations*, Rosa's teacher sees this as largely depending on obscurity and incomprehensibility) that is brought to the fore, 'As a compensation against their romance, Miss Twinkleton, reading aloud, made the most of all the latitudes and longitudes, bearings, winds, currents, offsets, and other statistics (which she felt to be none the less improving because they expressed nothing whatever to her)' (203–204).

Despite her comic anxiety Miss Twinkleton turns out to be partially right about the dangers of reading for impressionable minds. Jasper, who does have the capacity to assess the impact of the written word, makes several references to the role of his diary in recording his life as he wants it to be read, and it will also become 'evidence' of Edwin's fate. '"A line for a day would be quite as much as my uneventful life would need, Heaven knows", said Jasper, taking a book from a desk, "but that my Diary is, in fact, a Diary of Ned's life too"' (85). Significantly, having staged the argument between

Neville and Edwin he tells Crisparkle that 'I mean to burn this year's Diary at the year's end' (129), but then uses it to record his oath of vengeance after Edwin's disappearance. In then handing the diary to Crisparkle rather than reading the entry aloud, he both registers his stated belief in the murder of his nephew, a development that counteracts his expressed intention of burning the diary, and reminds Crisparkle of the hierarchical status of the written over the spoken word. Others will presumably be impressed by the apparently damning evidence of the dated diary entries leading up to Edwin's disappearance, and Crisparkle as the chosen reader is surely forced to admit this, based on the way he is affected himself. But on the confines of the text, the actual reader is encouraged to suspect that this 'evidence' is as misleading as the letter Bella Wilfer sends to her parents after her wedding and in her father's presence. Such a document is only trustworthy if it is written without prior consideration of the use to which it can be put, and there is no way of establishing that this diary was written without the intention of using it in this way, or even whether the dates are authentic.

Like Jasper or Mrs Clennam, Dickens himself uses private writing to tendentious ends, which further complicates the status of his personal correspondence. Unlike the carefully constructed diary that incriminates Neville Landless, Dickens's letters might be seen as providing a closed circuit, safe from the undesired interpretations of hostile critics. But even before this strategy spectacularly backfired with the negative publicity surrounding the 'violated letter' in 1858, the novels included narratives in which third-person narrators exploit or cross the private / non-private boundary line through the writing and reading of diaries and letters. Like *David Copperfield* and *Bleak House*, *Little Dorrit* and *Our Mutual Friend* explore the status of both letters and the characters who write them. In this context *Little Dorrit* warns against both self-absorption and self-aggrandising habits and the uses to which letters may be put.

Significantly Dickens was unable to control letters written about him or purporting to be written by him. By the late 1860s he seems to have been the victim of more sophisticated methods being adopted by begging letter writers, as he warned Georgina Hogarth in telling her, 'Forgery of my name is becoming popular. You sent me this morning a letter from Russell Sturgis, answering a supposed letter of mine' (To Georgina Hogarth, 14 December 1868. Pilgrim 12. 244–45). Sturgis had written to Dickens agreeing to contribute funds to a third person, supposedly at Dickens's request. Even the publication of some of his letters in 1880, in a two-volume edition edited by Georgina and Mamie, actually countermands his expressed wishes, albeit in the act of presenting a particular image of the writer.

Note

1. With thanks to Annie Deakin for this suggestion. Responsibility for the possibly strained translation of 'Marchons' as 'let us make progress' is entirely my own.

5 Afterlives

As Dickens's fame grew, he actively encouraged readers to conflate his authorial persona with his books, identifying himself first as the whimsical 'Boz' and subsequently as the more individualised and recognisable 'Charles Dickens'. Just this infusion of the writing into the image of the writer himself can be seen in the representation of Dickens by the journalist G. A. Sala, in his 1870 *Charles Dickens*. Sala writes unabashedly that 'he was my master; and but for his friendship and encouragement, I should never have been a journalist or a writer of books' (vi). Crucially in this account the figure of the literary teacher is known to his readers through particular fictions before he can be encountered as an actual person; as Sala explains, it may make him appear less fanatical if he states that:

> when he first came before the world as an author I was an illiterate child, gifted with a strongly retentive memory, but Blind; that the chief solace in my blindness was to hear my sister read the "Sketches by Boz;" that when I recovered my sight it was out of "Pickwick," and by the same loving teacher that I was taught to read; and that finally I knew him from 1836 upwards, and, in literature, served him faithfully for nineteen years. (98)

The two modes of relationship are intended to be largely interchangeable. As Slater reminds us, 'one of the main things that Dickens still represents in our culture is an ideal of perfect, blissful, quintessentially English, domesticity' (*The Great Charles Dickens Scandal* 191).

Forster later attributed Dickens's success largely to this inclusion of memorable features and recognisable linguistic markers; as he remarked of the characters in *Nicholas Nickleby*, 'They talked so well that everybody took to repeating what they said… and the sayings being the constituent elements of the characters, these also of themselves became part of the public' (vol 1. 96). George Eliot would notice a certain staginess in his demeanour, writing later that 'I heard him address various public assemblages, and I listened I think, to each of his Public Readings; and in all he had consciously an idea in his mind, up to which he may be said to have acted. … The situation in which he found himself for the time became an ideal one forthwith and his part a part with the rest'. Even on one dramatic occasion when he had helped a policeman in the act of arresting a thief, nearly being assaulted in the process, she recalled that 'his voice, his air, his walk made me think of some accomplished artist called upon to represent all this upon the stage' ('In the Chair' 101). Close friends might have added to this the obvious identification of writer with characters, for instance in the consciously ritualistic or theatrical making of punch in the style of Micawber.

'His Companion Oftener Than I Could Well Afford the Time for': *A Life of Charles Dickens*

Forster's *Life of Charles Dickens* was first published in three volumes between 1871 and 1874, beginning the year after Sala's diffidently expressed hope in his own *Charles Dickens*, 'His Life, in an extended, substantial, and, authorized form will, ere long, I doubt it not, be written; and I hope that the writer of such a Life may be either his constant and noble-minded friend John Forster, or his near connection and co-labourer in letters, Wilkie Collins' (94–95).

Given Dickens's ambivalence about disclosing details of his life, particularly after his separation from Catherine and the resulting rumours about his relationship with Ellen Ternan, there were obvious difficulties in taking it on at all. Forster was understandably keen to make the point that Dickens himself had invited him to write a history of his life after he abandoned the autobiographical fragment. As Bodenheimer argues in assessing Forster's achievement:

> Dickens emphasized what both friends knew: that in writing a Dickens biography Forster would continue to play the roles he had played throughout Dickens's life. He wold protect him from himself; he would attempt to restrain Dickens's excesses; he would interpose himself between Dickens and trouble, whether personal or professional; and he would be the primary witness to Dickens's artistic struggles and triumphs. In writing – and eliding – as he did, Forster implicitly told an important truth of Dickens's life: that he lived most fully in what we might call a homosocial world of men. ('Dickens and the Writing of a Life')

Less adulatory than Sala, who had rather hysterically claimed that Dickens's name would be known worldwide 'as the names of Shakespeare and Napoleon are known – as that of a Great Man' (6), he was also more tactful in his handling of the Dickens's separation in 1858; eschewing Sala's titillating allusions, he clearly agreed with his position, however sensationally expressed, that 'Those who have a right to speak, have not spoken; and the world has no right to inquire into the mystery – if any mystery there be – nor will have, any time these fifty years' (97).

This chapter is based on the two-volume edition first published in 1876, including Forster's revisions (and incorporating occasional responses to criticism of the original edition). On what is perhaps a somewhat defensive note, volume 2 of the new edition includes a reference to Forster's correspondence with Dickens's doctor, who had written to him, 'nor need I say with how much interest I have read the first volume of your late friend's Life' (364). Following adverse comments, he was also keen to stress that he had not deliberately intruded his own personality, in his decision to take the letters to himself as a key source. Rather Dickens's letters were inseparable from an account of his character and provided the text with an autobiographical element accessible only through this friendship. More importantly still, they provided an index to the writing which constituted the essential nature of the man:

> Though Dickens bore outwardly so little of the impress of his writings, they formed the whole of that inner life which essentially constituted the man; and as in this respect he was actually, I have thought that his biography should endeavour to present him. The story of his books, therefore, at all stages of their progress, and of the hopes or designs connected with them, was my fist care. With that view, and to give also to the memoir what was attainable of the value of autobiography, letters to myself, such as were never addressed to any other of his correspondents, and covering all the important incidents in the life to be retraced, were used with few exceptions exclusively. (vol 2. 377)

In the first instance Forster's biography of his friend derives much of its authority from Dickens's own sanction, but more obviously still from the dedication to his daughters Mary and Katey; however, as he acknowledges, it is largely based on letters written to Forster himself over a period of roughly 30 years. As he remarks with a degree of pride, 'The first letter I had from him was at the close of 1836' (65), at the period of his first fame. Tellingly he acknowledges the importance of the epistolary form to Dickens himself, giving as one example Dickens's use of an 'epistle' in his last edited issue of *Bentley's Miscellany* in 1839, before handing over responsibility to Harrison Ainsworth (vol 1. 93).

G. K. Chesterton noted approvingly that the effect of the *Life* is created 'more by reporting correspondence than conversation' (Introduction x), but writing it at all places Forster in an ambivalent position, given such heavy dependence on personal letters in the teeth of Dickens's known anxiety at the thought of his letters finding their way into the public domain. Perhaps for this reason variations on the phrase 'worth preserving' or 'worthy of being preserved' recur throughout the volumes in relation to the literary quality of Dickens's letters, used both to round out his published writing and to intimate his relationship with the biographer himself.

Gissing captures this double sense of the letters as both 'artistic' in themselves and a record of the literary relationship between writer and biographer, as 'Year after year, he keeps his friend minutely informed by letter of the progress he makes with every book; consults him on endless points, great and small; is inexhaustible in gossip about himself, which never appears egoistic because of the artistic earnestness declared in every syllable' (*Charles Dickens: A Critical Study* 60). Forster himself makes a similar point in guiding the readers of his biography in how to read Dickens's private correspondence, suggesting that 'one of the impressions left by the letters is that of the intensity and tenacity with which he recognised, realised, contemplated, cultivated, and thoroughly enjoyed, his own individuality even in its most trivial manifestations' (vol 2. 378).

Throughout the *Life* Forster invokes letters both as a means of understanding the writer, claiming that 'all of them are marvellously exact in the reproduction of his nature' (vol 2. 418) and as a counterpoint to the published work. Specifically he claims an authenticity and freshness for the travel letters that he feels is diminished by the demands of publication, commenting for instance that the *American Notes* lack the vitality of Dickens's original impressions:

> In the Notes there is of course very much, masterly in observation and description, of which there is elsewhere no trace; but the passages amplified from the letters have not been improved, and the manly force and directness of some of their views and reflections, conveyed by touches of a picturesque completeness that no elaboration could give, have here and there not been strengthened by rhetorical additions in the printed work. There is also a charm in the letters which the plan adopted in the book necessarily excluded from it. (vol 1. 219)

Discussing Dickens's intense response to the Niagara Falls, he claims that 'The first vividness is in his letter' (234). The function of these letters for the writer himself is presented as a semi-fictional engagement with adventurous travel. Referring to the family's Italian residence in 1844, Forster suggests that Dickens 'liked rest after his travel all the more for the little excitement of living its activities over again, week by week, in these letters to me' (vol 1. 363).

These letters are presented as somehow more 'real' because Forster has by his own account taken the decision not to edit them (a questionable enough claim, as the Pilgrim editors show). The reader is thus given the impression of a privileged view of raw material, comparable perhaps to the modern marketing device of including 'out takes' in the special editions of a DVD. At one point Forster tells the reader that:

> the letters, *from which I am now printing exactly as they were written*, have claims, as mere literature, of an unusual kind. Unrivalled quickness of observation, the rare faculty of seizing out of a multitude of things the thing that is essential, the irresistible play of humour, such pathos as only humourists of this high order possess, and the

unwearied unforced vivacity of ever fresh, buoyant, bounding animal spirits, never found more natural, variously easy, or picturesque expression. (vol 1. 221. Emphasis added)

As Slater has shown, Forster's light touch editing actually was at odds with the later ravages of Georgina and Mamey's 1882 edition of Dickens's letters, in which, 'Following editorial procedures that were pretty cavalier even by the standards of the day, Georgina and Mamie altered the texts of various letters, silently omitting anything deemed too personal or likely to give offence, and dovetailing together passages from letters of widely different date' (*The Great Charles Dickens Scandal* 42). The reception of this edition was predictably benign, as:

> Reviewers of successive volumes of this family-edited collection of Dickens letters were generally positive but convey no sense of new things about Dickens being revealed through them. In the main, reviewers were simply confirmed in their belief that Dickens was a great and good man, though perhaps neither a very deep-thinking nor an emotionally complex one. (Slater, *The Great Charles Dickens Scandal* 43–44)

The impression of Dickens as lacking complexity is precisely what Forster's biography tries to correct, and this is largely effected through analysing his impact on the imaginative faculty of his readers, including Forster himself. The life of the writer, it is suggested, can be as powerful in this sense as his actual writing. Beginning with a fairly conventional summary of Dickens's childhood, Forster initially focuses on his subject's extraordinary powers of recall:

> He has often told me that he remembered the small front garden to the house at Portsea. … He was carried from the garden one day to see the soldiers exercise; and I perfectly recollect that, on our being at Portsmouth together while he was writing Nickleby, he recognised the exact shape of the military parade seen by him as a very infant, on the same spot. (vol 1. 4)

By the end of the passage, the adult writer's ability to retain details of childhood experience has been transferred to the current biographer, who assures readers of the truth of the incident, which 'I perfectly recollect'. Occasionally Dickens's individual personality becomes momentarily lost in a structuring of the 'literary life', as when Forster cites the famous passage in *David Copperfield* where the neglected books become a 'glorious host' and means of solace during the Murdstone regime. Confirming that this passage is taken verbatim from the autobiographical fragment, Forster comments, 'The usual result followed. The child took to writing himself' (vol 1. 8).

162 *Afterlives*

In later passages, not only do the different forms of the written word become interchangeable, it can even be replaced with the vicarious memories of the biographer (while Forster must be referring to his ability to draw on conversations between himself and Dickens, this is not explicitly stated): 'There is here another blank, which it is, however, not difficult to supply from letters and recollections of my own' (26). In a similar strategy, a discussion of Dickens taking his father's books to the pawn shop is supplemented by a correlating passage from *David Copperfield*. An engagement with this written account of the writer thus becomes in itself an imaginative text demanding analysis, as suggested in the famous letter Thomas Carlyle wrote to Forster in February 1874, 'This Third Volume throws a new light and character to me over the Work at large… deeper than all if one had the eye to see deep enough, dark, fateful silent elements, tragic to look upon, and hiding amid dazzling radiances as of the sun, the elements of death itself' ('Maddest Nonsense and Tragic Depths'. Collins vol 1, 63). In reading this powerful invocation of a 'tragic' figure whose 'dazzling radiances' mask the 'elements of death', it is easy to forget that Carlyle is describing the biographical account and not the actual man he himself knew well.

In the *Life* the impact of the writing is such that readers themselves become actively imaginative, a model Dickens had promoted throughout his writing career. In this sense Forster sees the fiction as essentially egalitarian, insofar as the writer, while he can be seen as a moral guide or director of imaginative experience, also enables the reader to see what he himself sees, meaning that 'all the world whom Dickens attracted to his books could draw from them the same advantage as the man of wit and genius' (97), as his construction of the personal imaginative vision as communal experience ensured that 'There was no character created by him into which life and reality were not thrown with such vividness, that to his readers the thing written did not seem the thing actually done' (374).

In an extreme statement of the case, he claims at one point that the 'reality' of the characters was intended literally to supersede their status as imaginative creations. In stressing Dickens's sense of responsibility to readers, which he himself characteristically emphasised above his claims to literary genius, Forster locates the conscious creation of character as a vehicle of communion between writer and assumed audience, from the beginning, 'What I had most indeed to notice in him, at the very outset of his career, was his indifference to any praise of his performances on the merely literary side, compared with the higher recognition of them as bits of actual life, with the meaning and purpose on their part, and the responsibility on his, of realities rather than creatures of fancy' (vol 1. 70). This sense of the real is not incompatible, he insists, with the idiosyncratic presentation of character so often assailed by critics as simple 'caricature', given that 'the rough estimates we form of character, if we have any truth of perception, are on the whole correct; but men touch and interfere with one another by the contact of their extremes, and it may very often become necessarily the main business of a novelist to display the salient points, the sharp angles, or the prominences merely' (vol 2. 117).

The extent to which Forster himself became absorbed in the creative process is indicated by his rueful comment on the many rides he shared with Dickens in the 1830s, in the intervals of writing:

> I was his companion oftener than I could well afford the time for, the distances being great and nothing else to be done for the day; but when a note would unexpectedly arrive while I knew him to be hunted hard by one of his printers, telling me he had been sticking to work so closely that he must have rest... I could not resist the good fellowship. (vol 1. 74)

Replicating the style of Dickens's own constructions of the ideal reader, Forster claims a creative vision for himself as well as endorsing Dickens's self-portrait of himself as a precocious and easily hurt child when he writes, 'I have the picture of him here very strongly in my mind as a sensitive, thoughtful, feeble-bodied little boy, with an amount of experience as well as fancy unusual in such a child' (vol 1. 9–10). In discussing *David Copperfield* he goes further in assuming that even adult readers project themselves into the character, much as the child David himself impersonates the characters from his favourite reading, 'It can hardly have had a reader, man or lad, who did not discover that he was something of a Copperfield himself. Childhood and youth live again for all of us in its marvellous boy-experiences' (vol 2. 107). Forster's sustained faith in the author / reader contract first established by Dickens in the 1830s is nowhere more in evidence than in this assumption that readers can appropriate the childhood experiences of a David Copperfield without finding themselves unduly distanced by his subsequent rise to fame. By the end of the century the credibility of this figure was being questioned by another writer, who was nonetheless himself a deep admirer of Dickens.

'Bright Realities, for Weary Eyes to Look Upon': Gissing's *Charles Dickens: A Critical Study* (1898)

In some ways the natural successor to Dickens as chronicler of the urban poor, the more identifiably 'realist' George Gissing's meta-fictional response to the earlier writer was both admiring and critical. If 'it is a recurring pattern in Gissing's fiction that the virtuous are punished and the villainous end triumphant: a parodic and deliberate reversal of the paradigms of Dickensian fiction' (James, introduction to *Charles Dickens: a Critical Study* 5), Gissing's characters themselves can sometimes be seen debating this very point. The 1891 *New Grub Street* parodies not just Dickens but also Gissing's response to what he saw as the limitations of his work, in the figure of Biffen and what he acknowledges himself will be a wholly uninteresting novel, his proposed *Mr Bailey, Grocer*. Explaining his artistic vision to Reardon, he tells him, 'I want to deal with the essentially unheroic, with the day-to-day life of that vast majority of people who are at the mercy of paltry circumstance. Dickens understood the possibility of such work, but his tendency to melodrama on the one hand, and his humour on the other, prevented him from thinking of it' (*New Grub Street* 144).

By the time he came to write *Charles Dickens: A Critical Study*, published in 1898, Gissing had revised these criticisms, or at least subsumed them into a wider consideration of Dickens's aims. As David Parker puts it, 'Gissing found himself unable to deny talents very different from his own. Perhaps with a touch of surprise, indeed, he found himself defending Dickens against critics with whom he might otherwise have largely agreed' (afterword to *Charles Dickens: A Critical Study* 208). Where he does feel obliged to criticise perceived weaknesses in the novels, he shows an obvious impatience, at once fending off over-zealous partisans of a later realist mode and apologising to Dickens's admirers, with the warning that 'it is a thankless task to write of such a man as Dickens in disparaging phrase. I am impatient to reach that part of my essay where I shall be at liberty to speak with admiration unstinted, to dwell upon the strength of the master's work, and exalt him where he is unsurpassed. But it is necessary to clear the way' (59).

Unlike *Allbut's Rambles in Dickens Land*, Gissing's study of Dickens is not primarily concerned with literary tourism but with the positioning of his subject in an ongoing debate over the value of different styles of fiction. One of its strengths, as Parker notes, is the commitment to critiquing an approach very different from Gissing's own, from the perspective of a largely admiring fellow author rather than a professional critic, 'His very amateurism is an aspect of what it is that makes Gissing so stimulating on the topic of Dickens's books. He wrote, not primarily as an analytic scholar, but as one writer considering another, understanding him, and recognizing different methods of achieving common objectives. He wrote workshop criticism' (afterword to *Charles Dickens: A Critical Study* 213).

The book is deeply concerned with the mythology of Dickens as a creative figure, as mediated through Forster's *Life*. But as Simon James suggests in his introduction, the reader's imaginative engagement is predicated on memories of the reading experience itself, 'Since, as he writes, Gissing is removed from the physical context of Dickens's fictional world… his experience of reading Dickens while producing the *Critical Study* is one of imaginatively *re*-visiting this world. The pleasure to be gained from Dickens is in part that of rediscovery, of being reminded of that which is familiar to and cherished by the author and by his implied reader' (2).

But if Gissing draws on the shared memory of reading Dickens that he assumes in his own readers, he is also able to construct the form that memory should take in the sense of unifying a disparate audience and articulating a critical position for that audience to uphold. As Parker argues, 'He was able to undertake his defence of Dickens the more readily, because he was cultivating a field largely untilled. He could write without looking over his shoulder. His is the first book deserving to be taken seriously, devoted to Dickens's art as such, and as a whole' (Afterword to *Charles Dickens: A Critical Study* 211).

Intriguingly though Gissing also claims that readers who disparage Dickens's fiction are often doing so without close knowledge of the work itself, which they are misremembering based on childish encounters with his characters, 'I have heard it very truly remarked that, in our day, people for the most part criticise Dickens from a recollection of reading in their childhood; they do not come to him with mature minds; in general, they never read him at all after childish years' (76). Throughout the study Gissing constructs the type of reader who would be interested in Dickens's fiction, in the process of interpreting the character and status of the writer himself.

But despite his assumption that 'To-day the women must be very few who by deliberate choice open a volume of his works' (111), he emphasises the way in which the characters from Dickens's novels took on a significance beyond their respective texts, becoming a form of cultural exchange within and across individual households. Like other 19th-century commentators, Gissing elides the distinction between writer and fictional character in discussing this aspect of Dickens's popularity, 'I suppose that for at least five-and-twenty years of his life, there was not an English-speaking household in the world, above the class which knows nothing of books, where his name was not as familiar as that of any personal acquaintance, and where an allusion to characters of his creating could fail to be understood' (184). The assumption that Dickens's name is comparable to that of a family acquaintance echoes familiar accounts of the characters becoming welcome guests in the homes of readers.

Ironically Gissing implies that Dickens himself focused on writing at the expense of his own reading, 'After success came to him (and it came so early) he never had much time for reading, and probably never any great inclination' (31). Dickens himself would have strenuously denied this presentation of a closed circuit, in which readers access his work, but he does not reciprocate – indeed in his description of Dickens's summer holidays in Kent Forster confirms that 'his reading was considerable and very various at such intervals of labour' (vol 2. 57) – but lurking behind Gissing's incidental comment is an awareness that Dickens's education had been sporadic and unstructured. Elsewhere he recognises the importance to Dickens of recognising as well as directing the literary tastes of his readers, 'Sympathy with his readers was to him the very breath of life; the more complete that sympathy, the better did he esteem his work' (61). While Dickens did in fact read extensively throughout his working life, the sense of sympathy to which Gissing alludes was absorbed largely through the reading of and imaginative engagement with his numerous fan letters.

Throughout the study Gissing sustains a sense of Dickens's style as a means of executing an imaginative social programme. While Oliver Twist is fairly scathingly dismissed for being 'as remarkable for purity of mind as for accuracy of grammar' (165), he also reminds potentially critical readers that 'He could make people laugh; and if once the crowd has laughed with you, it will not object to cry a little – nay, it will make good resolves, and sometimes carry them out' (21). Usefully Gissing also infers from the novels that Dickens himself was closer to the imaginative level of his readers than is often assumed. *New Grub Street*'s Biffen concludes that 'The working classes detest anything that tries to represent their daily life. It isn't because that life is too painful; no, no; it's downright snobbishness. Dickens goes down only with the best of them, and then solely because of his strength in farce and his melodrama' (380). But the author of the critical study is more receptive to the vision of an imaginative working class, understood and translated by the act of genius, 'This was his task in life, to embody the dreams of ordinary men; to fix them as bright realities, for weary eyes to look upon' (73). In this formulation the creative capacity of the writer functions not to imagine what has previously been unseen, but to detect what is already latent in the minds of readers and give it tangible form. As James reminds us, 'his own sense of self as a writer was not confirmed by mass approval, but produced by it. Dickens was not a lonely *fin-de-siècle* artist like Gissing but a successful commercial practitioner in an expanding industry' (Introduction 12).

Gissing's assessment of Dickens's ability to draw out and embody 'the dreams of ordinary men' is subtly different from Sala's related comment that despite the myth of Dickens's quasi-miraculous attainment of fame with the early numbers of *Pickwick*, 'His triumphs were neither fortuitous nor accidental. They were premeditated, consummated, and deserved' (Sala 20). It was simply that:

> Everybody knew Mrs Gamp years before Dickens was born; but none had thought about painting her. Many had done business with Ralph Nickleby but none had thought of describing him. Mr. Squeers had figured in a dozen law-suits for cruelty and neglect ten years before "Nicholas Nickleby" was written; yet Dotheboys Hall was hailed as a country as newly brought within human cognizance as California or Queensland. (Sala 31)

An awareness of this literary context perhaps informs Gissing's defence of David Copperfield's unrealistic powers of written memory, while arguing that this first-person narrator should not be taken as a developed character and teller of his own story. In line with the conventions of mid-Victorian realism, Dickens can attribute a high degree of background knowledge to his character without compromising his standing as an authentic character, 'David relates in detail conversations which take place before he is born, and makes no apology for doing so. Why should he? The point never occurs to the engrossed reader' (52). However Gissing denies that David is even intended to represent a successful character in his own right, implying that the novel cannot fully contain both character narrator and the actual author whose voice is so clearly felt behind David's own:

> Had Dickens intended to show us a man of letters, he would here have failed most grievously; of course he aimed at no such thing; the attempt would have cost him half his public. And so it is that one never thinks of the good David as a character at all, never for a moment credits *him*... with that glorious endowment of genius which went to the writing of his life. (87)

By way of contrast, Gissing concludes that the fallible and deeply troubled Pip is convincing because his story in no way compares to that of the successful author, and 'No story in the first person was ever better told' (56).

Despite changes in literary trends, Dickens continued to provide a model for at least some of the next generation of writers both during his life and in the decades after his death. In 1867 the narrator of Rhoda Broughton's *Cometh up as a Flower* notes that a particular character 'reminds one somehow of the tone of Dickens's books, there is a broad, healthy geniality about him; he is like a wood fire on a frosty day' (136). In 1890 J. M. Barrie whimsically imagined a scene in which a latter-day Stylist, a Realist, a Romancist and an Elsmerian have called up the ghosts of Walter Scot, Henry Fielding, Smollett, Dickens and Thackeray for purposes of conversation and questioning. At one point an apparently bewildered Dickens tells them that 'I wrote for a wide public (*Stylist sighs*), whom I loved (*Realist sighs*). I loved my characters, too (*American sighs*), they seemed so real to me (*Romancist sighs*), and so I liked to leave them happy. I believe I wanted to see the whole world happy (*Elsmerian sighs*)' ('Brought Back from Elysium' 853). Over the next 15 years two younger writers who were themselves accused of cultivating an ephemeral populist style, Jerome K. Jerome[1] and Marie Corelli, would independently defend Dickens in their own work against the charge of 'vulgarity'. Corelli demanded in 1905:

> And what of dear Charles Dickens – he, whom certain superfine persons who read Yellow Journalism presume to call 'vulgar'? Is love, is pity, is tenderness, is faith 'vulgar'? Is kindness to the poor, patience with the suffering, tolerance for all men and all creeds 'vulgar'? If so then Charles Dickens was vulgar – not a doubt of it! Few authors have ever been so blessedly, gloriously 'vulgar' as he! (300)

Much as Dickens did in his letters of invitation to potential *Household Words* contributors, Corelli's essay tries to occlude the cash element in this reclamation of the term 'vulgar'.

By the 1912 centenary questions of Dickens's value as a writer were still polarising opinion, as Laurence Mazzeno has shown. It was in 1898 that

The Academy first printed a story about the collectability of Dickens, placing him firmly in the heritage category. It claimed that an unnamed collector, having overpaid for a supposedly rare early Dickens text it described only as 'a certain little booklet ... considered to have survived in only three or four copies', only to learn that a second-hand bookseller had obtained nearly 50 copies from the printer's warehouse, protected his investment by buying up the entire stock himself. According to *The Academy* 'The collector asked himself, "Shall I allow every one of my book-hunting rivals to possess a copy at a fifth of the price I originally paid, or shall I purchase the entire remainder. It is almost needless to say that he not only bought the whole, but that, with three or four exceptions, he consigned his purchase to the flames!' The same journal later recycled its own news item, repackaging the original story as a nostalgia piece for the 1912 centenary ('Morality in Book Collecting').

In the same year a very different feature in the *Bookman* asked a number of 'representative authors' for their memories and impressions of Dickens and his fiction, working on the premise that 'the appreciation of him is growing rather than diminishing' ('Charles Dickens: Some Personal Recollections and Opinions' 246). By far the majority of the writers represented had made their own reputations at the *fin de siècle* (Percy Fitzgerald and Mary Braddon being rare exceptions); too young to speak with authority on the mid-century literary landscape, by implication they have been chosen to speak on Dickens because they themselves represent a particular view of the Victorian past as constructed by a new generation. But rather than accepting this possible relegation to a literary moment that has now passed, many of the writers who responded (including Jerome K. Jerome) chose to define themselves through a continued response to Dickens as both readers and writers.

The questions they were asked to consider were: '(1) Any personal recollection they had of or connected with Dickens; (2) Whether their life or work owed anything to his influence; (3) Their personal opinions of the value of his novels; whether they considered his humour appealed as strongly to readers of our own time as of his own, and which they would rank as the greatest of his books' ('Charles Dickens. Some Personal Recollections and Opinions.' 247).

The answers are printed on consecutive pages, creating the sense that they are in dialogue with each other, as George Bernard Shaw concludes somewhat irascibly, 'My works are all over Dickens; and nothing but the stupendous illiteracy of modern criticism could have missed this glaring feature of my methods' (247), while in a wonderfully suggestive phrase, Jerome K. Jerome responds with, 'I should doubt the possibility of any living reader not having been influenced in life and work by Dickens' (252). Mary Braddon largely agrees, although interestingly she limits her discussion of influence to the time in which Dickens was actually writing, 'I think it is impossible for anybody to have lived in the Mid-Victorian age and not to have been influenced by that most powerful and remarkable writer' (249).

With classic acerbity the critic Andrew Lang wrote, 'I often wonder who the purchasers of his books can be' (249), a dismissal that seems to be answered in Chesterton's airy assumption, 'His novels have long been independent of anybody's personal opinion' (255). Not for nothing does Mazzeno comment that 'defending Dickens became for Chesterton something of a cottage industry' (48). F. Anstey admitted that he personally was so steeped in Dickens, he was unsure of the precise extent of the earlier writer's influence, but went so far as to say that 'I think it very probable that... both my life and work have been influenced by him' (249). Peter Merchant has recently confirmed that Anstey's memories of school 'were seamlessly bound up with the memories he derived from reading Dickens' (Merchant 137). Perhaps the most interesting letter was sent in by Israel Zangwill. In direct contrast to the *Academy*'s philistine collector with his focus on the worth of Dickens's 'little booklet' as a collectible but ultimately disposable item, Zangwill invokes the calibre of Dickens's writing as well as its enduring appeal, through a recollection of his childhood reading of 'a coverless book without a title-page' (*Bookman* 252), which he only discovered years later to have been a collected edition of Dickens's Christmas books. This story, whether authentic or not, raises the stakes for critics in assuming that intelligent readers will appreciate the quality of Dickens's storytelling even before learning whose work they have been enjoying. As a new humourist of the 1890s Zangwill himself had been strongly identified with Jerome K. Jerome's monthly *Idler* and its series of spoof articles on criticism of the day, one of which had specifically aligned the new humour's much-maligned innovative style with the ebullience of Dickens's early episodic fiction.[2] In raising questions about what engages an uninformed reader who can have no prior sense of whether a book is held in high regard or reviled as ephemeral holiday reading, Zangwill is essentially recreating the experience of the early readers of 'Boz' in ways that would otherwise be impossible. At the same time he obliquely undermines the authority of the critics who question the transcendent qualities of great fiction.

Harry Furniss, Dickens's posthumous illustrator, sums up the ways in which Dickens's readers continue to rewrite the author himself in explaining that he 'created for us delightful imaginary friends we seem to have known, and our mutual friend, Charles Dickens, is of these the greatest' (251).

Conclusion

As a close reading of Dickens's fiction, journalism and letters reveals, his huge output is sustained and regulated by a self-conscious engagement with both reading and writing as imaginative acts, and as his letters demonstrate, communicating with potential readers became increasingly important as part of the planning process itself. Forster offered the expected tribute in describing him after his death as 'the intimate of every English household, and a familiar friend where ever the language is spoken whose stores of harmless pleasure he has so largely increased' (vol 1. 314).

Dickens himself had put it rather better when he made the discreet boast, in defending a stylistic choice to Bulwer Lytton, '... I think it is my infirmity to fancy or perceive relations in things which are not apparent generally' (To Sir Edward Bulwer Lytton, [?28 November 1865]. Pilgrim 11. 113). Much to his pleasure, imaginative scenes could even anticipate actual events, as he recorded on one occasion in 1862 when 'I stood five hours on the end of the pier at Boulogne in the height of the fury of the storm, and it was a wonderful sight. To my great consolation I only saw one thing missed in the Copperfield storm' (To Mrs Brown, 24 October 1862. Pilgrim 10. 149–50).

The danger is that readers will fail to respond or that writing will not in the end be sufficient to effect change, 'Dickens's transformative style may seem to take the sting out of a threatening world, but he knew as well as his critics that this might only be a trick of the mind, a trick of the text' (Tyler, introduction 10). But in a literal sense, the reader is invited to participate in reading and responding to the text as an active practice, rather than a passive experience. In some cases particular or general readers are invited on a metaphorical journey through serialisation, as when *Pictures from Italy* equips readers with their own passport symbolically permitting them to travel, or when one friend is assured that 'Your company on the journey of twenty months, lightens the way believe me' (To Charles Kent, 6 October 1864. Pilgrim 10. 432–433) during the writing of *Our Mutual Friend* in monthly parts. Dickens presents himself as a literary critic, both officially for *Household Words* and *All the Year Round* and more informally at the request of friends and aspiring authors who were admirers of his books. But while he offers comments to friends on what he has been reading, allusions in the letters to reading as a specifically leisure activity are more sparse.

These letters themselves are written on a spectrum from informal missives to friends to answers to fan letters and business communications. But such divisions are themselves open to negotiation. Dickens often described himself attempting to keep up with his constantly expanding correspondence while writing his novels; the cross-fertilisation, as letters appear in the plots of his novels and fictional characters appear in his letters, surely justifies Gissing's comment that 'In his letter-writing alone, Dickens did a life's literary work. Nowadays no one thinks of writing such letters; I mean, letters of such length and detail, for the quality is Dickens's own. He evidently enjoyed this use of the pen' (*Charles Dickens: A Critical Study* 186).

In some cases friends are the recipients of business letters or apparently spontaneous descriptions of scenery that are nonetheless intended for later use in travel writing such as *Pictures from Italy*. Meanwhile the business correspondence itself often contains literary motifs, and Dickens's written disputes with publishers arguably contain fictional elements as he literally 'rewrites' former agreements. Most dramatically, the 'violated letter' derives its shock effect from its status as a supposedly private letter that was always intended for at least limited circulation before finding its way into the press without his consent. In the earlier publication of the 'Personal' article in *Household Words* in 1858, Dickens had already reworked the terms of his relationship with unseen readers. The 'personal' section of a journal suggests short and possibly coded pieces of text, often addressed to a particular individual and attributed by initials only. For Dickens to adopt this means of addressing his public therefore suggests that some kind of advertisement is being made to a circle of intimates, although the text itself exposes the contradiction at the centre of this relationship. While he assumes that his personal friends will retain absolute confidence in his honour, 'there is a great multitude who know me through my writings, and who do not know me otherwise; and I cannot bear that one of them should be left in doubt, or hazard of doubt' (490).

The private letters are already fictional in a number of ways, and there is a further sense in which the fiction can be seen as a series of letters to friends and the wider public. Despite warning other writers against the inclusion of prefaces to their novels, Dickens himself includes prefaces set out in a way that is suggestive of the letter format, albeit with the place and date at the bottom rather than the top. As if to reinforce the sense in which he is writing directly to a privileged readership, *Our Mutual Friend* ends with a 'Postscript in lieu of a Preface'. In response to requests from readers, Dickens would sometimes autograph a few lines from a favourite novel that might then be pasted into the reader's copy, potentially giving it something of the status of a presentation volume to a friend. Publishers were requested to send out bound copies and serial instalments as they appeared to chosen individuals, in a ritual suggesting elements of both the library list and the 'visiting list' used by ladies to keep track of their social responsibilities while also displaying their inclusion in an exclusive coterie. From the 1840s onwards Dickens wrote to friends inviting them to find coded messages in his novels or simply to appropriate any passages they happened to enjoy, as a substitute for delayed personal correspondence.

Within the novels letters are often of crucial importance in developing the plot and revealing character, but they may also be used as a meta-fictional device, as when the chambermaid in *Martin Chuzzlewit* first imaginatively completes Lewesome's letter confessing to his relationship with Jonas Chuzzlewit, which she is unable to see properly over the shoulder of the immediate reader, and then believes what she has herself invented as deriving clear authority from its status as 'written' word. As in Dickens's private letters, epistolary scenes in the fiction often draw attention to the mechanics of writing, as in the famous letter written by Fanny Squeers in *Nicholas Nickleby*, where she comically insists that her father cannot write himself, 'the doctors considering it doubtful whether he will ever recuvver the use of his legs which prevents his holding a pen' (175). A sophisticated – albeit largely comic – writer such as Micawber not only provides readers with a script for silent internal performing (to borrow Malcolm Andrews's phrase), but demonstrates how it should be performed in his final climactic scene with Uriah Heep.

In *Little Dorrit* characters metaphorically become the letters they help to circulate but do not themselves write. In *Our Mutual Friend* the written page reminds the reader that a letter is literally supposed to stand in for the writer, as Jenny gleefully sees Fledgeby's pain embodied in his writing (a code the innocent Riah is unable to crack). George in *Bleak House* intuitively resists meeting Smallweed's letter unprepared, staring at the envelope for some time in order to guess the enclosure before directly confronting it. The misappropriation of letters, on which the plot of the novel turns, similarly stands as a reminder that coded language is not available to the 'wrong' reader. This contextual knowledge is a key feature of Dickens's personal appeals to friends, as he encourages them to see private messages embedded in his novels. One of Dickens's own letters to Thomas Trollope augments the sense in which the written word can figuratively take one person to another, as he tells him that 'I saw your brother Anthony at the Athenaenum [sic] not long ago, who was in the act of reading a letter from you' (6 May 1869. Pilgrim 12. 350–51. 351). The inclusion of this detail unusually creates a circuit among the three figures, as Dickens writes a letter to Thomas confirming that his letter has been read by Anthony. In the fiction characters are rarely, by definition, able to realise the impact of their letters on the addressee.

The ideal letter is clearly supposed to mimic or at least invoke the human voice, as Esther reminds the reader when she insists that Jarndyce's proposal 'was written just as he would at any time have spoken to me' (*Bleak House* 638) or as Dickens himself implies when he expresses gratitude for a literary letter:

> On coming here just now (half past one) I found your letter awaiting me, and it gave me infinite pleasure – you can scarcely think how much pleasure; for to hold consultation on the quiet pursuits in which we have had so much common interest for a long time now – is a delightful and wholesome thing in the midst of this kind of life – in the midst of any kind of life. (To Wilkie Collins, 31 October 1861. Pilgrim 9. 489–90. 489)

Letters can even substitute for inadvisable speech or reveal the expressive aspect of a hidden face; the kindly Mrs Lirriper sizes up the situation of her young female lodger, abandoned by her presumed husband to face the birth of her child alone, without even reading the letter communicating the news, 'My dear I never looked at the face of the letter which was lying open by her, for there was no occasion' ('Mrs Lirriper's Lodgings' 516).

Some meanings are only available through writing, as when Micawber introduces a spontaneous pun, 'HEEP of infamy' (*David Copperfield* 731) or even in Dickens's use of 'etc etc', used both to avoid the immodesty of repeating a personal compliment and to signal an assumption that his correspondent knows the frequency with which he is asked to receive such verbal tributes. Dickens's letters often suggest a more individualised construct than is really the case, a facet that only emerges when they are read together and repeated images or anecdotes are visible on the page across consecutive letters. In some cases he dictates or suggests letters to others purporting to share information about him, while proforma letters were deployed to answer unsuccessful submissions to *All the Year Round* and impracticable requests for readings. In one personal letter declining a request made by proxy, Dickens explains that 'It is one the like of which is so often preferred to me, that my Secretary for the Readings is obliged to have a lithographed answer for the purpose' (To Austin Henry Layard, 29 November 1861. Pilgrim 9. 528).

In a symbolic fusion of the different levels of authority represented by writing and print, Dickens told his solicitor in 1861 that in making a new will 'I wish to write it in my own hand' (To Frederic Ouvry, 27 September 1861. Pilgrim 9. 464–65. 464). While the *All the Year Round* office sent out proforma rejection letters and Dolby seems to have been employed in sending out letters on Dickens's behalf during the 1867 American tour, he occasionally assures a particular correspondent that this practice has been suspended on their behalf, as 'I cannot receive so genuine and touching a letter as yours, without answering it in my own hand and from my heart' (To Mrs O. F. R. White, 22 November 1867. Pilgrim 11. 486).

In the final analysis, letters depend for their efficacy on both writer and reader, becoming in certain contexts less facilitators of understanding than statements of mutual trust, as when Dickens assumes that an old friend will be reassured by the sight of his handwriting even before reading the letter itself, 'I have owed you a letter for so long a time, that I fear you may sometimes have misconstrued my silence. But I hope that the sight of the handwriting of your old friend will undeceive you, if you have, and will put that right' (To the Hon. Mrs Richard Watson, 8 July 1861. Pilgrim 436–38. 436). Writing to another intimate friend, he trusts that even a reluctantly written letter will offer the promise of affection that he fears its brevity may seem to withhold, 'Here is a limping brute of a reply to your always-welcome Christmas letter! But as usual, when I have done my day's work, I jump up from my desk and rush into air and exercise, and find letter-writing the most difficult thing in my daily life' (To W. W. F. de Cerjat, 25 October 1864. Pilgrim 10. 443–445).

However this reciprocity can be short-circuited in a number of ways, for instance if the recipient is unable to understand what is written, or on occasion through the trope of the absent or missing letter. Dickens frequently cites the receipt of letters 'by the hundred' in order to explain gaps in his own correspondence, and in his novels the circuit breaks down when letters are not passed on (the petty revenge of Mrs McStinger on Captain Cuttle takes this form with fateful results) or when they are not posted – towards the end of *Bleak House* Richard Carstone's letters to Esther are half written before being turned into waste paper. In much the same way, the gravestone epitaphs devised by Joe Gargery and John Chivery are never carved (in a final irony, notes to the Pilgrim edition of Dickens's letters record that epitaphs he composed for dead friends and relations have since become illegible).

Like letters, manuscript sources are crafted by the author in numerous ways. In *The Mystery of Edwin Drood* Jasper plays on the assumption that a diary has greater integrity than a formal declamation because it is supposedly written without forethought or for public consumption, an attitude that enables him (presumably) to manufacture evidence before the disappearance of his nephew. The status of David Copperfield's writing is also complex: what David claims is a manuscript to be seen only by himself is experienced by the reader as part of an infinitely reproducible print series but really is based on a manuscript source (this multi-layered text becomes even more bewildering when that original manuscript is partly printed and partly rewritten in Forster's *Life of Dickens*). Signalling his awareness of the ms / print hierarchy, Dickens sometimes included hand-written excerpts from his fiction in letters to admirers, which they would be free to insert in to their personal editions of those books.

The demands of life as a writer are expressed in writing itself. Turning down an invitation shortly before the start of his second American tour Dickens complained that 'the regulation of my personal affairs, the six months' prospective management of a great periodical published every week, the course to be taken in America, the apportionment of 100 nights of hard work – tug at my sleeve and pull at my pen, every minute in the day' (To Mrs Elliot, 12 September 1867. Pilgrim 11. 424–26). Sometimes obstructive external events are recorded in writing and in turn are fed back in to letters 'I cannot imagine how that paragraph ever got into circulation, but it is just now overwhelming me with letters and causing me real annoyance' (To Charles Kent, 3 September 1867. Pilgrim 11. 420), while Dr Howe, who had educated the deaf, dumb and blind girl Laura Bridgeman is told that 'I fear I must regard my reading to your pupils, though it were but for ten minutes, as a thing not reasonably possible. It would bring down upon me such an avalanche of correspondence as would crush me out of recognition' (To Dr S. G. Howe, 22 November 1867. 485–86).

The impact of Dickens's ethos on the reader is intended to work beyond the text itself and designed to form lasting reading habits and culture. As he wrote in 1859, 'I hope I have done my part to make the rising generation "more childish", in rendering them a little more imaginative, a little more gentle, and a little less conceited and hard, than they would have been without me. I desire to do nothing better' (To Mrs Gore, 3 January 1859. Pilgrim 9. 10).

Winter locates the source of Dickens's authority in his ability to create a reading experience for individuals while also creating and sustaining a community of readers for whom his characters, and even an image of the author himself, would register as cultural exchange:

> readers and reviewers constructed Dickens's own mental attributes retroactively, through reflection on the experience of reading his novels, as the origin of both the effects that his novels seemed to produce

upon individual readers and the common interests and attachments that readers developed in relation to his fictions. According to this account, which would become a canonical representation of Dickens's influence, the author's inventive memory produces the common repertoire of associations – the specific form of cultural memory – accessible to readers through his novels and his public persona. (80–81)

In fact Dickens himself becomes part of this circle of engaged readers in his insistence that the scenes he writes are at least as real to him as they can be to anyone else. The sense of mutual trust he seeks to establish is reinforced not just by his habit of addressing unseen readers as intimate friends; notably his personal friends are invited to stand in for the public on occasion, allowing Dickens to test the efficacy of his writing on them in eliciting emotional responses to his reading. From 1858 his regular series of public readings allowed Dickens to become – literally – a reader of his own writing. Crucially these readings also collapsed the distance between writer, text and reader as Dickens memorised the adaptations of particular scenes and dramatically closed the book before he began to 'read'. According to Small:

> In the history of the reading public Dickens's platform career holds a special place, for he succeeded in bringing together unprecedentedly large numbers of readers for a genuinely public experience of reading. Normally an invisible constituency, on these occasions the fiction reading public was to a significant degree made visible to itself as a collectivity. (266)

Notably Dickens continues to describe these events in terms of shared reading rather than individual performance; in recalling one reading in Peterborough, he reported that 'I think everybody for the time forgot everything but the matter in hand. It was as fine an instance of thorough absorption in a fiction as any of us are likely to see ever again' (To Frank Stone, 19 October 1859. 138–39). He repeatedly describes his reading tours as if they were scenes or chapters in variations of the phrase 'This episodical life of mine'.

The imperturbable reader is one who is also beyond the reach of authorial influence, a figure that finds its ultimate expression in the machinistic Tulkinghorn. Concerns over readers failing to mark themselves with their reading is a double bind, as is the illicit reading by unintended audiences which is apparent also in Thackeray, 'If I leave this manuscript open on my table, I have not the slightest doubt Betty will read it, and they will talk it over in the lower regions tonight; and to-morrow she will bring in my breakfast with a face of such entire imperturbable innocence, that no mortal could consider her guilty of playing the spy' (*Pendennis* 385).

Such anxieties suggest the ultimate unknowability of the text, given its status as both story and – literally – work. Dickens puts his own spin on this idea in telling Angela Burdett Coutts somewhat disingenuously, 'As to my art, I have as great a delight in it as the most enthusiastic of my readers; and the sense of my trust and responsibility in that wise, is always upon me when I take pen in hand. If *I* were soured, I should still try to sweeten the lives and fancies of others; but I am not – not at all' (To Miss Burdett Coutts, 8 April 1860. Pilgrim 9. 233).

In assessing the significance of Dickens, the aim of his strongest admirers was to present him as incomparable (and therefore unique), but also as one of the key figures of his time. Sala's response to this dilemma was to compare him to non-literary pioneers of the 19th century, claiming with some justification, 'The record of Charles Dickens is an essential part of the nineteenth century and of the Victorian era; and it would be as difficult to obliterate from the chronicle of our time the remembrance of who he was and what he did, as to ignore Fulton or Stephenson, Brewster or Faraday' (7).

Dickens himself reveals an awareness throughout his writing that this status depends on actual rather than ideal readers – his characteristic response is to 'create' an ideal readership in both senses of the word, one that would first read his fiction and in the process, be morally altered by it. In one sense his career could be seen as the sustained attempt to record and embody his literary ethos in his own person, from the various prefaces to his novels and the editorial direction of *Household Words* and *All the Year Round*, to the enactment of characters in the public readings as recorded in numerous letters to family and friends.

In a rare admission that even in his own mind the characters in his books were not actually real, he once wrote to a friend, 'is it not a strange thing if writers of fiction never dream of their own creations: recollecting I suppose, even in their dreams, that they have no real existence? *I* never dreamed of any of my own characters' (To C. C. Felton, 1 September 1843. 547–551. 550). But in his accounts of 'recording' fictional events and reading his own work both to himself and to varied audiences of friends and the regional public, Dickens stresses both the autonomous status of his characters and the imaginative investment required in order for them to become familiar 'friends' who could be encountered by the group round the domestic hearth. In managing these contradictory demands over a period of more than 30 years, he ultimately confirms his position as his own ideal reader.

Notes

1. For a detailed discussion of Jerome's fictional response to Dickens and his work, including a scene in which the eponymous Paul Kelver unwittingly repeats this accusation to Dickens himself, see Carolyn W. de la L. Oulton, *Below the Fairy City: A Life of Jerome K. Jerome*. Brighton: Victorian Secrets 2012.
2. Barry Pain. 'If he had lived TO-DAY. A specimen of the New Criticism'. *TO-DAY*. 23 February 1894. 10.

Bibliography

Dickens's novels and non-fiction

American Notes. London: Penguin, 2004. Print.
Bleak House. Oxford: Oxford World's Classics, 1998. Print.
Christmas Carol and Other Christmas Books, A. Oxford: Oxford World's Classics 2008. Print.
David Copperfield. Oxford: Oxford World's Classics, 1999. Print.
Dombey and Son. Oxford: Oxford World's Classics, 2008. Print.
Glancy, Ruth, ed. *Charles Dickens: The Christmas Stories*. London: Everyman, 1996. Print.
Great Expectations. Oxford: Oxford World's Classics, 2008. Print.
Little Dorrit. Oxford: Oxford World's Classics, 2008. Print.
Martin Chuzzlewit. Oxford: Oxford World's Classics, 2009. Print.
"Mrs Lirriper's Lodgings". *The Christmas Stories*. 500–30. *The Mystery of Edwin Drood*. Oxford: Oxford World's Classics, 2009. Print.
Nicholas Nickleby. Oxford: Oxford World's Classics, 2008. Print.
Oliver Twist. Oxford: Oxford World's Classics, 2008. Print.
Our Mutual Friend. Oxford: Oxford World's Classics, 2008. Print.
Pictures from Italy. London: Penguin, 1998. Print.

Dickens's letters

House, Madeline, and Graham Storey, eds. *The Pilgrim Edition: The Letters of Charles Dickens*. Volume 1: 1820–1839. Oxford: Clarendon Press, 1965. Print.
———. Volume 2: 1840–1841. Oxford: Clarendon Press, 1969. Print.
Storey, Graham, and Kathleen Tillotson, eds. *The Pilgrim Edition: The Letters of Charles Dickens*. Volume 3: 1842–1843. Oxford: Clarendon Press, 1974. Print.
Storey, Graham, and K. J. Fielding, eds. *The Pilgrim Edition: The Letters of Charles Dickens*. Volume 5: 1847–1849. Oxford: Clarendon Press, 1977. Print.
———, Kathleen Tillotson and Nina Burgis, eds. *The Pilgrim Edition: The Letters of Charles Dickens*. Volume 6: 1850–1852. Oxford: Clarendon Press, 1988. Print.
———, Kathleen Tillotson and Angus Easson, eds. *The Pilgrim Edition: The Letters of Charles Dickens*. Volume 7: 1853–1855. Oxford: Clarendon Press, 1993. Print.
———, and Kathleen Tillotson, eds. *The Pilgrim Edition: The Letters of Charles Dickens*. Volume 8: 1856–1858. Oxford: Clarendon Press, 1995. Print.
——— ed. *The Pilgrim Edition: The Letters of Charles Dickens*. Volume 9: 1859–1861. Oxford: Clarendon Press, 1997. Print.
———. *The Pilgrim Edition: The Letters of Charles Dickens*. Volume 10: 1862–1864. Oxford: Clarendon Press, 1998. Print.

178 *Bibliography*

———. *The Pilgrim Edition: The Letters of Charles Dickens*. Volume 11: 1862–1864. Oxford: Clarendon Press, 1999. Print.
———. *The Pilgrim Edition: The Letters of Charles Dickens*. Volume 12: 1868–1870. Oxford: Clarendon Press, 1999. Print.
Tillotson, Kathleen ed. *The Pilgrim Edition: The Letters of Charles Dickens*. Volume 4: 1844–1846. Oxford: Clarendon Press, 1977. Print.

Dickens's journalism

Slater, Michael, ed. *The Amusements of the People and Other Papers: Reports, Essays and Reviews 1834–51*. London: Dent, 1996. Print.
Slater, Michael, ed. *"Gone Astray" and Other Paper from Household Words*. London: Dent, 1998. Print.
———. "Curious Misprint in the Edinburgh Review." *Gone Astray*. 413–20. Print.
———. "Personal." *Gone Astray*. 488–90. Print.
———. *Sketches by Boz and Other Early Papers 1833–39*. London: Phoenix, 1996. Print.

Non Dickens texts

Barrie, J. M. "Brought Back from Elysium." *The Contemporary Review*, 1890. 846–54. Reprinted in Nadel. Print.
Boyle, Mary. "Dickens's 'Dearest Meery' Remembers." *Interviews and Recollections*, Vol 1. 83–86. Print.
Broughton, Rhoda. *Cometh up as a Flower*. Sussex: Victorian Secrets, 2012. Print.
Burnett, Harry. "The Young Novelist at Work and Play." *Interviews and Recollections*, Vol 1. 21–24. Print.
Calthrop, Dion Clayton, and Max Pemberton, eds. The Dickens Souvenir of 1912. Print.
Carlyle, Thomas and Jane. "Maddest Nonsense and Tragic Depths." Collins Vol 1. 61–64. Print.
"Charles Dickens. Some Personal Recollections and Opinions." The Bookman. February 1912 (41). 246–55. Proquest: British Periodicals. Accessed 30 January 2015.
Cholmondeley, Mary. ms diary. Private archive. Print.
Cholmondeley, Mary. *Red Pottage*. London: Pickering & Chatto, 2011. Print.
Christian, Eleanor E. "Dickens on Holiday (1840) and Afterwards." *Interviews and Recollections*, Vol 1. 33–41. Print.
Collins, Philip. *Dickens: Interviews and Recollections*, Vol 1. London: Macmillan, 1981. Print.
Corelli, Marie. "The Power of the Pen." *Free Opinions Freely Expressed*. London: Archibald Constable & Co. 1905. 202–309. Print.
Eliot, George. '"In the Chair" George Eliot and Others.' Collins Vol 1. 96–104. Print.
Fitzgerald, Percy. 'Some Memories of Dickens and "Household Words."' Calthrop and Pemberton. 22–28. Print.
Gissing, George. *New Grub Street*. Oxford: Oxford World's Classics, 1993. Print.
———. *Collected Works of George Gissing on Charles Dickens*. Volume 2. *Charles Dickens: A Critical Study*. Ed. Simon James. Surrey: Grayswood Press, 2004. Print.

Macready, William. "Dear Dickens is a Most Extraordinary Man!" Collins Vol 1. 28–32. Print.
Masson, David. "Pendennis and Copperfield: Thackeray and Dickens." *The North British Review*, 1851. 57–89. Reprinted in Nadel. Print.
Nadel, Ira Bruce, ed. *Victorian Fiction: A Collection of Essays from the Period*. New York and London: Garland, 1986. Print.
Oliver, Owen. "A Christmas Bonus." *Cassell's Magazine* September 1911–March 1912. 339–46. Print.
Procter, Adelaide Anne. *Legends and Lyrics*. London: George Bell and Sons, 1892. Print.
de Quincey, Thomas. *Confessions of an English Opium-Eater and Other Writings*. Oxford: World's Classics, 2008. Print.
Roberts, W. "Morality in Book Collecting." (*Literature*, October 8, 1898). *The Academy and Literature*. 28 September 1912: 83, 2108. Periodicals Archive Online 412. Accessed 22 January 2015.
Sala, G. A. *Charles Dickens*. Farnborough: Gregg International, 1970. Print.
Thackeray, W. M. *Catherine, Snobs etc.* London: Caxton Publishing Company (date not given). Print.
——. *The Newcomes*. Oxford: World's Classics, 1995. Print.
——. *Pendennis*. London: Penguin, 1972. Print.
Trollope, Anthony. *The Three Clerks*. Oxford: World's Classics, 1989. Print.
——. *The Warden*. Oxford: World's Classics, 2014. Print.
Yonge, Charlotte. *The Heir of Redclyffe*. Oxford: World's Classics, 1997.

Bibliography of Secondary Sources

Ablow, Rachel, ed. *The Feeling of Reading: Affective Experience and Victorian Literature*. University of Michigan Press, 2010. Print.
——. *The Marriage of Minds: Reading Sympathy in the Victorian Marriage Plot*. Stanford, CA: Stanford University Press, 2007. Print.
Allbut, Robert. *Rambles in Dickens Land*. London: Chapman and Hall [1899]. Print.
Andrews, Malcolm. *Dickensian Laughter: Essays on Dickens and Humour*. Oxford: Oxford University Press, 2013. Print.
Birch, Dinah, and Mark Llewellyn, eds. *Conflict and Difference in Nineteenth-Century Literature*. Basingstoke: Palgrave Macmillan, 2010. Print.
Bodenheimer, Rosemarie. *Knowing Dickens*. Ithaca: Cornell University Press, 2007. Print.
——. Dickens and the Writing of a Life." *Charles Dickens Studies*. Ed. John Bowen and Robert L. Patten. Basingstoke: Palgrave Macmillan, 2006. 48–68. Print.
Bowen, John, and Robert L. Patten, eds. *Palgrave Advances in Charles Dickens Studies*. Basingstoke: Palgrave Macmillan, 2006. Print.
Bradbury, Nicola. "Dickens's Use of the Autobiographical Fragment." Paroissien. 18–32. Print.
Brake, Laurel, Bill Bell, and David Finkelstein. *Nineteenth-Century Media and the Construction of Identities*. Bastinstoke: Palgrave Macmillan, 2000. Print.
Brantlinger, Patrick. *The Reading Lesson: The Threat of Mass Literacy in Nineteenth-Century British Fiction*. Indianapolis: Indiana University Press, 1998. Print.
Chialant, Maria Teresa. "The Adult Narrator's Memory of Childhood in David's, Esther's and Pip's Autobiographies." Merchant and Waters. 77–91. Print.

Cordery, Gareth. "*David Copperfield.*" Paroissien. 369–79. Print.
Davis, Philip. *Why Victorian Literature Still Matters*. Oxford: Wiley-Blackwell, 2008. Print.
Demoor, Marysa. *Marketing the Author: Authorial Personae, Narrative Selves and Self-Fashioning, 1880–1930*. Basinstoke: Palgrave Macmillan, 2004. Print.
Di, Wu. "Child Readers in Dickens's Novels." Merchant and Waters. 167–82. Print.
Douglas-Fairhust, Robert. *Becoming Dickens: The Invention of a Novelist*. Cambridge, MA: Belknap Press of Harvard University Press, 2011. Print.
Drew, John. "Texts, Paratexts and 'E-texts'": The Poetics of Communication in Dickens's Journalism. *Dickens and Modernity*. Ed. Juliet John. Cambridge: D. S. Brewer, 2012. 61–93. Print.
Duncan, Ian. *Modern Romance & the Transformation: The Gothic, Scott, Dickens*. Cambridge: CUP 1992. Print.
Easley, Alexis. *Literary Celebrity, Gender, and Victorian Authorship, 1850–1914*. Newark: University of Delaware Press, 2011. Print.
Eliot, Simon, and Jonathan Rose, eds. *A Companion to the History of the Book*. Oxford: Wiley-Blackwell, 2007. Print.
Flanders, Judith. *The Victorian City: Everyday Life in Dickens' London*. London: Atlantic Books, 2012. Print.
Flint, Kate, ed. *The Cambridge History of Victorian Literature*. Cambridge: Cambridge University Press, 2012. Print.
Freedgood, Elaine. "Material." *The Cambridge History of Victorian Literature*. 370–87. Print.
Furneaux, Holly. *Queer Dickens: Erotics, Families, Masculinities*. Oxford: Oxford University Press, 2009. Print.
Gilbert, Pamela K. "Ouida and the Canon: Recovering, Reconsidering, and Revisioning the Popular." *Ouida and Popular Culture*. Ed. Jane Jordan and Andrew King. Aldershot: Ashgate, 2013. 37–51. Print.
Gordon, John. *Sensation and Sublimation in Charles Dickens*. New York: Palgrave Macmillan, 2011. Print.
Grass, Sean. *Charles Dickens's Our Mutual Friend: A Publishing History*. Farnham: Ashgate, 2014. Print.
Gregory, Gill. *The Life and Work of Adelaide Procter: Poetry, Feminism and Fathers*. Aldershot: Ashgate 1998. Print.
Grossman, Jonathan H. *Charles Dickens's Networks: Public Transport and the Novel*. Oxford: Oxford University Press, 2012. Print.
Hack, Daniel. *The Material Interests of the Victorian Novel*. Charlottesville, VA: University of Virginia Press, 2005. Print.
Hager, Kelly. *Dickens and the Rise of Divorce: The Failed-Marriage Plot and the Novel Tradition*. Aldershot: Ashgate, 2010. Print.
Hammond, Mary. *Charles Dickens's Great Expectations: A Cultural Life, 1860–2012*. Aldershot: Ashgate 2015. Print.
Hardy, Barbara. *Dickens and Creativity*. London: Continuum, 2008. Print.
Hedgecock, Jennifer. *The Femme Fatale in Victorian Literature: The Danger and the Threat*. New York: Cambria Press, 2008. Print.
Horne, Philip. "Style and the Making of Character in Dickens." Tyler. 155–75. Print.
John, Juliet. *Dickens's Villains: Melodrama, Character, Popular Culture*. Oxford: OUP, 2001. Print.

———. "Things, Words and the Meanings of Art." *Dickens and Modernity*. Ed. Juliet John. Cambridge: D. S. Brewer, 2012. 115–32. Print.

———. "Dickens and the Heritage Industry; or, Culture and the Commodity." Birch and Llewellyn. 157–70. Print.

Mazzeno, Laurence W. *The Dickens Industry: Critical Perspsectives 1836–2005*. New York and Suffolk: Camden House, 2008. Print.

Merchant, Peter. "'A Kind of Odour of Salem House': David Copperfield and Thomas Anstey Guthrie." Merchant and Waters. 131–47. Print.

Merchant, Peter, and Catherine Waters, eds. *Dickens and the Imagined Child*. Farnham: Ashgate, 2015. Print.

Mills, Victoria. "Bricabracomania! Collecting, Corporeality and the Problem of Things." Shears and Harrison. 33–47. Print.

Nelson, Claudia. *Precocious Children and Childish Adults*. Baltimore: John Hopkins University Press, 2012. Print.

Parker, David. *Charles Dickens and Christmas*. New York: AMS Press, 2005. Print.

Price Leah. *How to Do Things with Books in Victorian Britain*. Princeton: Princeton University Press, 2012. Print.

Paroissien, David, ed. *A Companion to Charles Dickens*. Oxford: Blackwell, 2008. Print.

———. "'Faithfully Yours, Charles Dickens': the Epistolatory Art of the Inimitable." Paroissien. 33–46. Print.

Patten, Robert L. "Publishing in Parts." *Palgrave Advances*. 11–47. Print.

Poovey, Mary. *Uneven Developments: The Ideological Work of Gender in Mid-Victorian England*. London: Virago, 1989. Print.

Purton, Valerie. *Dickens and the Sentimental Tradition: Fielding, Richardson, Sterne, Goldsmith, Sheridan, Lamb*. London: Anthem Press, 2012. Print.

Pykett, Lyn. *Charles Dickens*. Basingstoke: Palgrave, 2002. Print.

Raven, James, Helen Small and Naomi Tadmor, eds. *The Practice and Representation of Reading in England*. Cambridge: Cambridge University Press, 1996. Print.

Sadrin, Anny. *Parentage and Inheritance in the Novels of Charles Dickens*. Cambridge: Cambridge University Press, 2010. Print.

Saunders, Max. *Self-Impression: Life-Writing, Autobiografiction, & the Forms of Modern Literature*. Oxford: Oxford University Press 2010. Print.

Sen, Sambudha. *London, Radical Culture, and the Making of the Dickensian Aesthetic*. Athens: Ohio State University Press, 2012. Print.

Shears, Jonathon, and Jen Harrison. *Literary Bric-à-Brac and the Victorians: From Commodities to Oddities*. Aldershot: Ashgate, 2013. Print.

Slater, Michael. *Charles Dickens*. New Haven: Yale University Press, 2009. Print

———. *The Great Charles Dickens Scandal*. New Haven: Yale University Press, 2012. Print.

Small, Helen. "A Pulse of 124: Charles Dickens and a Pathology of the Mid-Victorian Reading Public." Raven, Small and Tadmor. 263–90. Print.

Stedman, Gesa. *Stemming the Torrent: Expression and Control in the Victorian Discourses on Emotions, 1830–1872*. Aldershot: Ashgate, 2002. Print.

Sutherland, John. *Victorian Fiction: Writers, Publishers, Readers*. Basingstoke: Macmillan, 1995. Print.

Tambling, Jeremy. *Going Astray: Dickens and London*. Harlow: Longman, 2009. Print.

Tyler, Daniel, ed. *Dickens's Style*. Cambridge: Cambridge University Press, 2013. Print.

———. Introduction to *Dickens's Style*. 1–25. Print.

———. "Spectres of Style." *Dickens's Style*. 93–109. Print.

Vincent, David. *Literacy and Popular Culture: England 1750–1914*. Cambridge: Cambridge University Press, 1993. Print.

Waters, Catherine. *Commodity Culture in Dickens's Household Words: The Social Life of Goods*. Aldershot: Ashgate, 2008. Print.

Waugh, Arthur. "Charles Dickens." *Cassell's Magazine*. September 1911–March 1912. 347–50. Print.

Winter, Sarah. *The Pleasures of Memory: Learning to Read with Charles Dickens*. New York: Fordham University Press, 2011. Print.

Index

Ablow, Rachel 28, 73
Academy, The 168
Alberti, Frau 22, 31
All the Year Round 21, 24, 26, 33, 60, 109, 110, 132, 134, 170, 176
Allbut, Robert 27
Allbut's Rambles in Dickens Land 27, 164
American Notes 5, 13, 30, 61, 64; author/reader relations in 65, 69
Amusements of the People and Other Papers, The: Reports, Essays and Reviews 1834–1851 (ed. Dent) 38
Andersen, Hans Christian 91, 106, 143
Andrews, Malcolm 7, 89, 128, 130
Anstey, F. 169
audience: Dickens' relationship with 13–14, 21, 27–8, 34, 88, 108, 151, 176; emotion of 2, 12; *see also* reader(s)
Austin, Henry 4, 20, 113
author/reader relationship 1, 15, 39; in *American Notes* 65, 69; in *A Christmas Carol* 55–60; in *Dombey and Son* 73–79; in *Martin Chuzzlewit* 61–72; in *Nicholas Nickleby* 47–55; in *Oliver Twist* 39–46; in *Sketches by Boz* 33–9
autobiography, *David Copperfield* as 80, 85–91, 102
Autobiography of a Working Man, The 24

Barnaby Rudge 71
Barrie, J. M. 167
Baylis, Thomas 104–5
Beadnell, Maria *see* Winter, Maria (Beadnell)
Beard, Thomas 109
Belcombe, Henry 15
Benson, E. F. 83
Bentley, Richard 5, 46
Bentley's Miscellany 40
Berwick (Miss) *see* Procter, Adelaide
Blanchard, Laman 58
Bleak House 12, 36, 73, 115, 134, 154; characters in 117, 119–20, 122–3; critique of the law in 100, 117–18; use of dual narrators in 115–17; heroes in 114, 115, 123; issues of literacy in 118–20; materiality of text in 104; mentions of writing in 117–18, 120, 123, 156; narrative voice in 114, 122–3; and the power of reading 15; preface to 115, 116, 137; references to letters and writing in 114–15, 120–3, 172; Thackeray's view of 115
'Boarding House, The' 3, 36
Bodenheimer, Rosemarie 24, 86, 99, 157
Bookman 168
Bowen, John 4
Boyle, Mary 111
Boz (character): as author of *Oliver Twist* 46; Dickens' identification with 157; as narrator 2–3, 7, 33; *see also Sketches by Boz*
Bradbury, Nicola 86
Braddon, Mary 168
Brantlinger, Patrick 40, 42, 148
Brookfield (Mrs) 31
Broughton, Rhoda 10, 167
Brown (Mrs) 170
Browning, Elizabeth 106
Bulwer Lytton, Edward 20, 21, 131, 109, 169
Burdett Coutts, Angela 2, 9, 19, 41, 74, 100, 112, 136, 137, 139, 175–6
Burnand, F. C. 17

Carlyle, Thomas 21, 162
Cassell's Magazine 60
Catherine (Thackeray) 43, 44–5
Cerjat, William de W. F. 19, 93, 105, 173

184 *Index*

characters: allusions to 16–17; in *Bleak House* 117, 119–20, 122–3; in *A Christmas Carol* 57, 60; in *David Copperfield* 89–92, 96–8, 100–1, 163; development of 104; Dickens' attachment to 73, 102, 176; Dickens' creation of 40, 54, 62, 78, 104, 108, 162, 165–7; in Dickens' letters 16–17, 159, 170; in *Great Expectations* 102, 125–7, 129–35; importance of reading to 11, 15, 41, 144, 148, 150; in *Little Dorrit* 138, 140–7, 171; in *Martin Chuzzlewit* 62–72, 171; in *The Mystery of Edwin Drood* 154, 156; in *Nicholas Nickleby* 47–52, 157; in *Oliver Twist* 41, 43–6; in *Our Mutual Friend* 138, 148–53, 171–2; readers' connection with 2, 10–12, 16, 26–30, 33, 36, 49–50, 55, 56, 58–9, 71, 73, 78, 86, 97, 106, 114, 162, 165, 174; Thackeray's 454–6
Charles Dickens (Sala) 157, 158
Charles Dickens: A Critical Study (Gissing) 163–9
Chesterton, G. K. 159, 169
Chialant, Maria 85
Chimes, The 12
Chittick Kathryn 7, 37, 47
Cholmondeley, Mary 45, 73, 83, 106
Chorley, Henry 139
Christian, Eleanor 61–2
Christmas Bonus, A' (Oliver) 60
Christmas Carol, A 10, 34; author/reader relations in 55–60; characters in 57, 60; as a Christmas book 57; Dickens' affinity for 31, 58–9, 102–3; expectations of the readers in 55–6, 58; heroes in 55; literary appropriations from 59–60; narrative voice in 55–6, 58, 108; shared reading in 56–8; Thackeray's view of 60
'Cleansing Fires' (Adelaide Procter) 83
Cometh up as a Flower (Broughton) 10, 167
Confessions of an English Opium Eater (de Quincy) 39
Corderey, Gareth 87
Corelli, Marie 72, 167
Cornwall, Barry *see* Procter, Brian
Costello, Dudley 14
Coutts, Angela Burdett *see* Burdett Coutts, Angela
Cranford 111

Dalglish, Andrew 16
Dallas, E. S. 108
Dames, Nicholas 9
David Copperfield 35, 116; allusions to 137; characters in 89–92, 96–8, 100–1, 163; critique of the law in 100–1; David as hero 35, 88–92, 98, 114; importance of reading in 92–4; letters in 94, 98–100; literary apprenticeship in 7; as literary biography 80, 85–91, 102; literary devices in 172; meta-textual strategies in 96; Micawber as hero 101; narrative voice in 10, 14, 89–90, 95–6, 98, 114, 161–3, 166–7; preface to 90, 91; references to writing in 174; role of the reader in 79, 95; shared response to 31
Day's Ride, A 110
Demoor, Marysa 3
Detective Police Party, A' 39
Devonshire (Duke of) 106
Di, Wu 11, 94
Dickens, Alfred 17–18
Dickens, Catherine 12
Dickens, Helen 133
Dickens, Henry 86
dinner at Poplar Walk, A' 34
Dixon, E. S. 32
Dombey and Son 59, 85, 91, 152; author/reader relations in 73–79; use of books and text in 73; emotional attachment with characters in 73; exploration of writing types in 74; heroes in 74; hierarchy of reading in 74–7; moralization in 79; narrative voice in 73, 76–9; preface to 73, 79; reader response to 78–9
d'Orsay, Alfred (Count) 98
Douglas-Fairhurst, Robert 7, 28, 35–6, 55, 108
Drew, John 33
Duncan, Ian 30

Easley, Alexis 3
Eden, Eleanor 24
Edinburgh Review 107
Edwin Drood *see The Mystery of Edwin Drood*
Eliot, George 25, 110, 157
Elliot (Mrs) 174

Felton, Cornelius 16, 58–9, 62, 71
Fechter, Charles 60

Fields, J. T. 17, 32
Fields, Mrs J. T. 17
Fitzgerald, Percy 15, 168
Flanders, Judith 119
Fletcher, Robert 82
Flint, Kate 8
Forster, John 15, 16–17, 28, 29, 37, 39, 100, 165, 169; as advisor 104; as biographer 85–7; letters to 2, 18, 22, 27, 31–2, 42, 59, 67, 71–2, 78–9, 90, 102, 103, 108, 159–61; see also *Life of Charles Dickens*
Freedgood, Elaine 104
'Friend Sorrow' (Adelaide Procter) 84
Furniss, Harry 169

Gaskell, Elizabeth 109, 111–12
'Ghost of Art, The' 38
Gilbert, Pamela 117
Giles, William 18
'Gin Shops' 37
Gissing, George 170; *Charles Dickens: A Critical Study* 163–9
Gleig, G. R. 21
Golden, Mrs. David C. 61
Gordon, John 116
Gore (Mrs) 174
Grass, Sean 116
Great Expectations 155; alteration of the ending 20, 111, 131; anonymous letter as plot device 136; characters in 102, 125–7, 129–35; compared to *David Copperfield* 102; dramatic representation in 130; expectations of the reader in 131; heroes in 114, 129, 131; issues of literacy in 126–7, 129, 132–4; materiality of text in 104; mentions of writing in 127–9, 156; narrative voice in 114, 124–5, 167; writing of 110
Grossman, Jonathan 2, 140

Hack, Daniel 37, 117
Hager, Kelly 44, 48
Haldimand, William 74, 105
Hall, Mrs S. C. 53–4
Hammond, Mary 130
handwriting 34, 100, 104, 107, 117, 128, 144–5, 173
Hard Times 11, 55
Hardy, Barbara 89
Heir of Redclyffe, The (Yonge) 30, 73
heroes, literary 25, 29, 45, 66, 103, 104, 111; in *Bleak House* 114, 115, 123; in *A Christmas Carol* 55; David Copperfield as 35, 88–92, 98, 114; in *Dombey and Son* 74; in *Great Expectations* 114, 129, 131; in *Little Dorrit* 147; in *Martin Chuzzlewit* 55, 63, 67; Micawber as 101; in *Nicholas Nickleby* 50, 53, 88; in *Oliver Twist* 40, 88
Hewitt, G. 138
Hill, Jane Seymour 100
Hogarth, George 6
Hogarth, Georgina 18, 133, 137, 156
Holland, Lady 22, 62
Holme, George 134
Hood, Thomas 21
Hook, Theodor 19
Horne, Philip 131
Household Words (journal) 10, 15, 22, 24, 26, 33, 39, 56, 60, 80, 84–5, 107–8, 110, 111, 112, 167, 170, 176
Howe, S. G. 174
Howitt (Mrs) 90
Hunt, Leigh 28, 116
Hunt, Robert 38

identity: creation of 3; group 36; shared 12; of the writer 3, 23, 81
Idler 169
imaginary, shared 13, 16, 30
Irving, Washington 21, 105

James, Simon 164, 166
Jerome, Jerome K. 103, 167, 168, 169
Jerrold, Douglas 24
John, Juliet 13, 43
journalism: Dickens' early 33–9; topical 33

Kent, Charles 170, 174
Kolle, Henry 34

Landor, Walter Savage 105
Lane, R. J. 138
Lang, Andrew 168
Langham Place group 82
Layard, Austin Henry 173
Lee, Richard 23
Leech, John 17
Legends and Lyrics (Procter/Berwick) 80, 82–3; Dickens' preface to 80–2, 84
Lemon, Mark 145

letters: alluding to previous works 71; from B. W. Procter 18; in *Bleak House* 114–15, 120–3, 172; in *David Copperfield* 94, 98–100; to Dickens 29; Dickens' burning of 80, 137, 138, 145; misappropriation of 136; in *Great Expectations* 114–15; invocation of the writer by 17; in *Little Dorrit* 137–47, 171; in *Martin Chuzzlewit* 171; in *Nicholas Nickleby* 171; *see also* letters from Dickens
letters from Dickens: to Frau Alberti 22, 31; to Hans Christian Andersen 106, 143; to Henry Austin 4, 20; to Thomas Baylis 104–5; to Thomas Beard 109; to Henry Belcombe 15; to Bentley 46; to Laman Blanchard 58; to Mrs Brookfield 31; to Mrs Brown 170; to Sir Edward Bulwer Lytton 109, 131, 169–70; to Dudley Costello 14; to Angela Burdett Coutts 2, 9, 19, 41, 74, 100, 112, 136, 137, 139, 175–6; to Thomas Carlyle 21; to Chapman 20; to Henry Chorley 139; to Andrew Dalglish 16; to E. S. Dallas 108; to William W. F. de Cerjat 19, 93, 105, 173; to Emile de la Rue 112; to the Duke of Devonshire 106; to Alfred Dickens 17–18; to Catherine Dickens 12; to Henry Dickens 86; to E. S. Dixon 32; to Alfred d'Orsay 98; to Eleanor Eden 24; to Mrs Elliot 174; to Charles Fechter 60; to Cornelius Felton 58–9, 71; to Mr. and Mrs. J. T. Fields 17, 32; to Robert Fletcher 82; to John Forster 2, 18, 22, 27, 31–2, 42, 59, 67, 71–2, 78–9, 90, 102, 103, 108, 159–61; to Elizabeth Gaskell 109, 111–12; to William Giles 18; to G. R. Gleig 21; to Mrs. David C. Golden 61; to Mrs Gore 174; to William Haldimand 74, 105; Mrs S. C. Hall 20, 53–4; to G. Hewitt 138; to Jane Seymour Hill 100; to George Hogarth 6; to Georgina Hogarth 18, 133, 137, 157; to Lady Holland 22, 62; to Thomas Hood 21; to S. G. Howe 174; to Mrs Howitt 90; to Leigh Hunt 116; to Washington Irving 21, 105; to Douglas Jerrold 24; to a journalist 7; to Charles Kent 170, 174; to Henry Kolle 34; to Walter Savage Landor 105; to R. J. Lane 138; to Austin Henry Layard 173; Richard Lee 23; to John Leech 17; to Mark Lemon 145; to Charlies Lever 110; to G. H. Lewes 24, 40, 46, 110–11; to Robert Lytton 145; to Maclise 69; to W. C. Macready 17, 39, 47, 56–7, 79, 97–8, 154; to Anne March 109–10; to Harriet Martineau 111; to Andrew McKean 54; to Thomas Mitton 31, 34, 59; to Mrs M'lan 24; to Captain E. E. Morgan 32, 139; to Samuel Newton 23; to Mrs Nichols 136; to Mrs Charles Eliot Norton 17; to Mrs Olliffe 19; to Miss Palfrey 124; to potential contributors to *Household Words* 109; to Marguerite Power 110; to W. H. Prescott 62; to Adelaide Procter 81; to Adelaide Procter's parents 82; to readers 6, 29, 32; to Arthur Ryland 102; to W. P. Snow 23; to Frank Stone 175; to Edward Taggart 15, 17; to Thomas Trollope 172; to unknown correspondents 106, 112; to unknown ladies of Plymouth, Massachusetts 65; to Samuel Ward 18; to Mrs Richard Watson (Lavinia) 105, 113, 124; to Mrs O. F. R. White 173; to William Wilkie Collins 172; to W. H. Wills 17, 84, 155; to Maria (Beadnell) Winter 14, 19–20, 102–3, 134; to Edward Wood 32; to Mrs Henry Wood 139; to C. M. Young 109
Lever, Charles 110
Lewes, G. H. 24, 40, 46, 110
Life of Charles Dickens (Forster) 59, 85, 87, 102, 157–63, 174
Little Dorrit 17, 152; characters in 138, 140–7, 171; critique of the law in 142–4; Dickens working on 139–40; heroes in 147; preface to 137; references to letters and writing in 137–47, 171; theme of public documents in 136; themes of reading and writing in 140–7
'Little Mermaid, The' (Andersen) 91
'London Recreations' 38
'A Lost Chord' (Adelaide Procter) 83
Lytton, Robert 145

Maclise, letter to 69
Macready, W. C. 17, 39, 56–7, 79, 97–8; dedication of *Nicholas Nickleby* to 47

Marsh, Anne 109
Martin Chuzzlewit: allusions to reading in 68; author/reader relations in 61–72; characters in 62–72, 171; construction of myth in 65; construction of the characters in 70; deception in 65; direct address to the reader in 63; expectations of the reader in 61, 64, 72; heroes in 55, 63, 67; on literature and imagination 67–9; meta-textual strategies in 65–7; narrative voice in 62; preface to 20, 61, 63; printing of in America 71; readers' expectations of the author 64–5; references to letters in 171; serialisation of 62; shared imaginary in 15
Martineau, Harriet 111
Masson, David 107
materiality: of books 10, 104, 153; of writing 37
May, Phil 17
Mazzeno, Laurence 167, 169
McKean, Andrew 54
melodrama 13–14, 49
Merchant, Peter 169
meta-textual strategies 10, 16, 37, 40, 96
Mills, Victoria 118
Mitton, Thomas 31, 34, 59
Monmouth College exposé 113
Morgan, Captain E. E. 32, 139
Morris, William 59, 153
'Mrs Lirriper's Lodgings' 172
'My Picture' (Adelaide Procter) 84
Mystery of Edwin Drood, The 17, 70; references to writing in 174; issues of writing and literacy in 153–6

naïve optimism 50–1
narrative presence 10–11, 58
narrative voice 2, 12, 15; in *Bleak House* 114, 122–3; in *A Christmas Carol* 55–6, 58, 108; in *David Copperfield* 10, 14, 89–90, 95–6, 98, 114, 161–3, 166–7; in *Dombey and Son* 73, 76–9; in *Great Expectations* 114, 124–5, 167; in *Martin Chuzzlewit* 62–3; in *Nicholas Nickleby* 10; in *Oliver Twist* 31, 39–40, 42; *see also* narrators
narrators: Boz as 2–3, 7, 33; companionable 35–6; first-person 114–15, 135; urban 36; see also *Bleak House*; *David Copperfield*; *Great Expectations*; narrative voice
New Grub Street 163, 166
New Woman fiction 44
Newcomes, The (Thackeray) 45, 46, 60, 97, 103, 114, 115, 138–9
Newgate School 43, 44, 45
Newhaven (Lady) 83
News from Nowhere (Morris) 59–60, 153
Newton, Samuel 23
Nicholas Nickleby 28, 154; author/reader relations in 7–55; characters in 47–52; 157; controlling of readers in 11; expectations of the readers in 47–50, 52–5; heroes in 50, 53, 88; melodrama in 49; moralizing in 2; naïve optimism in 50–1; narrator's voice in 10; preface to 20, 47; references to writing and letters in 171; self-mythologising in 48–50; status of the reader in 52–3; transfer of knowledge in 53–4
Nichols (Mrs) 136
Norton, Mrs Charles Eliot 17
novels: palimpsestic 153; serialisation of 8–9, 42, 62, 111, 113, 115, 170

Old Curiosity Shop, The 20
Oliver Twist 165–6; author/reader relations in 39–46; characters in 41, 43–6; controlling of readers in 11, 42–4; ending to 46, 73; heroes in 40, 88; meta-textuality in 40; moralization in 41; narrative voice in 31, 39–40, 42; as example of Newgate School 43, 45; preface to 20–1, 31, 41, 113; and the role of the reader 40–2; and the role of the writer 41; Thackeray's view of 43, 44–5, 115; Trollope's view of 43
Olliffe, (Mrs) 19
Our Mutual Friend 55, 131, 134; characters in 138, 148–53, 171–2; issues of writing and literacy in 137, 147–53, 171–2
Overs, John 23, 112

Palfrey (Miss) 124
palimpsestic novels 153
paratextual material 33–4, 79, 113
Parker, David 55, 56, 164
Parliamentary Sketch, A' 38
'Parlour Orator, The' 4

188 *Index*

Paroissien, David 15–16, 18
Patten, Robert 8, 113
Paul Kelver (Jerome) 103
Pendennis (Thackeray) 5, 7, 28–9, 45, 89, 92, 101–2, 114
'Pet Prisoners' 38
Pickwick Papers 166
Pictures from Italy 3, 13, 170; preface to 20
Poetry of Science, or Studies of the Physical Phenomena of Nature, The (Hunt) 38
Poole, John 154
Power, Marguerite 110
prefaces 29–30, 45, 73, 79, 113, 134–5, 171, 176; to *Bleak House* 115, 116, 137; to *David Copperfield* 90, 91; to *Dombey and Son* 73, 79; to *Legends and Lyrics* 80–2, 84; to *Little Dorrit* 137; to *Martin Chuzzlewit* 20, 61, 63; to *Nicholas Nickleby* 20, 47; to *Oliver Twist* 20–1, 31, 41, 113; to *Pictures from Italy* 20; to *Sketches by Boz* 34–5
Prelude (Wordsworth) 89
Prescott, W. H. 62
Price, Leah 10, 91–2
Procter, Adelaide (Miss Berwick) 80; poems by 83–4
Procter, B. W. 18
Procter, Brian (Barry Cornwall) 80
Purton, Valerie 12
Pykett, Lyn 128

Quincy, Thomas de 39

Rambles in Dickens Land (Allbut) 27, 164
reader(s): children as 11; creation of intimacy with 1, 27–30, 32–3, 97, 105, 170–1; engagement of 34, 174–5; imaginative response of 9–10; interaction with 3–4; male vs. female 27, 165; responses of 27, 78–9; role of 1, 4, 14, 22, 34; *see also* audience
reading: active 47–8; context of 8–9; in *David Copperfield* 92–4; hierarchy of 74; shared 11, 56, 175
Red Pottage (Lady Newhaven) 83
reviews 24, 28, 38, 58, 72, 107–8, 116, 161
Rue, Emile de la 112
Ryland, Arthur 102

Sadrin, Anny 40, 89, 127
Sala, G. A. 33, 86, 157, 166, 176
Saunders, Max 86–7
Sen, Sambudha 29, 37, 40, 116, 140
sentimental tradition 12, 48, 50, 117
serialisation 8–9, 42, 62, 111, 113, 115, 170
shared imaginary 15, 16, 30
Shaw, George Bernard 168
Sketches by Boz 1, 4, 23; author/reader relations in 33–9; collected sketches 35; engagement of the reader by 33–4, 37, 39; influence of 33; interactive strategies in 39; meta-textuality in 37; narrative voice in 35–8, 90; preface to 34–5
Sketches by Boz episodes: 'The Boarding House' 3, 36; 'A Detective Police Party' 39; 'A dinner at Poplar Walk' 34; 'The Ghost of Art' 38; 'The Gin Shops' 37; 'London Recreations' 38; 'A Parliamentary Sketch' 38; 'The Parlour Orator' 4; 'Pet Prisoners' 38; 'The Tuggses at Ramsgate' 36, 37; 'A Visit to Newgate' 38
Sketches by Boz and Other Early Papers 34
Slater, Michael 35, 62, 157, 161
Small, Helen 108, 175
Snow, W. P. 23
Sorrows of Satan, The (Corelli) 72
Stone, Frank 175
Stowe, Harriet Beecher 113
Sturgis, Russell 156

Taggart, Edward 15, 17
Ternan, Ellen 157
Thackeray, William Makepeace 5, 7, 24–5, 28, 43, 44–5, 46, 60, 89, 92, 95–6, 101, 103, 107, 114, 115, 117, 138, 140, 152, 175
'Third Poor Traveller, The' (Adelaide Procter) 84
Three Clerks, The (Trollope) 25, 43
Trollope, Anthony 25, 43, 117, 172
Trollope, Thomas 172
'Tuggses at Ramsgate, The' 36, 37
Tyler, Daniel 58

Uncle Tom's Cabin (Stowe) 113
Urania Cottage project 9

Vanity Fair (Thackeray) 46
Vicar of Wakefield, The 9

villains, literary 40, 43, 49, 52, 92
Vincent, David 23, 149
Visit to Newgate, A' 38

Ward, Samuel 18
Warden, The (Trollope) 25
Waters, Catherine 109
Watson, (Mrs) Richard (Lavinia) 105, 113, 124, 137
Watts, Richard 81
Waugh, Arthur 98
White, Mrs O. F. R. 173
Wilkie Collins, William 139–40, 172
Wills, W. H. 17, 24, 81, 84, 109, 111, 155

Winter, Maria (Beadnell) 14, 19–20, 102–3, 134, 137
Winter, Sarah 4, 7, 8
Wood, Edward 32
Wood, (Mrs) Henry 139
Wordsworth, William 89
writer(s): accessibility of 25; construction of 3; responsibility of 6–7; women as 80–2, 84–5; *see also* author/reader relationship

Yonge, Charlotte M. 30, 73, 109

Zangwill, Israel 169